The Dangers of Fashion

The Dangers of Fashion

Towards Ethical and Sustainable Solutions

Edited by Sara B. Marcketti and Elena E. Karpova

BLOOMSBURY VISUAL ARTS
LONDON • NEW YORK • OXFORD • NEW DELHI • SYDNEY

BLOOMSBURY VISUAL ARTS
Bloomsbury Publishing Plc
50 Bedford Square, London, WC1B 3DP, UK
1385 Broadway, New York, NY 10018, USA

BLOOMSBURY, BLOOMSBURY VISUAL ARTS and the Diana logo are trademarks of
Bloomsbury Publishing Plc

First published in Great Britain 2020

Cover design: Philippa Thomas

A catalogue record for this book is available from the British Library.

Library of Congress Cataloging-in-Publication Data
Names: Marcketti, Sara B., editor. | Karpova, Elena (Professor of apparel, textiles, and
merchandising), editor.
Title: The dangers of fashion: towards ethical and sustainable solutions / edited by Sara
Marcketti and Elena Karpova.
Description: London ; New York, NY : Bloomsbury, 2020. | Includes   bibliographical
references and index.
Identifiers: LCCN 2019037752 | ISBN 9781350052048 (paperback) | ISBN 9781350052055
(hardback) | ISBN 9781350052024 (pdf) | ISBN 9781350052031 (epub) Subjects:
LCSH: Clothing trade—Moral and ethical aspects. | Clothing trade--Environmental
aspects. | Fashion—Moral and ethical aspects. | Fashion—Environmental aspects.
Classification: LCC HD9940.A2 D36 2020 | DDC 338.4/774692—dc23
LC record available at https://lccn.loc.gov/2019037752

ISBN: HB: 978-1-3500-5205-5
       PB: 978-1-3500-5204-8
       ePDF: 978-1-3500-5202-4
       eBook: 978-1-3500-5203-1

Typeset by RefineCatch Limited, Bungay, Suffolk
Printed and bound in India

To find out more about our authors and books visit www.bloomsbury.com
and sign up for our newsletters.

Contents

Figures and Tables

Figures

Tables

Notes on Contributors

Elizabeth "Missy" Bye, Ph.D., is a professor in Apparel Design and the Head of the Department of Design, Housing, and Apparel at the University of Minnesota, USA. Bye co-directs the Wearable Product Design Center, which is an innovative, synergistic "think-tank" that allows researchers to explore methods and technologies that will change how we design, produce and wear clothing. Current projects include the co-design of culturally appropriate athletic wear and Minnesota Apparel manufacturers.

Huantian Cao, Ph.D., is a professor in the Department of Fashion and Apparel Studies, University of Delaware, USA. His research interests include sustainable design and development of textiles and apparel, functional apparel, and functional textiles. He conducts applied scientific research with a multidisciplinary approach to reduce environmental impacts or enhance functions of textile and apparel products.

Ting Chi, Ph.D., is an associate professor in the Department of Apparel, Merchandising, Design and Textiles at Washington State University, USA. His research focuses on strategic supply chain management and marketing in the textile, apparel, and retail industries. He has published more than eighty peer-reviewed journal articles and conference proceedings. His research has been funded by the USDA, the EPA, the California Agriculture Research Initiatives, the Walmart Foundation, Cotton Inc., and private companies.

Marsha A. Dickson, Ph.D., is Irma Ayers Professor of Human Services in the Department of Fashion and Apparel Studies at the University of Delaware, USA. She is recognized globally for her pioneering and prolific scholarship and impactful professional service on topics of social responsibility and sustainability.

Hallie Erdahl is a graduate of Iowa State University's Apparel, Merchandising, and Design Program where she received a Louise Rosenfeld Undergraduate Research Internship from the College of Human Sciences. Hallie is currently an Area Coordinator and Director of Student Activities at Waldorf University, Iowa, USA, and also a certified health coach and fitness instructor.

Denise Nicole Green, Ph.D., is a faculty member in the American Indian and Indigenous Studies Program and the Department of Fiber Science and Apparel Design at Cornell University, USA, where she also directs the Cornell Costume and Textile Collection. Her research investigates the cultural significance of clothing, textiles, and the fashioned body by triangulating anthropology, curation, and creative design scholarship.

Jung E. Ha-Brookshire, Ph.D., is professor in the Department of Textile and Apparel Management at the University of Missouri, USA. She teaches global sourcing, global supply chain management, and the capstone course for retail marketing and merchandising students. Her research interests include the moral responsibility of corporate sustainability, the global supply chain and sourcing strategies, and the sustainable production and consumption of textile and apparel.

Jana M. Hawley, Ph.D. serves as Dean of the College of Merchandising, Hospitality and Tourism at the University of North Texas, USA. She is a Fulbright Scholar to India, a HERS Fellow, ITAA Fellow, SEC Administrators Leadership Fellow, and a Kemper Fellow for Excellence in Teaching. Hawley's scholarly works focus on international craft development, textile recycling, and fashion industry sustainability. She earned her Ph.D. from the University of Missouri.

Kim Y. Hiller Connell, Ph.D., associate professor, Kansas State University, USA, completed graduate studies related to apparel and textiles, environmental science and policy, as well as international development. Her areas of expertise are sustainability within the fiber, textile, and clothing supply chain and consumer behavior. She has published in consumer behavior and sustainability education related journals and has received funding for research related to understanding and encouraging sustainable apparel consumption. She also teaches sustainability-focused courses at both graduate and undergraduate levels.

Nancy Hodges, Ph.D., is the Burlington Industries Distinguished Professor and Head of the Department of Consumer, Apparel and Retail Studies at the University of North Carolina, Greensboro, USA. Her research interests include examining the role of industry dynamics within community contexts.

Susan B. Kaiser, Ph.D., is a faculty member in the Departments of Gender, Sexuality, and Women's Studies, and Design at the University of California, Davis, USA. She is also active in the campus Textiles and Cultural Studies

Graduate Groups. Her research focuses on the interface between fashion and cultural studies, with a current interest in issues of time, place, and subjectivity.

Elena E. Karpova, Ph.D., is Putnam and Hayes Distinguished Professor in the Department of Consumer, Apparel, and Retail Studies at the University of North Carolina, Greensboro, USA. Research interests include trends in the global textile and apparel industries, trade, and markets; sustainability; and creative thinking. She is a co-author of *Going Global: The Textile and Apparel Industry*.

Melody L. A. LeHew, Ph.D., professor, Kansas State University, USA, completed graduate studies related to retail strategy and consumer behavior. Her research program is focused on sustainable behaviors at all levels of production and consumption as well as sustainability in higher education. She has received several federal grant awards for integrating sustainability knowledge and skills into the curricula. Dr. LeHew served as Project Director on a multi-institutional grant to create a professional development program to enhance educators' understanding of climate change. She also teaches graduate courses related to sustainability.

Rachel LoMonaco-Benzing, Ph.D., is an NTT Assistant Professor in the Fashion School at Kent State University, Ohio, USA.

Sheng Lu, Ph.D., is an associate professor in the Department of Fashion and Apparel Studies at the University of Delaware, USA. Dr. Lu's research focuses on the economic and business aspects of the textile and apparel industry, including international trade, trade policy, and governance of the global apparel value chain.

Sara B. Marcketti, Ph.D., is director of the Center for Excellence in Learning and Teaching and professor in the Apparel, Events, and Hospitality Management Department, Iowa State University, USA. Co-authored books include *Survey of Historic Costume*, with Phyllis Tortora, and *Knock-it-Off: A History of Design Piracy*, with Jean Parsons. She is the recipient of the International Textile and Apparel Association Teaching Excellence Award and is a Fellow of the Costume Society of America.

Ellen McKinney, Ph.D., is associate professor in the Department of Apparel, Events, and Hospitality Management, Iowa State University, USA. Her work is primarily in creative and functional worn product design, with specializations in patternmaking, creative design process, and wearable technology. She also engages in cultural exchange through apparel design, expressed in written and design-based forms.

Pamela S. Norum, Ph.D. is professor and Department Chair in the Department of Textile and Apparel Management at the University of Missouri, USA.

Jean L. Parsons, Ph.D., is professor in the Department of Textile and Apparel Management at the University of Missouri, USA. A recognized scholar in both design and history, her research includes digital textile and apparel design and the history of the apparel industry. She is co-author of *20th Century Dress*, with Jane Farrell-Beck, and *Knock-it-Off: A History of Design Piracy*, with Sara Marcketti.

Kelly L. Reddy-Best, Ph.D., is an assistant professor in Apparel, Merchandising, and Design at Iowa State University, USA. In her research she examines the socio-cultural aspects of appearance, specifically the interrelationships of identity, clothing, and inequality for stigmatized populations. She teaches courses related to the social/psychological and cultural aspects of appearance.

Eulanda A. Sanders, Ph.D., is the Donna R. Danielson Professor of Textiles and Clothing at Iowa State University, USA. She is also the Department Chair of Apparel, Events, and Hospitality Management. Her scholarly activities are in the areas of apparel and textile design processes, fashion cultural studies, and wearable technology.

Hayley Warren is an industry professional who has worked with NGOs, academia, and businesses in Asia, Europe and the USA, promoting social responsibility and transparency within the textile industry. She holds a masters in CSR and BSc (Hons) in Business and Sociology.

Introduction: The Dangers of Fashion

Sara B. Marcketti and Elena E. Karpova

Fashion is often perceived as glamorous. A new pair of shoes, a dress, makeup and perfume can make someone feel like a million bucks (see Figure I.1). Many people follow the latest celebrities in their extraordinary and sometimes outlandish fashions as they walk down the red carpets. The creation of the newest fibers and manufacturing processes, while not overly exciting on the surface, can yield opportunities never before dreamed of—such as fabrics that stop bullets and materials that help premiere athletes excel to the next level. For all of us as fashion consumers, textile innovation can make everyday life easier by not requiring ironing your favorite shirt after laundry or having stain-resistant fabrics. But, if you are a follower of fashion, you undoubtedly also know about the dangers of fashion. The tragic loss of over 1,000 lives at the Rana Plaza collapse in Bangladesh in 2013 made public the dubious business practice of creating clothing in inhospitable and downright dangerous conditions (see Figure I.2).

Drawing on both historical and contemporary examples, the contributors to this book examine harmful and ethically uncertain aspects of the fashion industry and offer existing and potential innovative solutions for each stage of the clothing lifecycle, from design to consumption to disposal. From sweatshops to fur farming, from polluting chemicals to eating disorders, from painful garments to modern time slavery, the fashion industry has engaged in activities which have had devastating effects on workers, consumers, communities, and the planet. This ground-breaking volume provides a framework for examining the ethical, social, and environmental dangers that arise as fashion products are designed, manufactured, distributed, and sold within retail outlets, consumed, and then disposed of.

A team of twenty-two fashion and apparel experts presents original perspectives on a wide range of topics, drawing on academic research and industry practices. Through a wide range of chapters, authors analyze fashion's

Figure I.1 Fashion occurs on and off of the runway. Photo by Dominique Charriau/ WireImage/Getty Images.

Figure I.2 A commercial building named Rana Plaza in Dhaka, Bangladesh, collapsed on April 24, 2013. The search for the dead ended on May 13, 2013 with a death toll of 1,132. Photo by Zakir Hossain Chowdhury/Anadolu Agency/Getty Images

negative consequences for individuals, companies, societies, and the global community. *The Dangers of Fashion* highlights the industry's darker side and provides pointers for more sustainable practices for businesses, individual consumers, and communities that seek to redefine the meaning and role of fashion in contemporary society. Readers are encouraged to further ponder the examined controversies and solutions through case studies included in each chapter.

Part 1 of the book, "The Moral and Ethical Dangers of Fashion," introduces a framework of moral development and how it relates to the world of fashion, and proceeds to explore the beginning of the fashion cycle: the creation of materials and designs that set the tone for the entire fashion industry as well as the controversy associated with stealing designs. Fashion is said to reflect the times; however, anticipating or predicting the future is more critical than ever due to the impact that current fashion is having on the environment, resources, and our wellbeing.

Part 2, "The Dangers of Making Fashion," explores the manufacturing process of fashion. Chapters in this section include the journey of natural and man-made fibers throughout the supply chain, focusing primarily on climate change; the pros and cons of offshore domestic manufacturing; as well as the role of human trafficking and modern-day slavery in the creation of the cut-and-sewn apparel.

Part 3 examines the dangers of consuming fashion. It begins with a discussion of fashion appropriation and cultural insensitivity. Next, the personal physical and emotional costs of striving to fit into a fashion culture that highlights beauty ideals from a Western perspective are presented. The section concludes with a discussion of the physical pain individuals endure as a result of the pressure to follow prevailing beauty ideas.

Finally, Part 4 explores the dangers of caring for and disposing of fashion from a consumer perspective, and the economic, environmental, and social costs. It presents the less known dangers associated with recycling textiles. Strategies to minimize the dangers at the end of the life of your old fashion styles are discussed.

We hope that upon reading this book, you will gain greater knowledge of the controversies and complexities of the fashion industry. While fashion can be glamorous, fun, and ephemeral, it is also a trillion-dollar global business that can be impacted by the decisions of consumers and the individuals who enter the business to pursue careers as fashion buyers, sourcing managers, designers, entrepreneurs, and historians! You will learn how you can make a difference through your own consumption habits and by educating your friends and family.

Part One

The Moral and Ethical Dangers in Fashion

1

Moral Dilemmas in the Fashion Business

Jung E. Ha-Brookshire

To start with . . .

In many situations in our lives, there are conflicting views of a person's moral (or amoral) behavior. Even in a business setting, a decision that seems to be detrimental to one group may save the livelihood of many people in another place. Something that is nearly harmless at home could result in morally-challenging situations in other areas. Furthermore, not everyone, not every culture, and not every society has the same set of moral values to recognize, judge, and act upon in complex situations. Especially where business profits are emphasized, morality is difficult to find. Shirley Anita Chisholm was an American politician, educator, and author who noted that "When morality comes up against profit, it is seldom that profit loses." This highlights the perception that, somehow, when we become business professionals, our morality loses out to profits. Is that a universal truth?

Given that the fashion industry is so widespread and involves so many people, from top executives of global brands to factory workers, professionals in the industry face many morally-challenging situations. For example, a model agency may encourage fashion models to stay thin even if it physically harms their bodies. A designer may take a company sample home without paying or telling others. An apparel buyer may have to work with factories that do not pay the workers on time because of the low costs the factory offers. A retail buyer may issue a chargeback to the vendors (or ask the vendor to give money back to the retail buyer) for mistakes that are not even the fault of the vendor. Are these all examples of bad behavior? To answer this question, one has to consider the boundaries of such behavior and evaluate the moral consequences.

Morality refers to principles related to right or wrong and good or bad behavior (Merriam-Webster, 2017). People start developing their morality from their childhood years via social learning; they do so by experiencing different stages of moral reasoning and moral behavior (Blasi, 1983). Lawrence Kohlberg (1987), an American psychologist, proposed that humans experience six stages of moral development. At each stage, people are able to judge different levels of good or bad, and act accordingly. Although his theory mainly focuses on children's development stages of moral development, this theory can also be applied to the moral development of professionals learning new workplace principles or norms. Indeed, many professions have their own codes of conduct, and college students or young professionals are required to learn discipline-specific principles and norms. So, what happens if business professionals are not morally sound and not able to make morally sound decisions? Other people would get hurt and suffer from such bad decisions. US buyers' decisions may negatively affect factory workers' lives. Retail buyers' chargeback decisions may hurt the vendor's financial performance. The next section explains the different stages of moral development which business professionals could experience while they are going through different stages of their careers.

Growing your morality

Kohlberg (1987) is one of the key psychologists who came up with the three levels and six stages of moral development that we all go through as we grow up. Level 1 can be described as pre-conventional. At this level, you just follow moral rules set by others. That is, moral rules and expectations are given to you and you must follow the rules. You don't have to figure out what the good or bad behavior is because the decision is already made for you by your parents or others. Level 2 is called conventional. At this level, you are now able to internalize the expectations that others have for you. That is, you are aware of and expected to follow their rules and you are motivated to do so because you do not want to upset your community. Finally, level 3 is called post-conventional. At this level, your own moral rules and what others expect from you are clearly distinguished. If these two are not consistent, you would be able to challenge others' rules and try to change their rules for the greater community. More specific descriptions of each of Kohlberg's levels follow below.

Stage 1: Do what you are told!

Stage 1 is called heteronomous morality. What that means is that, what is right or wrong is defined by people who have authority and power over you. For example, parents hold authority on moral issues over children; or, senior executives do so over a first-year associate at work. In this case, moral rules are not the products of collaboration with others; rather, they are given to the individual from the outside or from above. In this light, certain actions are completely good or completely bad in an absolute sense, depending on who performs the actions. At this stage, you are not or cannot be involved in constructing or developing your own moral rules.

In a business setting, we could see this level of moral judgment in a brand new employee. In the following example, Peter is a new employee and Max is his immediate supervisor. Because Peter has no prior experience in the field or in the company, Peter may seek all cues and norms from his supervisor. Max told Peter, "Do what you are told." To Peter, Max is the authority, so whatever Max does is right. For example, Peter saw Max accept a $500 gift card from a vendor. Peter didn't ask Max if it was appropriate to do so. Instead, Peter accepts Max's behavior as right and, therefore, Peter would also accept similar gift cards from other vendors. In this situation, one might say that Peter's behavior is morally challenging; however, Peter does not regard it as such because rules are made by "adults"—in this case, Max and other senior executives. Peter is simply following the rules. At this stage, Peter's morality could be said to be in its infant stage, without any thoughts or reasoning behind his actions. However, Peter's behavior, accepting a gift card in exchange for a favor for vendors, could perpetuate corruption and non-transparent transactions in business settings.

Stage 2: Let's make a deal!

In stage 2, you are now able to gain the social perspective of other individuals. Kohlberg (1987) thought that a person at this stage can understand that others have their own interests and desires, and these are as important and valid as your own interests and desires. Therefore, you now realize that other people may have different rules guiding their moral (or amoral) judgment, so you may have to solve conflicting interests between you and others. One way to tackle this problem is to come up with a reciprocal exchange agreement, such as "Let's make a deal," "If you scratch my back, I will scratch yours," or "If you get away with it, I should get away with it, too." In this case, there is no intrinsic value in good and bad. Rather, by exchanging equal goods or values, both the self and the others' needs and desires are satisfied in performing good or bad behavior (see Figure 1.1).

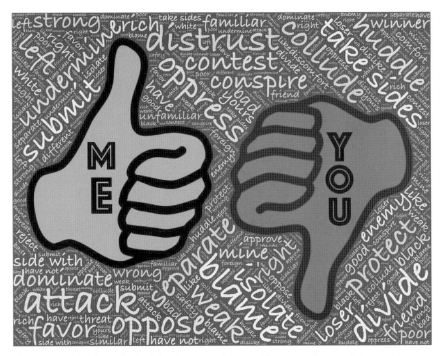

Figure 1.1 Making a deal with others to achieve self-interest is one of the main characteristics in stage 2 of moral development. Source: https://pixabay.com/illustrations/me-you-selfish-contest-compare-1767683/.

We can readily encounter examples of stage 2 in a fashion business setting. For example, Sally has been in the workplace for a few months and noticed another employee, Jenny, taking a fairly expensive Italian leather jacket sample home without anyone's approval. Sally asked Jenny if she could take one, too, and Jenny responded, "Let's make a deal. Why don't you take one, too, since I am taking one." Sally thought that was a good exchange in that she gets to have a jacket she loves, and Jenny also gets one that she wanted. If Sally's moral reasoning level had been at stage 1, she would have just followed Jenny's behavior and taken the sample without even asking. At this stage, Sally at least questioned Jenny's behavior; yet, her solution to this situation was to take another sample to have an equal transaction without contemplating the consequences of this action. Therefore, at this stage, Sally's morality can be said to be individualistic and does not extend beyond the boundaries of Sally herself. In Sally's mind, taking samples home does not pose a moral dilemma.

However, if all at work behave like Sally, then such a work environment could become dangerous because it would be made up of people who only think about their own interests. Taking a garment sample or even paper clips from the workplace seems harmless. However, using company real estate or vehicles for personal vacations is a misuse of company resources. When business professionals travel all over the world without close oversight via expense reporting systems, the result may be more challenging situations that require a more advanced level of problem evaluation.

Stage 3: Be nice to others!

At stage 3, your perspective is now extended to other people with whom you have relationships. This makes stage 3 the first part of level 2, in that social and community expectations affect your moral decisions. For example, when you meet with someone else and form a relationship, or "coupleship," you now operate with shared expectations and norms, which might be different from those of your own. For example, as a good person within the coupleship, you are expected to be faithful, loyal, altruistic, and committed to the other person, beyond being a good person in yourself. This is the stage of "Be nice and kind and then you will get along with others" (Rest, 1983). Hence, researchers refer to this stage as interpersonal normative morality.

Such couple-like relationships can also be found in business settings. For example, Janell and Lauren used to be colleagues in a business and recently founded a new start-up fashion company called Imagine. Janell has expertise in fashion business management while Lauren is known for her creativity. Before forming this new business, even when they worked together as colleagues, they did not have to watch each other's work schedules or work ethics. As co-owners of Imagine, they now realize that they must create new norms or expectations of the partnership to ensure that they are equally committed to the success of the new company.

To accomplish this, they discussed basic norms such as: 1) neither will look for another job or business opportunity as long as they are a co-owner; 2) they will be in the office at least four days a week in the morning to discuss new developments or business options; and 3) when meeting vendors or buyers, each must consider what the other would do before making any big decisions. Once these expectations were set, Janell and Lauren tried their best to honor these commitments as a good partner should do. At this stage, the coupleship expectations become the guiding principles of a new partnership. Any behavior that violates these expectations, such as looking for another partner without telling the other or making buying decisions without checking with the partner, are considered to be bad behavior.

There are many real-life business examples of partnerships breaking up or of the separation of personnel due to non-loyal behavior by the membership. There are many instances of CEOs resigning because of unacceptable or amoral behavior such as sexual harassment, covering up accidents, or even faking accounting books. When violations of interpersonal expectations within a company occur, the company could be in a dangerous moral position.

Stage 4: Morality becomes laws!

At stage 4, the coupleship boundary goes beyond friends or family. Morality now rules the whole society, which includes all who share general social institutions. In this case, moral norms are not just set by those who have close relationships, as in a partnership, but rather by legal codes, so they apply to all people within society, impartially. At this stage, the rights and obligations of social members as described in legal codes are equal before the law, and the sense of duty, loyalty, and faithfulness is not only applied to each other, but also to the entire society. At the same time, all citizens have a debt to society by virtue of participating in social institutions and receiving benefits from society. Therefore, "everyone is obligated and protected by the law" at this stage (Rest, 1983). Therefore you now have to make moral decisions based on the philosophy that your actions must meet all social standards and rules.

In a business setting, the moral expectations of stage 4 can be found in professional codes or employee handbooks. For example, Janell and Lauren's partnership grew and now they have more than fifty employees at Imagine. It is now much harder to control all employees' behavior but both partners want commitment and loyalty from all their staff. So, they created an employee handbook as a code of conduct for Imagine. This handbook clearly states that employees shall not accept any gift worth more than $100. It also states that the $100 limit applies to all employees and that any violations of this rule would be taken into account in employee performance evaluations. Peter, who thought Max's receipt of a $500 gift card from a vendor was good behavior, now operates under the rule that clearly states that accepting such a card is bad behavior. At the same time, because of the same rule, Peter feels it is morally safe to receive a gift to the value of $99. Therefore, receipt of a $99 gift card is not a moral dilemma, but a $101 gift card could be morally challenging to Peter because of the employee code of conduct. Peter is exercising "social system morality" (Lapsley, 1996, p. 71).

At this stage, public laws are very important for individuals' moral judgment. However, when such laws are not clear or not present, danger could emerge. For example, a sourcing manager, Kristen, noticed one of her textile mills in a developing country emitted dark smoke fumes into the air and that there was dirty water full of colorants surrounding the building. She consulted the handbook and code of conduct to see if it was acceptable to do business with this sort of factory. She found no guidance. She also checked if the textile mill was operating within the local environmental laws, but she found no legal regulations regarding what factories should or should not do. Therefore, despite her personal concerns about the environment near the mill, she did not raise any issues with the owner of the mill. The business carried on as usual. If all sourcing professionals were to make decisions in the way Kristen did, we would have justifiable concerns about the consequences for the local environment.

Stage 5: Fight for others!

At stage 5, you are able to differentiate between social norms and your own norms. When social norms or legal codes do not meet your own standards, such as Kristen experienced at stage 4, you now have the ability to criticize existing laws and social norms and ask "Is it right or moral?" At this stage, you seek to create new rules and policies to ensure that your principles are extended to all members of society and communities, upholding equal rights and being sensitive to social welfare needs. This stage is markedly different from stage 4, in which your goal was to follow existing codes or rules. At stage 5, you want to achieve the ultimate goal of an acceptable quality of life and liberty, and if existing rules and norms do not help to achieve that goal, you are willing to challenge that situation. This is why Kohlberg describes the focus of this stage as "human rights and social welfare morality" (Lapsley, 1996, p. 71). If Kristen had had the ability to process moral judgment at stage 5, she would have challenged the lack of relevant policies in the company handbook and the lack of local laws in order to develop new solutions to deal with factories that disregard the natural environment.

We often see people exercising this level of morality. In the fashion manufacturing industry, workers boycott or protest in order to change their working conditions or receive compensation. They often demand safer working conditions, better benefits, and even to have a voice in company rule-making. People who support such protests are concerned with equal rights, self-worth, and the dignity of all employees. For these people, to see others working for extremely low wages or in an unsafe environment poses a moral dilemma. However, people who have not developed to stage 5 may not find such situations to be morally challenging. For example, Kristen did not question the environmental harm done by the textile mill. If you are trained to focus on the "bottom line" and to ignore anything that does not directly contribute to the company's financial profits, poor working conditions would not present themselves as a moral issue. This is where other companies, human rights groups, and the general public detect gaps in such companies' moral standards and do not hesitate to criticize them for this failing.

Disagreements between workers and company executives are important elements in making progress. Without protests, demands, questions, and dialogue, rules remain unchanged and communities see no improvement. In the case in question, the concerns of workers or of Kristen could trigger a process that would lead to the establishment of new rules or laws to protect basic rights and improve conditions. People in the community must be encouraged to be part of new rule-making processes (Rest, 1983). Without this type of development, businesses might retain poor working conditions and low wages for their employees and continue to pollute the environment with dirty water and harmful emissions.

Stage 6: Fair to all!

The final stage, stage 6, is characterized as the moral point of view. That is, at this stage, you would be able to gain and integrate various perspectives into a self-reflective mode and be able to judge from the point of view of others. For example, when facing new morally challenging situations, you would be able to imagine yourself in a hypothetical situation and be able to discuss and evaluate that situation from other people's perspective. The objective is to come up with rules that will be fair and just to all people affected by the situation. Kohlberg said that this was the stage in which a person exercises prescriptive role-taking in order to test the validity of decision-making. This is the stage when the philosophy of "Treat others as ends in themselves and not as means to an end" (Lapsley, 1996, p. 75) is paramount in your moral decision-making. Universal justice and maximum utility (the greatest good for the greater number) are the guiding principles of moral reasoning. Kohlberg and his colleagues (1990) later pointed out that sympathy is one of the key components in making moral judgment, as it requires a true understanding of individuals and their physical and mental condition. Stage 6 is the final stage of moral development, an achievement that would not be possible without sympathy and an awareness of all perspectives (see Figure 1.2).

Suppose that Devonte is a sourcing manager at a major retailer, and there was unrest at the Cambodian factory he has been working with for several years:

Figure 1.2 How to devise the best way to satisfying everyone's needs and wants is a complicated and challenging task. Source: https://pixabay.com/illustrations/conflict-conflict-lens-lenses-1458437/.

workers were demanding better pay and better working conditions. Devonte's company executives were not interested in hearing about the workers' demands because they believed they were operating according to the law in terms of the pay rates offered to factory workers for garment orders and were also following the company's code of conduct (notice that this refers to stage 4). Therefore, as far as the executives were concerned, there was no moral dilemma and the business decisions they had made were entirely appropriate. Devonte understands this point of view because he is aware of the pressure on the executives to satisfy shareholder demands for higher profits in the short term.

However, Devonte also feels that the code of conduct does not address key problems at the factory level and that the retailer's payments to the factory are not sufficient to pay higher wages to workers and allow them a decent lifestyle, even if the wages are in accordance with the law. Thus, even though the sourcing decision is in line with company practice, Devonte faces a moral dilemma between profits and workers' lives, and he wonders what can be done to solve this dilemma (Devonte is now at stage 5). When addressing this problem, he tries to imagine what it would be like to live on such pay and work in such a factory, and he feels compelled to help the workers during their strike.

By assessing both sides' position and views, Devonte came up with a new proposal. He calculated the costs of finding and working with new factories. He also calculated the operating loss as well as the potential damage to the retailer's reputation because of the workers' protests. After assessing both costs, he proposed to work with this one factory on a long-term basis. This proposal would save his company approximately 5 percent of the total cost of goods sold due to having a committed workforce and no switch costs incurred. He also proposed that the savings be shared with the factory workers. He believed his solution would please his executives as the company would bear no additional costs while factory workers would benefit from their share of the savings. To reach this point, Devonte had to think about both the executives' and the workers' lives. In other words, he had to operate his moral reasoning in line with stage 6 of our process. Devonte definitely did more than Kristen, who was at stage 4, and more than a person at stage 5. He participated in making new rules based on his ability to empathize with both the factory workers and the company executives, resulting in solutions that would satisfy both groups. Without people like Devonte, danger will remain in the global fashion industry where many conflicts still exist.

Now what?

This chapter has shows that we all are learning and still in the development stage in terms of morality. Moral decision-making is not simply something you learn as a child and stop learning at the age of ten. We all continue to learn well into our professional lives. What is interesting is that depending on the level of one's moral ability, individuals may experience different moral reactions to the same event. In this chapter, Peter, Janell, Lauren, Sally, Jenny, Kristen, and Devonte made their business decisions at different moral stages, in which the scope of moral dilemmas were identified and evaluated in different ways. The type of dilemma that Devonte addressed was much more complex and difficult than that which faced Sally questioned. As we grow within our professions, we will continue to learn what is right or wrong in different situations.

In the fashion industry, professionals face various morally uncertain situations. Some are as simple as taking paper clips from the company without permission. Others are as complex as whether to reduce unnecessary waste and consumption in the world. It is difficult to navigate such a world when we all have different levels of moral judgment and standards. That being the case, sometimes certain acts are perceived to be right while at other times they are not.

Therefore, rather than rushing to judgment on who or which company is (a)moral, (un)ethical, or (ir)responsible, perhaps we should consider why this person or that company made a certain decision at that point in time and whether there are any signs that the person or the company has learned from their mistakes. It behoves us to bear in mind the specific context of any morally questionable situation and to suggest solutions for the future. Rather than reach a simple verdict that those in question are either without fault or are evil incarnate, we should evaluate each situation carefully as part of the learning process in which we are all engaged. It is important here that all of us, whether company representatives or professionals, grow and learn by experiencing the type situations depicted in this chapter. Sometimes, as Shirley Chisholm pointed out, morality will lose to profits. However, the hope is that we all apply the highest level of morality throughout our professional careers so that morality eventually trumps profits, without any dilemma.

References

Blasi, A. "The self and cognition: The role of the self in the acquisition of knowledge and the role of cognition in the development of the self." In B. Lee and G. Noam *Psychosocial Theories of the Self*, pp. 189–213. New York: Plenum, 1983.

Kohlberg, L. "The development of moral judgement and moral action." In L. Kohlberg (ed.), *Child Psychology and Childhood Education: A Cognitive Developmental View*, pp. 259–328. New York: Longman, 1987.

Kohlberg, L., Boyd, D., and Levine, C. "The return of Stage 6: Its principle and moral point of view." In T. Wren (ed.), *The Moral Domain: Essays in the Ongoing Discussion between Philosophy and the Social Sciences*, pp. 151–81. Cambridge, MA: MIT Press, 1990.

Lapsley, D. K. *Moral Psychology*. Boulder, CO: Westview Press, 1996.

Merriam-Webster (2017). "Moral." https://www.merriam-webster.com/dictionary/moral.

Rest, J. "Morality." In P. Mussen (ed.), *Handbook of Child Psychology*, 4th edn., vol. 3, J. Flavell and E. Markman (eds.), *Cognitive Development*, pp. 556–628. New York: Wiley, 1983.

2

Sustainability Must Drive Design

Elizabeth Bye

Fashion reflects the values, resources, and culture of a society during a given period, thus the roles and responsibilities of a fashion designer change over time. Designers understand the process of making a garment that meets the physical and emotional needs of a consumer and promotes a successful business. They are critical to making decisions that drive industry practices and consumer behavior. Though awareness about the environment and quality of life on earth has been a concern for decades, our society is beginning to address sustainability issues in more deliberate and committed actions. As a result, fashion designers must consider people, planet, and profit from local and global perspectives when making choices about their work. Design is increasingly moving towards positive change, offering a perspective that considers global impact rather than just an individual's desire.

History of designing fashion

Fashion styles and the way fashion is produced have evolved with new technology and a more democratic social structure. Historically, royalty and the wealthy used fashion to convey their status. Fabric and clothing were valuable assets. For example, trade along the Silk Road or cotton production in the early textile mills built national economies and wealth for many.

Prior to the Industrial Revolution, clothing was made in the home, including weaving fabric or knitting garments. The position of "fashion designer" did not exist. However, with a society growing in wealth, the original couturiers, including Charles Worth and Paul Poiret, introduced haute couture in the nineteenth century and developed new methods of design, business, and promotion (Bye, 2010). Their clientele were the wealthy who could afford the materials, attention to detail, and service that insured their status. Industrialization created employment opportunities outside the home and a reduction in the effort required to clothe a family. By the mid-nineteenth century the ability to purchase ready-made fabrics contributed to a growing interest in fashion. Paris fashion magazines and fashion dolls were popular, and women eagerly waited for news of the latest styles that they could make at home or have made by a local dressmaker.

The role of the early Paris couturiers was to dictate fashionable details and silhouettes. In addition to private appointments, they presented shows to clients and buyers. Clients typically did not generate enough income to support the business, so couturiers sold toiles of their designs that could be copied or reinterpreted by another manufacturer.

Paris haute couture was considered the driver and pinnacle of fashion until the mid-twentieth century, surviving though great political and economic change. Women's lifestyles and fashions began to change dramatically in the 1960s as more women worked outside the home. A growing and influential youth culture that was more open, casual, and political contributed to new ideas about fashion. Ready-to-wear fashion grew in demand, affordability, and originality. The job of fashion designer emerged from those who started by copying couture toiles. Stylists considered what the average women wanted to wear and designed with a more modern, casual sensibility. These new designers presented an original point of view that supported the acceptance and growth of the ready-to-wear industry. Designers including Mary Quant, Kenzo Takada, and Issey Miyake along with Halston, Stephan Borrows, and Anne Klein, were accepted in Paris, but shared a more global, wearable vision of fashion. The role of the new fashion designer was to produce fashion that was modern, affordable, and met the needs of a rapidly changing society.

Though accessibility to our mass-produced fashions is much more democratic than haute couture, the true cost of that accessibility is not equally shared. Today, most textiles and apparel are considered disposable, as they are considered inexpensive to produce and do not hold long-term worth. There has been economic pressure on designers and manufacturers to produce fashion faster and cheaper under a relentless demand for new ideas and innovation (Fletcher, 2014). The motivation to purchase is rarely to replace an item that is worn out or to invest in an object of value. Many designers are disillusioned by the drive to produce profitable designs quickly and cheaply. There is little time to consider the needs of the person wearing the garment or make decisions about the materials, production, care, and afterlife of the garment. There is also little time to encourage the development of truly innovative ideas.

Historically, the average person had a small wardrobe that was worn repeatedly, for many occasions, and repaired so that the garments were serviceable for an extended time. Garments could be remade as fashions or bodies changed or were repurposed for other products. In the early twenty-first century, the average person has a rather large wardrobe, though this varies according to an individual's budget. Fashion is available at multiple price points and the fashion cycle has increased from two to four collections a year to a demand for new fashion every few days. Fast fashion has made clothing disposable, and created a pattern of overconsumption that we cannot maintain (Fletcher, 2014). Closets are huge yet still overflow, and we wear only 20 percent of what we own. With the average American producing over 80 lbs. of textile waste a year, the search for novelty must change. Current levels of consumption have a negative impact on our environment and the quality of life for those making fashion and those consuming fashion.

Countertrends to overconsumption

While many fashion businesses support this pattern of overconsumption, grassroots responses are gaining strength and visibility. Consumerism was a rising trend in the 1950s as a growing middle class wanted new products to enhance the quality of their lives. There was little concern about any negative implications from this trend. However, in response to emerging concerns about pollution and our collective impact on nature the Hippie movement promoted the concept of "love mother earth" and celebrated the first Earth Day on April 22, 1970. Sustainability is not a trend or a countertrend, but the adoption of practices that result in "development that meets the needs of the present without compromising the ability of future generations to meet their own needs" (World Commission on Environment and Development, 1987). Expanding our frame of reference from the notion of pollution to our current understanding of sustainability has advanced the urgency of our responses as designers.

Slow fashion is related to a trend called voluntary simplicity, which is an approach to life where individuals choose to live with few material objects. Slow fashion has emerged as a practice in response to fast fashion and the rapid pace of pursuing the next new fashion trend. Individuals who embrace slow fashion value knowing where materials originate and how the garment is made; knowing that workers are fairly paid and safe from human rights violations; knowing that clothing is of high quality; and knowing that environmentally friendly care and disposal is part of the design (Fletcher, 2014). With a focus on sharing responsibility for the earth's resources, the idea of the quality of a fashion product over the quantity is gaining acceptance. Eileen Fisher is committed to sustainability with the goal of becoming 100 percent sustainable by 2020. In addition to timeless, classic designs, they are increasing use of sustainable, organic fibers and natural dyes, and have started a take back program to promote a circular business model, designing ways to include the discarded garments into new designs.

Two increasingly important elements of garment quality are also in response to the disposable nature of fashion and the trend towards global homogeneous design. Emotional attachment to a garment and the location in which it is made or purchased seem to give fashion a personality or heirloom qualities, making it worthy of investment and special care.

Fashion that is designed or encourages an individual to create value and meaning in a garment is likely to be kept for a long time. The meaning in a wedding dress, a lucky shirt, or a military uniform is clearly understood and is strong justification for saving and caring for such pieces. Some people might have a favorite garment that they refuse to give up, continuing to wear it for years while other items are easily disposed. There are a variety of reasons for this that range from it being a memorable gift or something purchased with a first pay check, to a piece that makes someone feel confident every time they wear it (DeLong et al., 2013). How can designers influence similar feelings of attachment in garments that do not have an obvious emotional connection? Custom-made garments or those made with consumer input through technologies such as co-design and mass-customization are likely to create a stronger attachment because they are designed specifically for an individual. The experience of purchasing a garment, including great customer service or careful fitting, may also build attachment.

A distinct location or origin provides uniqueness, authenticity, and meaning to a garment. There is a disappointing amount of homogeneity in fashion around the world; however, the movement to buy local products is a countertrend to that sameness. Building a connection to place celebrates a unique culture that has meaning for local and visiting consumers (DeLong et al., 2013).

An interest in do-it-yourself projects has inspired many consumers to upcycle or redesign garments that may have once been disposed of without a second thought. Local classes and tutorials on social media provide directions and inspiration to turn a dated formal gown into a chic cocktail dress, or a man's dress shirt into a baby romper. Fashion swaps connect people to trade unwanted garments and often have sewing machines and advice for simple alterations.

During these events, it quickly becomes evident which garments have been designed for easy alterations, and which are not worth the time. This is an opportunity for designers to provide custom, individualized services to those who may not be able to imagine and construct a new garment.

The tenets of slow fashion translate into the accepted understanding that to have the most impact on overall sustainability, reducing the amount of clothing that we purchase and extending the useful life of our garments are the best practices. However, this does not mean an end to fashion. Change is the very nature of fashion. While the idea of sustainable fashion once recalled images of beige, shapeless, serviceable garments, now sustainable fashion is trend setting and chic. Innovators including Stella McCartney, Yvon Chouinard, the founder of Patagonia, Livia Firth, the founder of Eco-Age, Tyson Toussant, the co-founder of Bionic Yarn, and Hannah Jones, chief sustainability officer at Nike Inc. are at the forefront of developing sustainable best practices for the fashion industry (Talbot, 2017). For example, working with partners outside the apparel field can produce valuable interdisciplinary solutions. Patagonia was the first company to move to 100-percent organic cotton by working with farmers and scientists to develop new agricultural processes and was the first to make fleece using recycled bottles. McCartney is partnering with Bolt Threads to produce a new protein fiber, similar to spider silk, that is biodegradable (Shilling, 2017). Leading by example, Firth wears recycled, upcycled, vintage, and worn-out fashion on the "red carpet" as part of her Green Carpet Challenge.

On a local scale, the slow fashion movement may foster smaller, independent fashion companies that support local economies and diversify choice (Jung and Jin, 2013). On a more global scale, it will take a committed fashion industry and committed consumers to impact the multifaceted challenges of sustainability. However, it is the designer who has the most control, opportunity, and duty to innovate and move fashion in a new direction.

These grassroots countertrends have occurred on a relatively individual, small scale, creating awareness and encouraging consumers to act, though the overall impact has been limited. Collective collaboration on a global scale, from all facets of the textile and fashion industry, is needed to shift the current industry paradigm. The Sustainable Apparel Coalition (SAC) developed a standardized supply chain measurement tool, the Higg Index. Designers can use this tool to measure the impact of their design and supply chain decisions to move towards best practices. The index does not provide solutions but encourages companies to set measurable standards and goals. For example, are products designed to include the identification of each individual material type so they can be separated for end of use recycling streams? To comply, designers can select materials that are easier to recycle, such as fabrics made from 100 percent of the same fiber, polyester zippers, or sustainable buttons.

Another effort is the GFA, www.globalfashionagenda.com/, a platform to share and promote industry standards on fashion sustainability. They support a new economy where fashion is designed differently, worn longer, and recycled and reused more often. GFA has called for a commitment to accelerate the transition to a circular fashion system. One partner developed designforlongevity.com as a toolbox with stories, best practices, and access to helpful tools for designers

Regardless of the sustainable best practices that a company uses, consumers must want to buy fashions produced by a company, which needs to make a profit. What will be the role of fashion designers as the twenty-first-century paradigm of sustainable fashion unfolds? How can they design products that meet multiple, and often contradictory, environmental, social, and economic demands while pleasing consumers and fulfilling their own need for expression and creativity?

The sustainability-driven designer

The fashion designer's role is to be both the creative leader and a problem solver. The term 'multidimensional designer' describes designers with diverse interests outside of fashion. Interests might range from writing to science, or coding to film, and often enhance the designer's main job. These broad, fresh points of view are essential to creating the future.

Starting with framing the concept, the fashion designer touches almost every step of the process to bring fashion to the consumer. Depending on the scale of the business, it is likely that the designer will be working with a team from across the company with a variety of expertise and resources to support a common goal. Understanding the company's priorities and developing a strategy to move those forward is essential. Independent designers or small companies usually have a mission to guide their decision-making; however, their access to research and resources is generally more limited. Sustainable design can be achieved in many ways, though the choices are not always clear.

The designer's daily focus is on the visual and functional details of a garment, fabric choices, production and quality, and evaluating how the garment fits the model. Once a garment has been approved for production, it moves out of the designer's area of responsibility. This is a narrow focus given the far-reaching impact of many design decisions. Independent designers or small companies have more control over the full process, and can often talk directly to customers and see them wearing the garments. There is growing interest in helping all designers think beyond the next deadline and consider the "product life cycle." Of interest is how the consumer wears and cares for a garment and what happens to it once they are ready to dispose of it. A closed loop or circular model for the fashion industry means developing a strategy that extends the useful life of garments, and then recovers the materials to make new products when the garment has exceeded its useful life. A closed loop vision must start with design, both individual garment designs and the design of macro systems that support a full circular model.

The vast options to support more sustainable design decisions can be overwhelming. Currently, there is no one model or checklist for designing sustainable, circular fashion. The Ellen MacArthur Foundation and IDEO have developed a Circular Design Guide intended to use the design process to imagine circular solutions to a variety of product and service categories ("Circular Design Thinking," n.d.). Designers are encouraged to build feedback loops into their work, know the life cycle of materials, partner with interdisciplinary stakeholders, and, as with all design, consider unintentional outcomes. The first point is to expand our view of the user. Who else might benefit from the product or system in addition to the initial consumer? For example, Nike recycles shoes and then sells the Grind material to surface playgrounds. The second point is to reimagine viability by looking beyond our own ability to reuse materials to partner with someone who will also reap added value. When wool is cleaned and processed, fiber for new textiles may be the priority, but the lanolin by-product is used in lotions and creams. Design for evolution is the third point and encourages designers to think beyond a "finished" product. What could that pair of jeans become? To change society's mindset, designers must build a strong narrative and share prototypes of possible innovations ("Circular Design Thinking," n.d.) The stories about the life-saving properties of a Mylar blanket can be hard to believe until one experiences the warmth. Solutions come from many perspectives and change as new processes and technologies develop. Prioritizing change based on a company's goals and their unique consumer will have the most positive impact.

Sustainable design strategies

Designers are faced with the challenges and opportunities presented from the current thinking that reducing the amount of clothing we purchase and extending its useful life are the practices best positioned to make the industry more sustainable. Materials, patterns, fit, assembly and use, care, and disposal are factors of our current system that can be improved on a micro level, and as a possible step towards full circular design. Designers must be aware of all the variables, know enough to ask questions, and actively collaborate with specialized experts to make the best possible decisions. For example, a designer can't meet consumer demand for the most popular organic cotton T-shirts. Will consumers be just as likely to purchase and be satisfied if they change the fabric to 50 percent organic cotton/50 percent recycled polyester?

Materials

As the main component of a fashion product, the selection of materials is paramount in designing sustainable fashion. While there is debate over the impact of using natural or synthetic fibers, there is no clear choice. Quality that supports longevity, performance, and appearance retention along with cost are key factors for consumers. Care requirements bring in another factor, as use and care of a garment is considered to have the most environmental impact across the life cycle. Finally, a closed loop model requires that there is a cost-effective way to recover the fibers and convert them into new products.

One of the main challenges with closed loop fiber recovery is that materials made of blended fibers, for example cotton and polyester, or cotton and spandex, are hard to separate and recover. Other promising technologies are finding ways to improve the quality and feel of short recycled cotton and wool fibers. New processes for dyeing and finishing that reduce water usage are being explored, and new biological fibers are being developed that are 100 percent biodegradable. For example, Natsai Audrey Chieza is a bio-artist who created a collection of textiles using dyes that come from bacteria. Modern Meadow is using protein collagen to produce bio-fabricated leather (Schilling, 2017). Designers need to seek out these innovations.

Textiles require a range of chemical finishes that can impact sustainability by improving performance and longevity. Color, stain resistant, self-cleaning, antimicrobial, and anti-static finishes serve a valuable purpose, though may contribute to environment and health risks, and prevent closed loop recycling. So, there are choices to be made that are not always clear. For example, is it more sustainable to use a self-cleaning finish that will reduce laundering, or does the application and afterlife of the self-cleaning finish cause more environmental harm?

Designers need an intimate knowledge of textiles and must be able to translate textile testing results and specifications into the quality factors that consumers value. Tear strength, shrinkage, pilling, and colorfastness tests are examples of quality measures that provide a level of longevity, performance, and appearance retention for each garment. For example, consider the difference between a pair of workman's jeans and a pair of fashion jeans. The specifications and requirements for the denim would be very different depending on the end use.

Patterns, fit, and assembly

In the process of bringing a two-dimensional sketch to life as a three-dimensional garment, the vision of the designer drives the technical design team. The sample patternmaker must understand the designer's intent in terms of silhouette, proportion, details, and fit. An experienced patternmaker can offer suggestions on placement of seams, details, and shaping that will preserve the visual intent of the designer while making sure the garment can be cut to minimize material waste and easily run through production. Three-dimensional computer aided design (CAD) systems offer a new approach to sample making. Patterns can be "sewn" digitally and fit on a digital avatar to create a 3D virtual sample (see Figure 2.1). The avatar can be the scan of an individual customer or the company's fit model. The potential to save time and resources is great as the need to make actual samples is reduced.

Some designers have explored the concept of zero waste in their designs. Draped and wrapped garments such as the sari are historically zero waste. The approach uses every possible part of the material so that there are no scraps to contribute to the average 15 percent cutting waste that ends up in landfills. This is achieved by reconfiguring pattern shapes and putting them back together like a puzzle. Though the concept may work well for smaller manufacturers, it has not been embraced by mass producers as styles tend to be avant-garde and more difficult to size. Another approach to zero waste is knit garments that are fully fashioned, meaning every garment is knit to size and design. There are no fabric scraps.

Though not zero waste, garments can be made from digitally printed fabrics where the printing is engineered to the shape and scale required. This greatly reduces the amount of dyeing and finishing required, and is thus more sustainable than cutting patterns from yards of printed fabric.

Most companies have standardized block patterns and size specifications to guide the patternmaking and grading process, and insure fit quality. To address

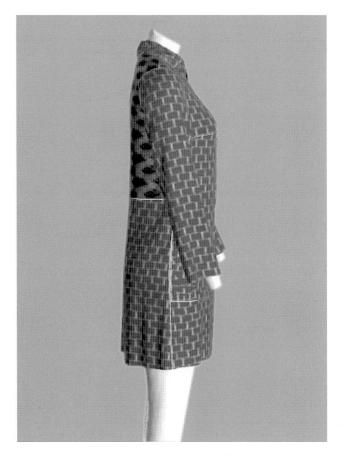

Figure 2.1 3D virtual sample, *c.* 2017. Courtesy Rachel V. Meyers.

longevity goals, garments can be engineered so alterations and repairs are easy to do. This might require wider seam allowances, more generous hems, different seam types, or a change in assembly procedures. A superimposed seam with a one-inch allowance, or a sleeve set in the round rather than flat allow for easy alterations. Some choices will be more expensive, so there needs to be a way to share this added value with the consumer. Adjustable options for waistlines or lengths can support greater longevity, and children's garments often incorporate growth features. Historically, men's shirts were designed with detachable collars for ease of laundering and replacement as they tend to be the first areas to show signs of wear. This practice may be valuable again as we try to design for longevity.

Good fit is challenging for many consumers. Fashionable knitwear and woven fabrics with spandex have eased some fitting issues. However, one of the most common reasons for discarding undamaged garments is that they no longer fit (Bye and McKinney, 2007). If consumers were able to purchase garments that fit well, either off the rack with alterations or custom fit, would they be willing to spend more money and take care of their investment? The technology needed for digital custom fitting has been developing over the past forty years, but is still not at a level needed for mass customization. There is such great variety in the human body that for consumers to expect that a garment will fit well "off-the-rack" is a real misperception. Consumer expectations would also need to adapt to customized garments, as there will be a wait for the garment rather than immediately availability.

Use, care, and disposal

The use, care, and disposal of our garments have the most environmental impact of any part of the product life cycle, as discussed in other chapters in this book. The size and flexibility of our wardrobes, how we launder and maintain our garments, and what we do with garments we no longer want are ingrained in our daily behavior. Even though consumers may be aware of the most sustainable choices, our behaviors are difficult to change. What choices can a designer make that will encourage more consumer best practices?

Having a wardrobe with great variety can make it a challenge to put together outfits. We only wear a fraction of our wardrobes, forgetting what we have in the back of the closet, and even having garments with sales tags that we have never worn. Testimonials from consumers who have edited their wardrobes to the pieces that they love, that fit well, that work together, and are well made report greater satisfaction with the way they look, less stress, and an overall freedom from the constant problem of having "nothing to wear" (Roes, 2013). Shifting the consumer's mindset to purchase a small number of well-made garments rather than a large variety of fast fashion is difficult, but the wellbeing of the individual and the planet are at stake. This is also a very different business model for companies that is not without risk. Selling fewer, more expensive garments requires a consumer who understands the value of their purchase. Their expectations for quality and service will increase, and retailers will need to adjust to lower volumes at a higher profit. For most, this would be a dramatic shift in behavior, making it a risky venture.

Designers can offer well-made garments created to wear in multiple ways and combinations, with the option to purchase coordinating pieces that span several seasons. Consistent dye lots might allow a consumer to purchase a jacket and pants one year, and then purchase the complimentary skirt and a new top the following year. The capsule collection concept was coined by Susie Faux in the 1970s and was popularized by Donna Karan's "Seven Easy Pieces" in the 1980s. Capsule wardrobes are popular, and many services will build and maintain a collection for consumers. Convertible designs that offer the ability to change the length of a jacket, add sleeves, or be worn in a different way by changing the way it is positioned on the body offer flexibility and novelty. Twelve Ways makes a garment that can be configured into twelve different tops, skirts, and dresses.

New technologies have the potential to offer variety in a single garment. A shirt that can change color or pattern would reduce the number of shirts required in a wardrobe. Hussein Chalayan, Chromat, and Behnaz Farahi' are designers who make garments that can shape shift, presenting multiple design options by using sensor technologies. Dresses can change silhouette and length, a sports bra can open ventilation based on body temperature, and a vest reacts to the environment using a shape memory alloy. Though innovators have been working on ideas like these, the technology is not ready for mass production.

Selecting fabrics and components that minimize laundering requirements and reduce or eliminate dry-cleaning must be core considerations for a designer. Textile testing provides a starting point for the likely performance of a fabric and suggested care. When comparing the energy required to care for a cotton T-shirt or a polyester T-shirt with wicking properties, the polyester T-shirt is the more sustainable choice. Sometimes a single component can change the care instructions. For example, a cotton blouse with wooden buttons that can't be laundered is an unfortunate combination. What could have been a washable garment now requires dry-cleaning.

Though not as engaging as talking about their inspiration, if designers could give a stronger voice to care options and help consumers know that they don't need to wash a garment after every wear it could have a substantial impact. For example, awareness is growing among denim devotees that jeans will mould to the body and last longer without traditional laundering. Once or twice a year a quick soak in the bathtub while wearing the jeans and hanging them to dry is enough.

The decisions designers make are important at the garment level and contribute to the goal of a closed loop life cycle. The bigger potential for impact needs to come from developing innovative macro solutions that disrupt the whole system of how we produce and wear fashion.

Designing systems

The most core function of a designer is to imagine something that doesn't exist in response to a problem that does exist. This could mean an individual garment design or imagining new systems of consumption or garment services that support a more sustainable fashion industry. When Sara Blakely developed Spanx, she popularized shapewear for a generation of women unfamiliar with foundation garments and responded to women who wanted to look their best in current fashion. Looptworks repurposes materials headed to the landfill into "meaningful, long-lasting and limited-edition products," such as converting airplane seats into soccer balls, purses, and bags (Hower, 2016). The basic systems of producing and caring for clothes have changed very little over time, even with advances in technology. Though we owned fewer garments, the average budget for clothing was about 14 percent of income in 1900, and today it is closer to 4 percent. The global scale and efficiencies of mass production allow us to have numerous fashion choices for a fraction of the cost. Though saving resources and time are still critical to profits, designers need to lead us out of a system that supports the disposable mindset of consumerism.

Systems thinking focuses on the structures and components that interact with behaviors and processes. How might designers disrupt current production and consumption systems with the goal of dressing people in a sustainable manner while improving the quality of their lives? Many are working to innovate different segments of our current process such as developing the critical link between discarded garments and new garments. What other questions do we need to ask that will lead us to redefine fashion and transform the market?

Rental systems offer an alternative to purchasing and owning a garment. Designers of rental garments should consider a variety of ways to allow for easy alterations and durability including adjustable features, generous seam allowances, assembly that allows ease of access, and fabrics that are forgiving when alterations are made. For example, VIGGA is changing the way we dress our children by making quality, organic kids' clothing available through a subscription model. Each piece has multiple life cycles as it is worn by many different children. They also offer maternity clothing under the same model ("Doing Business as Usual," n.d.)

During great economic recessions and political conflicts, temporary system changes have been made. In 1942, the US War Production Board (WPB) ordered a 15 percent reduction in the amount of fabric used in women's fashion as wool and silk were needed for uniforms and parachutes during World War II. After the establishment of the People's Republic of China, the Mao suit was worn as a symbol of proletarian unity, and temporarily halted Chinese fashion. Historically, sumptuary laws were used to control consumption though primarily to protect the status of the upper classes. Living and dressing under limitations is possible. Though restrictions often feel constraining, they can propel designers to be more creative and encourage innovation. For example, developing a viable alternative to leather has introduced new bio-materials and forms for shoes and bags.

Futurists have created scenarios of future fashion which tend to include sleek space and technology inspired uniforms. It is useful and critical to imagine how we might dress later in the century considering the real challenges that are present. Designers have an opportunity and a responsibility to offer alternative scenarios and systems that provide an improved quality of life and reduce the current system's impact on the environment while concurrently supporting society's economic and social wellbeing. Fashion will change and disruptions to the status quo are certain. Designers can and must drive the transformations needed to benefit people, planet, and fashion companies.

Case study: Winsome

Winsome (winsomegoods.com) is a line of women's wear created from a foundation of sustainability established by Kathryn Sieve in Minneapolis. By using a range of sustainable best practices and emphasizing a nurturing work environment, Sieve has organically grown a thriving small business. Her designs are wearable, versatile, and easy care. The Winsome woman makes intentional decisions about her clothing purchases and the modern, minimal style complements many wardrobes.

Winsome produces the garments in a studio located behind a small storefront (see Figure 2.2). The small team of sewers works a flexible schedule in a bright, open space, and are paid a living wage, well above minimum. Each signs the tag of every garment to remind the customer that the garment was individually made. Emphasizing the significance of sewing as a craft and trade, and respecting the contributions of employees are core values.

Two collections a year are wholesaled across the country, sold online, and at the studio. Sieve has been selective in building relationships with the retailers. A shared vision for the future of the fashion industry is important. Winsome is part of a shift towards an infinite number of finite market niches which is altering the way fashion is retailed, worn, and discarded (Lewis, 2016). Sieve hopes to

Figure 2.2 Winsome Studio, *c.* 2017. Courtesy Kathryn Sterner. Photography by Cameron Wittig.

shift the consumer culture of disposable fashion to one with more intention and thought for the people who produce fashion and the environment we share.

Sieve believes that sustainability must drive design at Winsome and so this frames her overall lifestyle. Part of her commitment is seen in community classes on sustainable fashion she offers with friend Emily Bryngelson of abrahamlabel. com. This includes learning to do basic hand-sewing, hems, and repairs. Future plans for Winsome are to develop a production facility to train and employ local people with an interest in sewing and production as a trade. This is a way to create better jobs and can support other independent designers developing their own market niches.

Sieve has learned that choices need to be made to balance Winsome's mission with remaining a viable business. Though initially the plan was to use all organic fabrics, sourcing these presented limitations. Natural, washable fibers form the core of the designs, though synthetics are considered if they offer the possibility of saving textiles from being sent to a landfill. Winsome is experimenting with their first made-to-order limited-edition collection in collaboration with a like-minded partner. On-demand manufacturing presents a new retail paradigm for designers, retailers, and consumers.

Many small fashion businesses are challenged when the business starts to grow, presenting problems with scaling production and delivery. What design strategies will best support Winsome's commitment to sustainability in the future?

References

Bye, E., *Fashion Design*. Oxford: Berg, 2010.

Bye, E. and McKinney, E. "Sizing up the wardrobe: Why we keep clothes that do not fit." *Journal of Fashion Theory* 11, no. 4 (2007): 483–98.

"Circular Design Thinking." *Design for Longevity*. https://designforlongevity.com/articles/circular-design-thinking

DeLong, M., Goncu-Berk, G., Bye, E., and Wu, J. "Apparel Sustainability from a Local Perspective." *Research Journal of Textiles and Apparel* 17 (2013): 59–69. doi.org/10.1108/RJTA-17-01-2013-B006.

"Doing Business as Usual." *Design for Longevity*. https://designforlongevity.com/videos/doing-business-as-unusual?c=czQ2OGRveEVGWEcxTWQyOVpVcUM0eURpcX FhMkV1YjlXM2JtTXVLc0ZxYkh6eU4v&s=czl2dmNJOUxTU2ExTm96b01FcUM 0eURpcXFhMkV1YjlXM2JtTXVLc0ZxYkh6eU4v.

Fletcher, K. *Sustainable Fashion and Textiles, Design Journeys*, 2nd edn. Milton Park, Abingdon, UK: Routledge, 2014.

Hower, M. "8 companies to watch in the circular economy." *Green Biz*, August 10, 2016. https://www.greenbiz.com/article/8-companies-watch-circular-economy.

Jung, S. and Jin, B. "A Theoretical Investigation of Slow Fashion: Sustainable Future of the Apparel Industry." *International Journal of Consumer Studies* 38 (2014): 510–19. doi: 10.1111/ijcs.12127.

Lewis, R. "The Long Tail Theory Can Be Reality for Traditional Megabrands." *Forbes*, May 31, 2016. https://www.forbes.com/sites/robinlewis/2016/05/31/the-long-tail-theory-can-be-reality-for-traditional-megabrands/#4fade7446372.

Roes, D. "What is a Normal Size Wardrobe?" *Recovering Shopaholic*, February 12, 2013. https://recoveringshopaholic.com.

Schilling, M. K. "Stella McCartney Weaves a New Way Forward." *Fast Company*, November 2017.

Talbot, L. "The 12 Forward Thinkers Changing Style and Sustainability." *Marie Claire*, July 19, 2017. http://www.marieclaire.com/fashion/a28282/fashion-forward/.

United Nations World Commission on Environment and Development. "Our Common Future." *The Brundtland Report*. Oxford: Oxford University Press, 1987.

3

Stealing Designs: Fashion Piracy and Counterfeiting

Sara B. Marcketti, Jean L. Parsons, and Hallie Erdahl

The practice of copying has existed since the beginning of fashion itself. The nature of fashion means that there must be desirable styles that are originated, then copied, and then abandoned in favor of newer creations. The fast speed of fashion change and need for repetition of fashion ideas at different price points, from the very high to the very low, makes intellectual property protection for fashion very difficult. The terms "counterfeiting" and "design piracy" are often used interchangeably in the fashion press. However, these words represent two distinct concepts. Design piracy describes the process of imitating fashionable goods without trying to pass or palm off the newly created product as a designer or brand that it is not. For example, if you purchased a dress from Forever 21 for $14.99 that looked remarkably like the multi-thousand-dollar Givenchy dress Beyonce wore on a red carpet this would be an example of design piracy. The designers or interpreters at Forever 21 imitated a style that Beyonce wore, but used lesser quality materials, changed the style so that it would be less complicated, and then marketed and sold it under the umbrella company Forever 21, not the designer name Givenchy. Design piracy is legal in the United States (European countries in the EU abide by the "Community Design Regulation" that provides both registered and unregistered protection to designs). Counterfeiting, on the other hand, is the creation of a product that is then palmed off or marketed as a particular brand. An infamous example is purchasing a supposed "Coach" purse out of the trunk of someone's car or at a "purse party" in which someone hosts the selling of counterfeit handbags. The purse would have the label Coach and may look strikingly similar to an authentic product. However, it is not actually produced and sold by the Coach Company. Oftentimes, counterfeit goods are less expensive, made of low-quality materials, are not properly packaged, and are sold in outlets where you might not normally expect to find higher-end goods,

Figure 3.1 Counterfeit shoes at a Beijing clothing market, 2004. Photo by FREDERIC J. BROWN/AFP/Getty Images.

such as an informal selling environment such as a flea market or sidewalk vendor with lots of other "designer" products (see Figure 3.1) (Marcketti and Parsons, 2016).

Counterfeiting

With the ubiquity of the internet today, consumers can easily be fooled by professional looking websites hawking fake goods. "Super copies" or the confusingly termed "genuinely fakes" can fool even the savviest consumer and even sometimes the original designer (Carpenter and Edwards, 2013). Creating and selling counterfeit goods is illegal in the United States because these goods violate trademark laws. Trademarks are the names, signs, or symbols that identify a product. These are often the most recognizable aspect of a brand: for instance, the double "C" logo of Chanel, the D & G symbol of Dolce and Gabanna, or the Nike "swoosh." In the United States, trademark laws provide protection against counterfeiters that create look-alike products passed off as the true original; they do not protect the design of the goods themselves. While trademark law may be used to prevent counterfeiting, it does not prevent pirating. Copyists of designs do not violate trademark laws when they copy the design without using the name or trademarks of the works they have copied. Fashion pirates often place their own identification on the copies. When it gets confusing is when a garment has an uncanny resemblance to the original, such as in the example of buying a seemingly genuine Ralph Lauren Polo shirt with a sewn-in authentic tag, but realizing the symbol embroidered on the front of the shirt is of a man riding a giraffe rather a horse!

Counterfeit goods represent a concern economically for businesses as well as present potential safety issues. It is easy to understand why counterfeit prescription drugs or baby formula would be a health risk. However, fake merchandise, even designer clothing, jewelry, and accessories, can pose a threat to consumer safety. Certain dyes have been found on counterfeit apparel that are known to be toxic and could cause cancer in animals. Dyes containing naptha-like substances are an active ingredient in lighter fluid ("How expensive are these shoes?" 2018). Counterfeit cosmetics have contained substances such as arsenic, cyanide, mercury, and rat droppings (Hoffower, 2018). People who wear or use these counterfeit products have reported allergic reactions, even chemical burns, because of the deleterious effects of the counterfeit goods on their skin.

Counterfeit products can be made in sweatshop conditions by individuals, including children, who are not paid fair wages and work in unsafe and harmful conditions. Sweatshops are found in almost all industries, but are most often associated with the garment trade (Garrin and Marcketti, 2015). The term "sweatshop" became a part of the general English language around the late 1880s to early 1890s and described the abusive labor practices carried out by ready-to-wear manufacturers (Liebhold and Rubenstein, 1999). Regardless of the type of work, sweatshops have remained, "an exploitative workplace associated with the garment trades and still synonymous with the lowest most degrading kind of American employment" (Hapke, 2004, p. 1). Sweatshop conditions often violate child labor laws and general labor laws, as well as basic human rights. In her 2007 book, *Deluxe: How Luxury Lost its Luster*, Dana Thomas describes the horrific conditions she witnessed in international sweatshops:

> I remember walking into an assembly plant in Thailand a couple of years ago and seeing six or seven little children, all under 10 years old, sitting on the floor assembling counterfeit leather handbags. The owners had broken the children's legs and tied the lower leg to the thigh so the bones wouldn't bend. [They] did it because the children said they wanted to go outside and play.

Consumers can also find themselves in unsafe environments when purchasing counterfeit goods, particularly if they are in building violate codes, such as when fire exits are locked to prevent workers from leaving or are blocked by boxes of merchandise.

In addition to the human pain caused by counterfeits, the production of counterfeit goods draws potential profits away from legitimate companies, causing lost jobs and billions of dollars in lost sales due to fake merchandise ("How expensive are these shoes?" 2018). Cities and states lose opportunities to collect tax revenue, meaning less money for public services. A report from 2003 revealed that New York state lost over $2 billion in just one year from unpaid sales tax, personal income tax, and business income tax revenue from the sale of counterfeit goods (Dash, 2004). Even more harmful than the financial losses are reports that proceeds from counterfeit rings have helped finance terrorist attacks, including the 1993 truck bombing of the World Trade Center (Ehrenfeld, 2003). Terrorist organizations may use the profits from counterfeits to fund their more nefarious operations as criminal networks often use similar routes to move counterfeit goods as they do to smuggle drugs and traffic humans (US Government Accountability Office, 2018).

With globalization and the internet shrinking the world, it makes it easier for counterfeiters to gain access to factories and create the supply chain to sell their goods. Unscrupulous companies can steal logos and manufacturing specifications when unsuspecting companies seek bids for the manufacture of their trademarked products. Using real logos and "tech specs," as they are called in the fashion industry, copies are created that are seemingly identical to the authentic product. Sometimes this occurs with manufacturers that steal information, sometimes it occurs with manufacturers who stop authorized production of brand name products and then fire up their factories later to produce more of the same goods for cheaper sale (Ceniceros, 2001). Along with actual counterfeit manufacturers, there is also a sophisticated sub-sector of support businesses offering counterfeit printing and packaging services.

Online marketplaces such as Amazon, WalMart, and eBay make it easy for international counterfeiting distribution networks to set up shop (Henkel, 2019). On Amazon alone, there are 2.5 million independent merchants with goods for sale. These merchants pay to list their products and can purchase additional services such as advertising, shipping, and warehousing. In 2017, more than half of the items customers bought were purchased from these third-party sellers (Matsakis, 2017). In a 2018 report by the United States Government Accountability Office, of the forty-seven products—from Nike Air Jordan shoes to Urban Decay makeup—investigators bought from online sellers, twenty were counterfeit (Hoffower, 2018)!

With all of the negative evidence against counterfeit goods, why would anyone purchase something counterfeit? Well, sometimes an individual might not know that they are purchasing a counterfeit product. Counterfeits have become so prevalent that "[a]ny brand that's hot is going to get copied—that's just the way it is," according to Barbara Kolsun, senior vice president and general counsel for Seven for All Mankind (Felgner, 2005). In addition to being easy to find, counterfeit goods might not be easy to identify. With technological advances, "super copies" are nearly identical (and sometimes better made) than the authentic product. Days before the 2019 Super Bowl face-off between the Los Angeles Rams and New England Patriots, US Immigration and Customs Enforcement officials seized $24 million worth of fake tickets and merchandise. Many of the fake tickets and merchandise appeared real. According to the National Football League senior counsel Michael Buchwald, "Every year we see fans who arrive at the stadium on game day only to be turned away at the gates because they bought counterfeit tickets. The quality of counterfeit tickets can be very sophisticated" (Giaritelli, 2019).

With peer pressure to dress fashionably, as well as the easy consumption of high-end counterfeit goods, some believe that it is their right to have the same access to high fashion and luxury as the wealthy. Additionally, some consumers believe that the genuine product prices are too high and not worth the additional cost for authenticity (Stewart, 2005). While it may be easy for some to decide not to purchase counterfeit goods on the streets of New York or Italy, it may be easier to rationalize purchasing a counterfeit product at a friend's house in suburbia. Counterfeits have a large market in developing nations, where labor laws are weak and the need or desire for fashionable clothing is high (Brenner and Harmon, 2007). Additionally, one might not know they are buying counterfeit items when purchasing online.

Throughout the years there have been numerous attempts to limit counterfeiting. Police sting operations and vendor alert programs are possible proactive methods to curb counterfeiters. In a recent six-year investigation, the US federal government seized enough counterfeit Gucci bags, Hermes belts, Tory Burch purses, and Louis Vuitton accessories to fill twenty-two shipping containers. The goods originated in China, with products to be shipped to retailers as far away as Illinois and California. In addition to fashion goods, Chanel perfume was also found, which investigators believed contained animal urine instead of the perfume company's formula (Robbins, 2018). Often these large operations are a result of coordination among a range of government agencies; for example, almost twenty US organizations play a role in intellectual property rights enforcement including the Department of Homeland Security's US Customs and Border Protection, US Immigration and Customs Enforcement, the Federal Bureau of Investigation, the US Food and Drug Administration, and the Consumer Product Safety Commission. You may have seen more local sting operations, however, particularly if you have traveled to a country in Europe and witnessed the police sirens approaching and sellers wrapping up their counterfeit wears in blankets and running away. These efforts provide control over counterfeit products to a degree, but without more organized efforts by government and industries committed to aggressive enforcement of the law at both the manufacturing and sales ends of these illegal operations, within days of raids, arrests, and seizures, counterfeit activities will inevitably resume.

With any intellectual property laws, it is incumbent upon those being copied to find the copyist and bring legal action against them. Hence, despite the competitive marketplace, once rival brands, such as True Religion, Abercrombie & Fitch, and Seven for All Mankind, now work together to bring to light counterfeit operations. Companies have also tried to use marketing to help consumers realize the importance of buying authentic merchandise. The advertising agency for Levi's created an ad campaign that highlighted the "mythology and romance of denim" to sway consumers away from counterfeit denim jeans (Voight, 1999).

Other methods of identifying and limiting counterfeit goods include fiber typing that can verify the authenticity of goods. Companies such as Tagover have developed labels using technology that demonstrate a product's authenticity— from wine, to food, to luxury apparel items. The problem, of course, is when authentic labels are stolen and used on fake goods (Robbins, 2018). Consumers can educate themselves about counterfeit goods and recognize that if something seems too inexpensive or is sold somewhere that is probably not a legitimate shop, then that product may be counterfeit.

Not to confuse matters, but there are also products sold in the parallel or grey market. This refers to suppliers or distributors creating a genuine branded garment in one country and then distributing these goods outside of the official distribution channel without the trademark holder's knowledge or permission. Companies can engage in this process, as can individuals, by purchasing luxury items in one country and then selling them online or in another country. The products are often cheaper because they are not being sold through official channels. According to Brian Buchwald, chief executive of US consumer intelligence company Bomoda, buyers need to take care, as "there are black market sellers selling counterfeit products, legitimate brands selling legitimate products, and a grey market where you have authentic products sold by unlicensed resellers" (Menon, 2016). When purchasing electronics or watches, the implications of buying grey goods include receiving older models or those without full warranties. In a complicated twist, a few upper end brands, such as Fendi and Gucci, actually participate in the grey market, offloading unsold seasonal merchandise, such as designer purses, to discount chains like T.J.Maxx and Marshalls.

Design piracy

While there are trademarks that can protect the labels of goods, legally designers and manufacturers have had tenuous success in proving their garments to be "original and novel" as required by United States (US) patent laws. Even though design patents can apply to the protection of decorative designs, there are challenges to their use. To be awarded a design patent, one must prove that there is novelty tantamount to invention. It is not enough that the design represents an original arrangement of materials; it must also be the result of an inventive gift, which has been extremely difficult for the courts to determine. The underlying technology or functional design of a garment can receive a utility patent, but there is nothing to prevent a copyist from designing a garment with a similar appearance but different underlying technology. Copyright laws that protect music, books, and movies have not applied to apparel since the courts have consistently judged that garments and fashion protect the wearer from the elements, decorate the body, and provide modesty, which are all viewed as useful and thus not able to be protected (Marcketti and Parsons, 2015). All intellectual property protection requires time to obtain, also limiting its usefulness for the fashion industry.

Due to limitations in US intellectual property laws, design piracy is currently legal in the United States. Rather than trying to imitate authentic goods, pirated goods look similar to the original, without claiming originality (see Figure 3.2). While it is allowable, piracy continues to be a controversial subject. Some individuals in the apparel industry believe that pirated goods, often called "knock-offs," provide good value and fashion to those that cannot afford high-fashion originals, while others believe piracy undermines the earning potential of the originating designer or manufacturer (Marcketti and Parsons, 2015).

Figure 3.2 A Mary McFadden designer dress on the left and a close copy by the Joan Leslie Company on the right, both from 1993. Courtesy of the Missouri Historic Costume and Textile Collection, University of Missouri.

Design piracy most often turns high-end designer goods into less expensive copies as epitomized by Forever 21, Zara, and other fast-fashion brands. High fashion and haute couture designers have also copied one another as well as other fine artists, such as painters. Piracy particularly impacts apparel manufacturing, unlike other goods, because firms entering the fashion business need little other than a popular garment style to be successful. In other less fashion-oriented manufacturing industries with standardized products, capital requirements are much greater. The firms need to maintain large production plants and consistently seek improvements in technical efficiencies—not necessities in the fashion industry. In recent years, the Council of Fashion

Designers of America and the American Apparel and Footwear Association have sought legal remedies to curb piracy. Such efforts are nothing new. Since the beginning of the US ready-to-wear apparel industry, businesses and organizations have tried to limit the copying practice, but with little impact.

Because pirated goods do not claim to be someone else's goods, there is a great deal of variation between how similar they look to the "original" article of clothing. Indeed, the degree of separation between the original and the knock-off has been one of the barriers to the apparel industry obtaining legislation against design piracy. For example, making very minor changes to a sleeve, a hemline, the neckline, or the fabric can have dramatic changes to the overall look of a garment. Courts have been hesitant to weigh in on the piracy debate, particularly as fashion means that there is a particular style that is worn by a large group of people and origination is difficult to prove. Take, for instance, ripped jeans. Ripped and tattered jeans have been popular in recent years and companies would be foolish not to capitalize on the trend by making variations on the ripped-jeans look at various price points to satisfy a wide swath of consumers. However, if you are a student of fashion history, you will remember that the ripped look was in fashion in the 1980s when Comme des Garçons' Rei Kawakubo created jackets, pants, and jumpers with gaping holes. If you look even further back in European fashion history, small all-over slits were popular in the fifteenth century!

As the above examples illustrate, determining originality is virtually impossible. Consider the little black dress. Some historians give the credit to Coco Chanel, when her short, simply designed black dress was published in *Vogue* magazine in 1926. The fashion editors likened it to Henry Ford's Model T because it was accessible to women from a cross-section of socio-economic classes, and represented an easy to mass produce design. Today, the little black dress can be found in countless variations – short, long, with sleeves, without, in any material imagined, and so on, but the similarities between the black dresses are quite clear. The little black dress has become such a standard style and idea in fashion, that to gain intellectual property protection for it would be virtually impossible.

In the twenty-first century, the pace of design piracy has quickened as an individual with the right industry connections need only email a picture of a garment to a factory and say they want something similar or a silhouette made just so. A knock-off can be delivered months before the "original" even hits stores for purchase (Wilson, 2007). Teri Agins explained the process in a 1994 article in the *Wall Street Journal*:

A photograph snapped at a fashion show in Milan can be faxed overnight to a Hong Kong factory, which can turn out a sample in a matter of hours. That sample can be Fedexed back to a New York showroom the next day, ready for retail buyers to preview. Stores order these lower-priced "interpretations" for their own private-label collections even as they are showing the costly designer versions in their pricier departments.

It should be noted that today, with digital photographs and emails, the speed of piracy is even faster than in the above example!

One of the reasons that knock-off products are inexpensive is because of the money the manufacturer has saved not having to research the product, in development and production. The copy-cat manufacturer has also avoided the failures of the many unsuccessful product lines that most businesses have to endure. The ubiquity of design piracy has created an environment in which many manufacturers do not want to spend money on designing costs (such as for creative designers) when copying is so easy and profitable.

Although some consumers believe that there is cachet in having a high-priced garment designed by a renowned design house or designer, other consumers are thrilled to have something that resembles (even moderately) a fashionable garment. Magazines and internet sites often promote this desire for the lower priced copy in their "steal vs. splurge" features that identify an original high-priced garment (splurge) and its lower-priced copy (steal). Piracy is so rampant that for many consumers, keeping track of the original is beyond their time, energy, or interest. For example, have you ever purchased something from a store and then gone into a different store and seen something extraordinarily similar? This is piracy in action.

Piracy also runs rampant because of the desire of consumers to keep up with ever-changing styles. Today, quality seems less important than stylishness, and some consumers purchase hundreds of garments each year with the expectation of only wearing them once or twice (Simpson and Karpova 2019). Many consumers who purchase this quantity of goods are more interested in low prices than in originality. The need for continual purchases and "new-ness" speeds up the pace of the industry, meaning more designs created, more fashions bought by consumers, and greater end-product waste as consumers tire of garments worn only once or twice. Long gone is the idea of shopping from one's closet to mix and match items to get greater and more versatile use, and seemingly forever gone is the idea of purchasing just one or two high-quality items every season that can be integrated into one's wardrobe for a lifetime!

Possible solutions

Possible solutions to the counterfeiting problem can be relatively simple. Be sure that what you are buying is from a reputable retailer. This can be very difficult, however, when shopping on the internet, as websites can look very professional. When shopping on Amazon and other internet sites that allow third-party dealers, some good ways to avoid counterfeits are to narrow down your shopping search to products sold by the site itself, read the reviews that are posted, and check for poor spelling and grammar, or similarly staged user photos or similarly worded phrases. Additionally, once you purchase a product, examine the packaging and check for missing tags, typos, and misspellings. Packaging should include all of the typical retail tags found on a new product, such as UPC barcodes and care instructions (Hoffower, 2018). No matter where you purchase the garment from, use your senses to determine if something is truly of the quality that you are expecting at the price that you pay. For example, if you are wanting to purchase a $2,500 Louis Vuitton bag and find one at an online retailer selling for $50, it is most likely a counterfeit.

To limit counterfeiting on its site, Amazon announced Project Zero, a program designed to reduce the number of fake products on its site. The initiative includes a tool that will allow some sellers to automatically remove counterfeit listings, without Amazon needing to intervene. Previously, brands had first to report counterfeits to Amazon in order for the company to investigate and take action. Amazon will also allow brands to assign a unique manufacturer number to every item they make. That way, each time Amazon sells one of their products, it can confirm its authenticity by checking that it came with a legitimate code. The "product serialization" program, as Amazon calls it, is akin to the identification numbers that often come with luxury watches (Matsakis, 2019).

One of the factors that may impact consumers who regularly purchase counterfeit (and grey) goods is overconsumption. Consuming more than one needs (overconsumption) can lead to personal financial debt and contribute to landfill waste. The late nineteenth–early twentieth century economist Thorstein Veblen created the terms "conspicuous consumption" and "invidious comparisons," noting that people often purchase products to show off their social status, and compete with one another. We know from our own experience and from countless studies that continuously acquiring new possessions, whether it be toys, clothes, or jewelry, does not add to a person's happiness. Actually, it can make someone feel less happy, with increasing social discontent and anxiety to keep up with ever-fancier and newer lifestyle choices (Brown, 2018). All consumers can find ways to shop within their closets to pair garments in new ways to achieve new looks. Some authors conducted a study in which participants refrained from purchasing garments to add to their wardrobe for ten weeks. In this "fashion detox," the authors found that shopping from one's closet rather than purchasing new items increased participants' creativity and satisfied consumers' needs for novelty and change (Ruppert-Stroescu, LeHew, Hiller, and Armstrong, 2015).

Design piracy is a bit more challenging of a problem to solve as it is not illegal in the United States. Some within the apparel industry believe that there are opportunities to enact more strict laws, similar to the EU system of design protection. However, there are many issues to resolve, particularly the length of time something would be protected, as well as the amount of time it would take to seek protection. Currently, intellectual property rights can take several months to several years to obtain. As such, by the time something is protected, a fashion design would likely have already completed its life cycle: it will have been created, marketed, sold, and possibly even disposed of. Some fashion designers have sought to limit piracy by making their garments so complicated through patternmaking and detailing that they are difficult to copy. However, this approach often works better for higher-priced garments and those that are for more expensive, once-in-a-lifetime events, such as wedding gowns. In today's ready-to-wear athleisure environment of leggings and T-shirts, the overly complex design philosophy would not sell very many garments.

Other designers and manufacturers have created lower-priced garments copied from their higher-priced designs. In the 1980s, Anne Klein introduced diffusion lines of garments called Anne Klein II, using less expensive material and retailing at much reduced prices. In the 1990s, this practice continued with bridge lines from Emanuel Ungaro (Emanuel), Donna Karan (DKNY), and Ellen Tracy (Tracy), and in the 2000s with CK by Calvin Klein and Marc by Marc Jacobs. Also in the 2000s, designers from Isaac Mizrahi to Vera Wang to Viktor & Rolf found new outlets for their diffusion lines by exclusively partnering with lower priced retailers such as Kohl's, Target, and H&M (Marcketti and Parsons, 2015).

Some brands have become even more creative in highlighting the counterfeit and piracy problem, while promoting their own brands. In 2018, Diesel, a company best known for T-shirts and denim jeans, opened a fake store on Canal Street in downtown Manhattan selling what seemed to be counterfeit products. The brand even misspelled its own name—Deisel—on the store front and on the goods, which were wrapped in individual plastic bags and piled messily on the shelves. When Diesel revealed that the store was in fact full of authentic products, consumers rushed to the business. Some consumers resold the goods purchased, with one "Deisel" sweatshirt that had been sold for $60 in the Canal Street shop resold for $500. The stunt was revealed on social media with footage of consumers buying the products, and shop assistants trying to convince those that passed by that the goods were genuine. According to Diesel founder Renzo Rosso, "There are so many fake products in the world. The fake products bring the brand down. So how can we use this to bring the brand up? We came up with this fantastic idea" (Richards, 2018).

Case study

Imagine that you are a recent college graduate from Iowa State University's (ISU) apparel, merchandising, and design program. During your undergraduate career, you were able to study abroad in Europe and complete several internships. Of your internships, two were your favorites: one was in a small family-owned store in Des Moines, Iowa, and the other in a large, corporate organization in Manhattan, New York City. You have now been offered a full-time position at both companies. However, there is much to consider. The salary offer in New York City is higher; however, so is the cost of living. The company in New York is also a global brand, with opportunities for international travel and possible promotions. While Des Moines is the state capital of Iowa, it is located in the Midwestern United States and is a much smaller city than NYC. There would be fewer travelling opportunities with the Iowa company, whose business is largely concentrated in the Midwest.

The last remaining consideration is that with the company in Des Moines you would be creating "original" goods. Your job would be to design garments targeted at the middle to upper-middle class consumer looking for unique fashion pieces for once-in-a-lifetime events such as high school proms, college graduation parties, weddings, and galas. You would have the opportunity to work closely with clients in designing custom-pieces tailored to their specifications. You would have the opportunity to choose the colors, the styles, the fabrics all to the client's tastes and whims. The company in New York creates sleepwear for large retailers targeted for mass production and consumption. During your internship in New York, one of your least favorite activities was when your supervisor tossed sleepwear on your work station and asked you to design and create garments that were similar, if not identical, except for the trademark. Recently, one of your friends, an ISU alumna, hinted to you her concern that the company in New York may be producing counterfeit labels in their overseas factory. What factors would most influence you when deciding which of these companies you would work for?

References

Agins, T. "Fashion knockoffs hit stores before originals as designers seethe." *Wall Street Journal*, August 8, 1994, p. 1.

Brenner, T. and Harmon, A. "Keeping it real: Brands take the right against counterfeiters from Canal Street to Congress." *DNR*, October 22, 2007, p. 16.

Brown, C. "Why over-consumption is making us unhappy." *Psychology Today*, March 26, 2018. https://www.psychologytoday.com/us/blog/buddhist-economics/201803/why-over-consumption-is-making-us-unhappy.

Carpenter, J. M. and Edwards, K. E. "US consumer attitudes toward counterfeit fashion products." *Journal of Textile and Apparel, Technology and Management* 8, no. 1 (2013): 1–16.

Ceniceros, R. "Counterfeit crackdown." *Business Insurance* 35, no. 37 (September 10, 2001): 1, 55.

Dash, E. "The handbag? Total knockoff. The price tag? All too real." *New York Times*, November 23, 2004. https://www.nytimes.com/2004/11/23/nyregion/the-handbag-total-knockoff-the-price-tag-all-too-real.html.

Ehrenfeld, R. *Funding Evil: How Terrorism is Financed and How to Stop it.* Los Angeles: Bonus Books, 2003.

Felgner, B. (2005, November 28). "Knock-offs just won't quit." *Home Textiles Today*. http://www.hometextilestoday.com/article/386997-knock-offs-just-wont-quit/.

Garrin, A. and Marcketti, S. B. "Teaching social justice through three periods of sweatshop history." *International Journal of Costume and Fashion* 15, no. 1 (2015): 75–85.

Giaritelli, A. "ICE snatches $24M in counterfeit NFL gear ahead of the Super Bowl." *Washington Examiner*, January 31, 2019. https://www.washingtonexaminer.com/news/ice-snatches-24m-in-counterfeit-nfl-gear-ahead-of-the-super-bowl.

Hapke, L. *Sweatshop: The History of an American Idea.* Piscataway, NJ: Rutgers University Press, 2004.

Henkel, R. "Product piracy: What sports retailers and brands can do about it." April 23, 2019. https://www.ispo.com/en/markets/product-piracy-what-sports-retailers-and-brands-can-do-about-it.

Hoffower, H. "Fake products sold by places like Walmart or Amazon hold risks of everything from cyanide to rat droppings —here's how to make sure what you're buying is real." *Business Insider*, March 29, 2018. https://www.businessinsider.com/how-to-find-fake-products-online-shopping-amazon-ebay-walmart-2018-3.

"How expensive are these shoes?" US Customs and Border Protection. 2018. https://www.cbp.gov/FakeGoodsRealDangers.

Liebhold, P. and Rubenstein, H. R. "History of sweatshops." In P. Liebhold and H. R. Rubenstein (eds.), *Between a Rock and a Hard Place: A History of American Sweatshops, 1820–present*, pp. 1–14. Los Angeles: UCLA Asian American Studies Center and Simon Wiesenthal Center Museum of Tolerance, 1999.

Marcketti, S. B. and Parsons, J. L. (). *Knock it off! A History of Design Piracy in Women's Ready-to-Wear Industry*. Lubbock: Texas Tech University Press, 2016.

Matsakis, L. "Amazon wants brands to fight fake products themselves." *Wired*, March 1, 2019. https://www.wired.com/story/amazon-fake-products-project-zero/.

Menon, B. "Are grey goods the real deal." *Guardian*, July 9, 2016. https://www.theguardian.com/money/2016/jul/09/grey-goods-real-deal-imported-sold-unofficially-consumers.

Richards, K. "Why Diesel opened a deceptive NYC pop-up store selling knockoffs of its own clothes." *AdWeek*, February 12, 2018. https://www.adweek.com/brand-marketing/why-diesel-opened-a-deceptive-nyc-pop-up-store-selling-knockoffs-of-its-own-clothes/.

Robbins, L. "Investigators seize fake luxury goods worth half a billion dollars." *New York Times*, August 16, 2018. https://www.nytimes.com/2018/08/16/nyregion/fake-luxury-goods-handbags.html.

Ruppert-Stroescu, M., LeHew, M. L. A., Hiller, K. Y., and Armstrong, C. M. "Creativity and sustainable fashion apparel consumption: The fashion detox." *Clothing and Textiles Research Journal* 33, no. 3 (2015): 167–82.

Simpson, L. H. and Karpova, E. "Understanding barriers to sustainable fashion industry: Everyday consume practices when shopping, storing, and disposing fast fashion." Regent's and International Textile and Apparel Association Joint Conference, London, 2019.

Stewart, C. "Brand piracy: A victimless crime?" *Gallup*, March 1, 2005. https://news.gallup.com/poll/15088/brand-piracy-victimless-crime.aspx.

Thomas, D. *Deluxe: How Luxury Lost its Luster*. London: Penguin Books, 2007.

United States Government Accountability Office. "Intellectual Property." 2018. https://www.scribd.com/document/373967329/Agencies-Can-Improve-Efforts-to-Address-Risks-Posed-by-Changing-Counterfeits-Market#fullscreen&from_embed

Voight, J. "Red, white, and blue: An American icon fades away." *Adweek* 40 (April 26, 1999): 28–35.

Wilson, E. "Before models can turn around, knockoffs fly." *New York Times*, September 4, 2007, pp. A1, A15.

Part Two

The Dangers of Making Fashion

4

Fibers and Materials: What is Fashion Made of?

Huantian Cao

Fashion products are mainly made of textile materials, which start from fibers. Textile fibers include natural fibers that are agricultural products from plants (e.g. cotton) or animals (e.g. wool), and manufactured fibers that are industrial products. Manufactured fibers can be further categorized into regenerated fibers that use natural polymers (e.g. cellulose from wood or bamboo) as the starting material in fibers production and synthetic fibers that are synthesized from small molecules. In 2014, the total global fibers demand was about 85.8 million tons, including 25.4 million tons of natural fibers, 5.2 million tons of regenerated fibers, and 55.2 million tons of synthetic fibers. From 1980 to 2014, the fibers demand growth was 55.7 million tons, of which 73.4 percent was polyester (Textile World, 2015). Fibers are spun into yarns, which are woven or knitted into fabrics. In addition to fibers-based materials, leather made from animal skin is another important material for fashion products. Textiles are dyed and finished to meet the aesthetic and functional requirements of fashion products. Fashion material production, especially fibers and leather production, dyeing, and finishing, uses large quantities of chemicals and generates huge amounts of wastewater contaminated with chemicals. Chen and Burns (2006) analyzed the productions of commonly used textile materials including cotton, wool, rayon, lyocell, nylon, polyester, and leather, and found that all of these materials caused adverse environmental impact. This chapter discusses the impact of textile and leather materials on the environment and human health.

Natural fibers

Cotton

Cotton is the second most commonly used fiber, accounting for 27 percent of all fiber consumption in 2015 (Textile Exchange, 2016). Cotton textile is soft, hydrophilic, and has good heat conductivity. It is widely used in fashion products such as pants, shirts, T-shirts, jackets, and underwear.

Cotton is an important fiber crop cultivated in more than seventy countries (see Figure 4.1). However, the cotton plant is susceptible to about 162 species of insects, which cause the main losses in cotton production (Shivanna et al., 2011). In Brazil, insects cause 10 percent (or 155,500 tons) of cotton production loss with an economic loss of US$400.14 million (or US$592 per hectare) (Oliveira et al., 2014). Using pesticides to protect the plant helps increase cotton production. It is estimated that cotton cultivation uses 11 percent of the world's pesticides while the plant is grown on only 2.4 percent of the world's arable land (Bevilacqua et al., 2014).

To effectively manage pest control, it is required to rotate among various classes of pesticides such as organophosphate (OP), carbamate, and chloronicotinyl (Mississippi State University Extension, 2016). Many of these pesticides are neurotoxic and harmful to the environment, wildlife, and human beings. OPs and carbamates inhibit the central nervous system and cause neurobehavior impairment such as memory impairment, confusion, anxiety, drowsiness, depression, and reduction in verbal attention and body movement

Figure 4.1 A field of cotton. Courtesy of Huantian Cao.

(Colosio, Tiramani, and Maroni, 2003). Organochlorine (OC) pesticides, another type of neurotoxin, include some of the most widely used pesticides in history such as dichloro-diphenyl-trichloroethane (DDT), dieldrin, and endosulfan. Endosulfan is effective against a broad number of pests and has been widely applied to a variety of crops, including cotton, in many parts of the world for about five decades (Weber et al., 2010). Endosulfan is extremely toxic to most fish and is bioaccumulative, building up in the food chain (Naqvi and Vaishnavi, 1993). Due to their toxicity, many OC pesticides have been banned: for example, DDT was banned in the US in 1972 (Stokstad, 2007) and endosulfan was banned in the US in 2010 (Lubick, 2010). However, OCs are persistent in the environment. Even though OC pesticides have not been applied to crops in the lower Namoi Valley in New South Wales, Australia, since 1982, they are present up to a depth of 1.2 meters in the soils, suggesting they may move into the groundwater and be consumed by human beings and livestock (Weaver et al., 2012).

Many pesticides are found in the World Health Organization (WHO) categories of highly hazardous (category I) and moderately hazardous (category II) chemicals (Mancini et al., 2005). Pesticides used in cotton cultivation have negative impacts on the health of wildlife and human beings, especially in developing countries where fewer toxic pesticides are banned, banned pesticides are still used illegally, the waste management of pesticides is inadequate, and protective equipment and practices are not sufficiently adopted (Mancini et al., 2005; Azandjeme et al., 2014). In cotton cultivating regions, pesticide residues have been found in wildlife, for example in bats in Benin (Stechert et al., 2014) and in fish in Egypt (El-Kady et al., 2017). Pesticides significantly impaired the endocrine regulation and caused severe damage to the liver and gonads of fish living in a cotton basin in Benin (Agbohessi et al., 2015). Mancini et al. (2005) conducted a season-long pesticide poisoning assessment among cotton farmers in three villages in India and found that 83.6 percent of the 323 reported poisoning events were associated with mild to severe poisoning symptoms, and 10 percent were associated with three or more neurotoxic/systemic signs typical of OP poisoning.

Genetically modified (GM) crops have been grown in the world since the mid-1990s (Coupe and Capel, 2016), and GM cotton is the third largest GM crop in terms of acreage, with 68 percent of the global cotton area occupied by GM cotton in 2014 (Burkitbayeva, Qaim, and Swinnen, 2016). One GM technology is to introduce insecticidal properties by inserting a gene from the soil bacterium *Bacillus thuringiensis* (Bt) into cotton's DNA so the cotton tissues can produce toxic proteins (Bt cotton) (Coupe and Capel, 2016). The Bt cotton plant resists bollworm, a major cotton-damaging insect, so it can significantly reduce pesticide use. In Pakistan, Bt cotton plots used an average of 2.73 liters of pesticide per acre with an average yield of 972.50 kg/acre, while the non-Bt cotton plots used an average of 3.46 liters of pesticide per acre with an average yield of 659.28 kg/acre. This represents a 21 percent reduction in pesticide use and 28 percent increase in yield for Bt cotton (Kouser and Qaim, 2013). In India, Bt cotton reduced total pesticide applications by 50 percent and category I pesticide uses by 70 percent, and helped to avoid at least 2.4 million pesticide poisoning cases each year (Kouser and Qaim, 2011).

Animal hair fibers: wool, cashmere and mohair

Wool fibers are obtained from sheep, and cashmere and mohair fibers are obtained from goats. Sheep and goats generate several products—meat, wool, milk, and skins—but generally, the main products are meat and milk, while hair and skins are by-products (Dýrmundsson, 2006). Sheep and goat farming causes greenhouse gas (GHG) emissions, uses more land for fiber production, and may lead to land degradation. Since fiber is one product of sheep or goats, fiber production accounts for a portion of the overall environmental impact of livestock (Opio et al., 2013).

Ruminants, including sheep and goats, have a continuous fermentation system in their rumen, a large fore stomach. The microbial fermentation of hydrolyzed carbohydrates generates methane (CH_4), a potent GHG (Broucek, 2014). Sheep and goats' GHG emissions are mainly from enteric CH_4 (with twenty-five times the global warming potential of CO_2) and nitrous oxide (with 298 times the global warming potential of CO_2) from manure (Opio et al., 2013). Wiedemann et al. (2016) studied GHG emissions in three wool producing regions in Australia—the high-rainfall zone in New South Wales, the Western Australian wheat-sheep zone, and the southern pastoral zone—and found no significant difference between regions or wool types. Biswas et al. (2010) identified that GHG emissions from wool production was about three times higher than the GHG emissions of the wheat-sheep production from the same types of land plots. More land is needed for wool production than other natural fibers. In the Western Australian wheat-sheep zone, the average land allocation for wool production was 93.6 m^2/kg of greasy wool (a yield of 107 kg of greasy wool per hectare) in arable pasture land and 92.1 m^2/kg of greasy wool (a yield of 109 kg of greasy wool per hectare) in non-arable pasture land (Wiedemann et al., 2016). In comparison, cotton yield in Australia has been in the range of

2,063 to 2,610 kg of cotton lint per hectare between 2008–9 and 2015–16 (Cotton Australia).

The small cloven hooves of sheep and goats destroy vegetation cover and are thus extremely damaging to the surface soil, greatly increasing erodibility (Taddese, 2001). Unsustainable grazing or overgrazing is one of the most widespread global land management problems and is regarded as putting significant pressure on the natural environment, leading to land degradation and desertification (Kairis et al., 2015). Sheep and goat overgrazing is a problem in many countries. For example, in a small area of the Central Palestinian Mountains, it was estimated that a total of 45,870 sheep and goats existed on 9,400 hectares of grazing land, though this amount of livestock would require about 76,450 hectares of natural grazing land, the result being an increased risk of erosion and land degradation (Hammad and Tumeizi, 2010).

Manufactured fibers

Regenerated fibers: rayon and lyocell

Viscose rayon is the first manufactured fiber, patented in England in 1892, produced from natural cellulose materials such as tree trunks and plant stalks (Monosson, 2016). In viscose rayon production, cellulose is treated with sodium hydroxide and carbon disulfide (CS_2) to form a cellulose xanthate spinning solution (viscose). The viscose solution is spun through spinnerets into a sulfuric acid bath to convert it back to cellulose in the fiber form (Gelbke et al., 2009). While it is safe for consumers to use rayon textile, during production, CS_2 and hydrogen sulfide are released and cause health problems for workers. The most important health effects of occupational CS_2 exposure include coronary heart disease, coronary risk factors (e.g., cholesterol, blood pressure, blood glucose, and blood coagulation), eye disease (bleeding in the eye and blurred vision), impairment of color vision, damage to the central and peripheral nerve systems, psychophysiological and behavior alterations (e.g., anxiety and depression), and male and female fertility and hormonal problems (Gelbke et al., 2009). It should be noted that most bamboo textiles are produced by the viscose rayon process using CS_2 to form cellulose xanthate.

To develop environmentally-benign regenerated cellulose fibers, Courtaulds, a UK company, developed a new fiber called lyocell (trade mark Tencel®) in the 1990s. In lyocell production, solvent N-methyl morpholine-N-oxide (NMMO) is used to directly dissolve cellulose without forming cellulose xanthate. NMMO is the only major chemical used in lyocell production and it can be recovered and recycled, which makes lyocell more environmentally friendly than viscose rayon (Woodings, 1995). The Tencel® brand is currently owned by the Lenzing Group (Austria).

Synthetic fibers: polyester

Polyester is the most commonly used of fibers, accounting for 55 percent of all fiber consumption in 2015 (Textile Exchange, 2016). As a synthetic fiber, polyester is available in filament and staple forms, and can be made into different widths from very small microdenier to high denier. Polyester fiber is hydrophobic and has relatively high strength. It is also a versatile fiber with a wide range of applications in fashion, home textiles, and industrial textiles. In fashion application, polyester can be used in any season from summer and aesthetic clothing (e.g., Nike Dri-FIT) to fiber-fill in winter coats. Most polyester materials we use today are synthesized from condensation polymerization using two organic feedstocks, an acid and an alcohol, derived from petroleum. However, using a depleting resource to produce polyester is a major environmental concern. There have been efforts to synthesize polyester using bio-based materials from renewable resources. The DuPont Company uses a fermentation process to produce 1,3-propanediol (PDO), an alcohol feedstock for polyester, from corn. PDO can react with an organic acid feedstock derived from petroleum to produce Sorona® poly(trimethylene terephthalate) (PTT, a type of polyester) (Kurian, 2005). Since one feedstock PDO is from the renewable resource corn and the other acid feedstock is derived from petroleum, Sorona®'s renewable content by weight is 37 percent (DuPont Company). The production of bio-PDO generates 40 percent less GHGs than petrochemical PDO, and polymerization and downstream processing, for example the dyeing of Sorona®, save energy compared to conventional polyester PET (Kurian, 2005). The generic name of Sorano® fibers is triexta, which is used in fashion and carpet products (see Figure 4.2). To further increase the bio-based renewable content in polyester, Colonna et al. (2011) synthesized the acid monomer from bio-limonene (derived from lemon skin), and the alcohol monomer from bio-succinic acid (obtained from corn), to create polyester containing 94 percent of bio-based materials.

Synthesizing polyester often uses antimony trioxide (Sb_2O_3) as a catalyst since it has a high catalytic activity, does not cause undesirable colors, and has a low tendency to catalyze side reactions (Duh, 2002). Antimony compounds have

Figure 4.2 Carpet made from triexta fibers. Courtesy of Huantian Cao.

harmful efforts on health: chronic exposure may cause severe irritation of the eyes, skin, and lungs, while long-term inhalation may lead to pneumoconiosis, stomach pain, diarrhea, vomiting, and stomach ulcers (Cooper and Harrison, 2009). Shanawany et al. (2017) studied workers in a polyester polymerization company in Egypt and found DNA damage among Sb_2O_3-exposed workers, indicating that Sb_2O_3 may have a genotoxic impact on occupationally exposed workers.

Polyester is not biodegradable, so recycling polyester via melting is a widely accepted method to deal with post-consumer polyester products such as soda bottles. Polyester is the most highly recycled plastic material, and recycled polyester fibers have been successfully used in textile products. Many fibers made from recycled polyester bottles are in the staple (short fiber) form. Polyester staple fibers made from recycled PET bottles have properties equivalent to those of virgin polyester (Gurudatt et al., 2005).

Polyester fleece, a commonly used fabric for jackets, is often made from recycled polyester staple fibers, which are easily separated from the garment to form microplastic lint. Researchers are increasingly worried about microplastic fibers entering soils, rivers, and oceans to damage wildlife and possibly ending up in the human food supply (Bomgardner, 2017). Sediment samples collected from eighteen shoreline sandy beaches in six continents indicated an abundance of microplastic content ranged from two fibers (Australia) to 31 fibers (Portugal and UK) per 250 mL of sediment, consisting of 56 percent polyester, 23 percent acrylic, 7 percent polypropylene, 6 percent polyethylene, and 3 percent polyamide (Browne et al., 2011). Fibers are the most common form of microplastics in the marine environment (Wright, Thompson, and Galloway, 2013), and the laundering of staple polyester textiles is one of the main reasons that microplastic fibers enter rivers and oceans (Hartline et al., 2016; Browne et al., 2011). Some marine organisms such as benthic holothurians may selectively ingest microplastics, showing a preference for fibrous shapes. Microplastics were found in myctophid fish and Hooker's sea lions/fur seal scats, indicating that microplastics may transfer through pelagic food chains (Wright, Thompson, and Galloway, 2013).

Leather

Leather is another important fashion material. The average annual world leather production between 2009 and 2011 was 551,000 tonnes of heavy bovine leather, 14,137.6 million square feet of light bovine leather, and 5,276 million square feet of sheepskin leather (Food and Agriculture Organization of the United Nations, 2013). In 2005, 55 percent of leather was used in footwear and 11.4 percent in clothing, while other major leather product sectors included furniture upholstery (13 percent), leather goods (9.2 percent), vehicle upholstery (7 percent), and gloves (4.4 percent) (United Nations Industrial Development Organization, 2010).

Converting animal skin to leather uses large quantities of chemicals and generates huge amounts of wastewater and solid wastes that are harmful to the environment and human health. BOD (Biochemical Oxygen Demand), COD (Chemical Oxygen Demand), and TSS (Total Suspended Solid) are important wastewater parameters. High BOD and COD levels are related to more organic pollutants in water, resulting in the quick consumption of dissolved oxygen in water and the death of fish and aquatic creatures. High TSS means more solid pollutants in water. In India, leather industry wastewater contained an average of 2,533 mg/L COD, 977 mg/L BOD, and 1,244 mg/L TSS, which are significantly higher than the Indian standard for inland surface water with 250 mg/L COD, 30 mg/L BOD, and 100 mg/L TSS (Mandal et al., 2010).

The leather production process can be divided into three sub-processes: the preparation stage/beam house stage (including more than ten steps to restore moisture and swell the raw hide, remove hair, tissues beneath skin and fat, bleach, and adjust pH); the tanning stage; and the crusting stage (including more than ten steps to dye, thin, retan, and lubricate the leather) (Dixit et al., 2015). Many of the beam house processes intensively use chemicals and water for "do-undo" operations, such as curing-soaking (adding salt to remove moisture and adding water to restore moisture) and liming-deliming (adding chemicals to swell the skin and remove liming chemicals) (Saravanabhavan et al., 2005). To detach hair from the skin and open up the collagen fibrous structure, a lime-sulfide process (liming and unhairing) is used, which significantly increases COD, BOD, and TSS loads in leather processing effluent (Jian, Wenyi, and Wuyong, 2011). Ammonium sulfate or ammonium chloride is used to remove lime (deliming) and generates ammonia (NH_3) gas which potentially causes a brain disorder associated with advanced liver disease and a blood disorder among leather production workers. Effluent from the deliming process has a high content of NH_3-N, providing nutrients for autotrophic bacteria, stimulating wildlife production in water, and causing eutrophication (algae overgrowth and the death of aquatic life) in lakes and rivers (Deng et al., 2015).

Untreated animal skins are susceptible to bacterial attack when wet and become inflexible if they are dried. Tanning is the process used to convert skin into a stable material that is resistant to microbial attachment and has enhanced resistance to wet and dry heat (Covington, 1997). More than 90 percent of global leather production uses chromium (Cr) salts, mainly chromium sulfate, in the tanning process (Sundar, Rao, and Muralidharan, 2002). Conventional chromium tanning has only about 55–60 percent chromium uptake and the tanning exhaust bath has a high concentration of chromium, which is toxic and carcinogenic, causing DNA mutation and disturbing the development of the embryo and fetus (Belay, 2010). Though only Cr(III) is used in tanning, oxidation of Cr(III) in leather production forms more toxic Cr(VI) and causes allergic contact dermatitis in consumers wearing leather products such as boots (Hansen et al., 2002).

Environmentally friendly leather processing has been intensively studied in recent decades, with Saravanabhavan et al. (2004) applying biotechnology in the beam house and tanning stages to treat goatskins: using enzymes for unhairing and fiber-opening to replace lime, sulfide, and ammonium chloride in the conventional liming–unhairing–deliming beam house processes, and using vegetable tannins in the tanning process. Environmentally friendly leather processing reduced 83 percent of BOD and 69 percent of COD, while the leather performance was similar to conventionally processed leather (Saravanabhavan et al., 2004).

Dyeing and finishing

Greige goods (undyed and unfinished fabric) just removed from a loom or knitting machine looks like a muslin and has very limited use in fashion products. Dyeing, printing, and finishing processes add color, pattern, aesthetics, and functions to textiles, which result in a wide range of fashion applications. The textile industry uses more than 8,000 chemicals, including more than 3,600 dyes, in the dyeing, printing, and finishing processes (Kant, 2012). Azo dyes, the largest and most versatile dye class, account for more than 50 percent of worldwide dye production (Chung, 2016). Azo dyes themselves carry only a minimum human health risk; however, they can be reductively split to form aromatic amines in the environment through degradation and by human beings in contact with sweat, saliva, or gastric juice (Pielesz et al., 2002). A number of aromatic amines formed from azo dyes reduction have been found to have carcinogenic risks in experimental animals and humans (Ahlström, Eskilsson, and Björklund, 2005). Chemical/dye workers have a higher incidence of bladder cancer due to occupational exposure to aromatic amines. It was estimated that 10 percent of bladder cancer in men and 5 percent of bladder cancer in women was caused by this occupation (Golka et al., 2002). One aromatic amine, benzidine, is classified as the most dangerous Group 1 carcinogen by the International Agency for Research on Cancer (IARC). According to IARC's classification, all azo dyes metabolized to benzidine, including at least forty-three dyes, were classified as Group 1 carcinogens (Chung, 2016). The European Union listed twenty-two confirmed or suspected carcinogenic aromatic amines, and banned azo dyes that may form one or more of these aromatic amines after reduction (Ahlström, Eskilsson, and Björklund, 2005). Some azo dyes themselves can be carcinogenic without being reduced to aromatic amines (Chung, 2016). For example, C.I. Acid Red 114 and Direct Blue 15 are classified as Group 2B carcinogens (possibly carcinogenic to humans) by IARC. (Note: the IARC carcinogen classification can be accessed at http://monographs.iarc.fr/ENG/Classification/ClassificationsAlphaOrder.pdf.)

Textile dyeing and finishing processes are conducted in water solution and there are multiple washing cycles. In a typical dyeing and finishing factory, about 150 m^3 of water are used to produce one ton of textile (Lu et al., 2010). This is equivalent to using approximately 22.5 liters of water to dye and finish one T-shirt (about 150 grams). A large quantity of clean water is used as influent, and wastewater contaminated with many chemicals and high BOD and COD loads is discharged as effluent, which negatively impacts the environment and human health.

Case study

In 2011, six major sportswear and fashion companies—Nike, Adidas, Puma, Li-Ning, C&A, and H&M—collaborated to produce a Joint Roadmap to Zero Discharge of Hazardous Chemicals (ZDHC). They identified eleven priority groups of well-known hazardous chemicals, such as alkylphenol and alkylphenol ethoxylates (AP/APEOs), phthalates, azo dyes, and perfluorinated chemicals (PFCs), and made a commitment to eliminate these chemicals from their supply chains and products by 2020 (Greenpeace International). These eleven groups of chemicals are widely used in textile production, especially the dyeing and finishing processes. For example, AP/APEOs are surfactants in detergents, scouring agents, dye-dispersing agents, and wetting agents. Phthalates are plasticizers to make synthetic leather softer, and are also commonly used in textile screen printing and coating. PFCs are water repellent and soil resistant agents.

Since its establishment, more brands and organizations joined the collaboration, and as of August 2017, twenty-three signatory brands, thirty-three value chain affiliates, and fourteen associates are members of the ZDHC Programme. In 2015, the ZDHC Programme published its Manufacturer Restrictive Substance List (MRSL) Version 1.1. In addition to the original eleven priority groups, a few other hazardous chemical groups, such as disperse (sensitizing) dyes, polycyclic aromatic hydrocarbons (PAHs), and volatile organic compounds (VOCs), have been added to MRSL Version 1.1. The ZDHC Programme also published the MRSL Conformance Guidance to assist companies to find processes and chemical formulations that are in conformance with MRSL. A summary of the ZDHC Programme and MRSL is available on the

ZHDC Programme website: www.roadmaptozero.com. Some ZDHC member companies have publicly reported their progress towards the elimination of hazardous chemicals in MRSL. They have asked facilities/factories in their supply chains to test the existence of hazardous chemicals in wastewater and publish those test results on a public platform: the Institute of Public and Environmental Affairs (IPE) DETOX Disclosure Platform (Puma; H&M).

In 2016, Puma asked forty-four of its largest wet (dyeing and finishing) processing facilities to test their wastewater samples, and thirty-four of them have published their test results on the IPE platform. Of the fourteen hazardous chemical groups, five were classed as 100 percent non-detected (i.e. completely eliminated from the facilities), five others were non-detected in more than 90 percent of the samples, and four chemical groups were non-detected in 77.6 percent to 86.4 percent of the samples (Puma).

In 2016, sixty-nine factories in H&M's supply chain tested incoming water and wastewater and all of them disclosed their test results on the IPE platform. In wastewater, of the eleven hazardous chemical groups, three were 100 percent non-detected, four were non-detected in more than 90 percent of the samples, and four were non-detected in 75 percent to 88 percent of the samples. H&M also noted that five chemical groups were detected in incoming water, indicating a challenge for compliance due to an already polluted water source (H&M).

ZDHC member companies are making progress in eliminating the most hazardous groups of chemicals in their product and supply chains. Some of these chemicals remain in the fashion products and affect consumers' health. Phthalates, which are present in fashion products such as footwear, raincoats, and screen printed T-shirts, can enter the human body through direct contact and cause development and reproductive problems (Heudorf, Mersch-Sundermann, and Angerer, 2007). Though some of these chemicals, such as AP/APEO, do not remain in the final fashion products, using them in textile production will cause health problems to workers, while discharging them will be harmful to the environment, wildlife, and the community near the production site. Eliminating ZDHC priority hazardous chemical groups in fashion production will be beneficial to consumers, workers, the community, and the environment.

References

Agbohessi, Prudencio T., Imorou Toko, Ibrahim, Ouédraogo, Alfred, Jauniaux, Thierry, Mandiki, S.N.M., and Kestemont, Patrick. "Assessment of the Health Status of Wild

Fish Inhabiting a Cotton Basin Heavily Impacted by Pesticides in Benin (West Africa)." *Science of the Total Environment* 506–7 (2015): 567–84.

Ahlström, Lars-Henric, Sparr Eskilsson, Cecilia, and Björklund, Erland. "Determination of Banned Azo dyes in Consumer Goods." *Trends in Analytical Chemistry* 24 (2005): 49–56.

Azandjeme, Colette S., Delisle, Hélène, Fayomi, Benjamin, Ayotte, Pierre, Djrolo, Francois, Houinato, Dismand, and Bouchard, Michèle. "High Serum Organochlorine Pesticide Concentrations in Diabetics of a Cotton Producing Area of the Benin Republic (West Africa)." *Environment International* 69 (2014): 1–8.

Belay, Alebel Abebe, "Impacts of Chromium from Tannery Effluent and Evaluation of Alternative Treatment Options." *Journal of Environmental Protection* 1 (2010): 53–8.

Bevilacqua, Maurizio, Ciarapica, Filippo Emanuele, Mazzuto, Giovanni, and Paciarotti, Claudia. "Environmental Analysis of a Cotton Yarn Supply Chain." *Journal of Cleaner Production* 82 (2014): 154–65.

Biswas, Wahidul K., Graham, John, Kelly, Kevin, and John, Michele B. "Global Warming Contributions from Wheat, Sheep Meat and Wool Production in Victoria, Australia—A Life Cycle Assessment." *Journal of Cleaner Production* 18 (2010): 1386–92.

Bomgardner, Melody M. "The Great Lint Migration." *Chemical & Engineering News* 95, no. 2 (2017): 16–17.

Broucek, Jan. "Production of Methane Emissions from Ruminant Husbandry: A Review." *Journal of Environmental Protection* 5 (2014): 1482–93.

Browne, Mark Anthony, Crump, Phillip, Niven, Stewart J., Teuten, Emma, Tonkin, Andrew, Galloway, Tamara, and Thompson, Richard. "Accumulation of Microplastic on Shorelines Worldwide: Sources and Sinks." *Environmental Science & Technology* 45 (2011): 9175–9.

Burkitbayeva, Saule, Qaim, Matin, and Swinnen, Johan. "A Black (White) Hole in the Global Spread of GM Cotton." *Trends in Biotechnology* 34 (2016): 260–3.

Chen, Hsiou-Lien and Davis Burns, Leslie. "Environmental Analysis of Textile Products." *Clothing and Textiles Research Journal* 24 (2006): 248–61.

Chung, King-Thom, "Azo Dyes and Human Health: A Review." *Journal of Environmental Science and Health*, Part C: *Environmental Carcinogenesis and Ecotoxicology Reviews* 34 (2016): 233–61.

Colonna, Martino, Berti, Corrado, Fiorini, Maurizio, Binassi, Enrico, Mazzacurati, Marzia, Vannini, Micaela, and Karanam, Sreepadaraj. "Synthesis and Radiocarbon Evidence of Terephthalate Polyesters Completely Prepared from Renewable Resources." *Green Chemistry* 13 (2011): 2543–8.

Colosio, C., Tiramani, M., and Maroni, M. "Neurobehavioral Effects of Pesticides: State of the Art." *NeuroToxicology* 24 (2003): 577–92.

Cooper, Ross G. and Harrison, Adrian P. "The Exposure to and Health Effects of Antimony." *Indian Journal of Occupational and Environmental Medicine* 13 (2009): 3–10.

Cotton Australia, "Statistics." http://cottonaustralia.com.au/cotton-library/statistics.

Coupe, Richard H. and Capel, Paul D. "Trends in Pesticide Use on Soybean, Corn and Cotton since the Introduction of Major Genetically Modified Crops in the United States." *Pest Management Science* 72 (2016): 1013–22.

Covington, Anthony D. "Modern Tanning Chemistry." *Chemical Society Reviews* 26 (1997): 111–26.

Deng, Weijun, Chen, Donghui, Huang, Manhong, Hu, Jing, and Chen, Liang. "Carbon Dioxide Deliming in Leather Production: A Literature Review." *Journal of Cleaner Production* 87 (2015): 26–38.

Dixit, Sumita, Yadav, Ashish, Dwivedi, Premendra D., and Das, Mukul. "Toxic Hazards of Leather Industry and Technologies to Combat Threat: A Review." *Journal of Cleaner Production* 87 (2015): 39–49.

Duh, Ben. "Effect of Antimony Catalyst on Solid-State Polycondensation of Poly(ethylene terephthalate)." *Polymer* 43 (2002): 3147–54.

DuPont Company, "Sorona® Environmental Data Sheet." http://www2.dupont.com/ Sorona_Consumer/en_US/assets/downloads/PS-1_Sorona_Environmental_Data. pdf.

Dýrmundsson, Ólafur R. "Sustainability of Sheep and Goat Production in North Europe Countries—From the Arctic to the Alps." *Small Ruminant Research* 62 (2006): 151–7.

El-Kady, Ahmed A., Wade, Terry L., Sweet, Stephen T., and Sericano, José L. "Distribution and Residue Profile of Organochlorine Pesticides and Polychlorinated Biphenyls in Sediment and Fish of Lake Manzala, Egypt." *Environmental Science and Pollution Research* 24 (2017): 10301–2.

Food and Agriculture Organization of the United Nations. "World Statistical Compendium for Raw Hides and Skins, Leather and Leather Footwear 1993–2012." 2013. http://www.fao.org/fileadmin/templates/est/COMM_MARKETS_ MONITORING/Hides_Skins/Documents/COMPENDIUM2013.pdf.

Gelbke, Heinz-Peter, Göen, Thomas, Mäurer, Mathias, and Sulsky, Sandra I. "A Review of Health Effects of Carbon Disulfide in Viscose Industry and a Proposal for an Occupational Exposure Limit." *Critical Review in Toxicology* 39, no. S2 (2009): 1–116.

Golka, Klaus, Prior, Verena, Blaszkewicz, Meinolf, and Bolt, Hermann M. "The Enhanced Bladder Cancer Susceptibility of NAT2 Slow Acetylators towards Aromatic Amines: A Review Considering Ethnic Differences." *Toxicology Letters* 128 (2002): 229–41.

Greenpeace International. "Progress and Hurdles on the Road to Detox." http://www. greenpeace.org/international/en/campaigns/detox/fashion/about/progress-and-hurdles-on-the-road-to-Detox/#a0.

Gurudatt, K., De, P., Rakshit, A. K., and Bardhan, M. K. "Dope-dyed Polyester Fibers from Recycled PET Wastes for Use in Molded Automotive Carpets." *Journal of Industrial Textiles* 34 (2005): 167–79.

H&M. "H&M Discharge Data Summary Report 2016." http://sustainability.hm.com/ content/dam/hm/about/documents/masterlanguage/CSR/Policies/HM%20 Discharge%20Data%20Report_2017.pdf.

Hammad, A. Abu and Tumeizi, A. "Land Degradation: Socioeconomic and Environmental Causes and Consequences in the Eastern Mediterranean." *Land Degradation & Development* 23 (2010): 216–26.

Hansen, Malene Barré, Rydin, Stefan, Menné, Torkil, and Johansen, Jeanne Duus. "Quantitative Aspects of Contact Allergy to Chromium and Exposure to Chrome-tanned Leather." *Contact Dermatitis* 47 (2002): 127–34.

Hartline, Niko L., Bruce, Nicholas J., Karba, Stephanie N., Ruff, Elizabeth O., Sonar, Shreya U., and Holden, Patricia A. "Microfibers Masses Recovered from Conventional Machine Washing of New or Aged Garments." *Environmental Science & Technology* 50 (2016): 11532–8.

Heudorf, Ursel, Mersch-Sundermann, Volker, and Angerer, Jürgen. "Phthalates: Toxicology and Exposure." *International Journal of Hygiene and Environmental Health* 210 (2007): 623–34.

Jian, Song, Wenyi, Tao, and Wuyong, Chen. "Kinetics of Enzymatic Unhairing by Protease in Leather Industry." *Journal of Cleaner Production* 19 (2011): 325–31.

Kairis, Orestis, Karavitis, Christos, Salvati, Luca, Kounalaki, Aikaterini, and Kosmas, Kostas. "Exploring the Impact of Overgrazing on Soil Erosion and Land Degradation in a Dry Mediterranean Agro-forest Landscape (Crete, Greece)." *Arid Land Research and Management* 29 (2015): 360–74.

Kant, Rita. "Textile Dyeing Industry and Environmental Hazard." *Natural Science* 4 (2012): 22–6.

Kouser, Shahzad and Qaim, Matin. "Impact of Bt Cotton on Pesticide Poisoning in Smallholder Agriculture: A Panel Data Analysis." *Ecological Economics* 70 (2011): 2105–13.

Kouser, Shahzad and Qaim, Matin. "Bt Cotton, Damage Control and Optimal Levels of Pesticide Use in Pakistan." *Environment Development Economics* 19 (2013): 704–23.

Kurian, Joseph V. "A New Polymer Platform for the Future—Sorona® from Corn Derived 1,3-propanediol." *Journal of Polymer and the Environment* 13 (2005): 159–67.

Lu, Xujie, Liu, Lin, Liu, Rongrong, and Chen, Jihua. "Textile Wastewater Reuse as an Alternative Water Source for Dyeing and Finishing Processes: A Case Study." *Desalination* 258 (2010): 229–32.

Lubick, Naomi. "Endosulfan's Exit: U.S. EPA Pesticide Review Leads to a Ban." *Science* 328, no. 5985 (2010): 1466.

Mancini, Francesca, Van Bruggen, Ariena H. C., Jiggins, Janice L. S., Ambatipudi, Arun C., and Murphy, Helen. "Acute Pesticide Poisoning among Female and Male Cotton Growers in India." *International Journal of Occupational and Environmental Health* 11 (2005): 221–32.

Mandal, Tamal, Dasgupta, Dalai, Mandal, Subhasis, and Datta, Siddhartha. "Treatment of Leather Industry Wastewater by Aerobic Biological and Fenton Oxidation Process." *Journal of Hazardous Materials* 180 (2010): 204–11.

Mississippi State University Extension. "Insect Control Guide for Agronomic Crops." (2016). https://extension.msstate.edu/sites/default/files/publications/publications/p2471_0.pdf.

Monosson, Emily. "Toxic Textiles." *Science* 354, no. 6315 (2016): 977.

Naqvi, Syed M. and Vaishnavi, Chetana. "Bioaccumulative Potential and Toxicity of Endosulfan Insecticide to Non-target Animals." *Comparative Biochemistry and Physiology*, Part C: *Comparative Pharmacology* 105 (1993): 347–61.

Oliveira, C. M., Auad, A. M., Mendes, S. M., and Frizzas, M. R. "Crop Losses and the Economic Impact of Insect Pests on Brazilian Agriculture." *Crop Protection* 56 (2014): 50–4.

Opio, C., Gerber, P., Mottet, A., Falcucci, A., Tempio, G., MacLeod, M., Vellinga, T., Henderson, B., and Steinfeld, H. "Greenhouse Gas Emissions from Ruminant Supply Chains – A Global Life Cycle Assessment." Food and Agriculture Organization of the United Nations (FAO), Rome. 2013. http://www.fao.org/docrep/018/i3461e/i3461e.pdf.

Pielesz, A., Baranowska, I., Rybak, A., and Włochowicz, A. "Detection and Determination of Aromatic Amines as Products of Reductive Splitting from Selected Azo Dyes." *Ecotoxicology and Environmental Safety* 53 (2002): 42–7.

Puma, "Zero Discharge of Hazardous Chemicals: Puma Progress Report 2016." http://about.puma.com/en/sustainability/environment/zero-discharge-of-hazardous-chemicals.

Saravanabhavan, S., Aravindhan, R., Thanikaivelan, P., Raghava Rao, J., Nair, Balachandran Unni, and Ramasami, T. "A Source Reduction Approach: Integrated Bio-based Tanning Methods and the Role of Enzymes in Dehairing and Fiber Opening." *Clean Technologies and Environmental Policy* 7 (2005): 3–14.

Saravanabhavan, Subramani, Thanikaivelan, Palanisamy, Rao, Jonnalagadda Raghava, Unni Nair, Balachandran, and Ranasami, Thirumalachari, "Natural Leather from Natural Materials: Progressing toward a New Arena in Leather Processing." *Environmental Science & Technology* 38 (2004): 871–9.

Shanawany, Saffa El, Foda, Nermine, Hashad, Doaa I., Salama, Naglaa, and Sobh, Zahraa. "The Potential DNA Toxic Changes among Workers Exposed to Antimony Trioxide." *Environmental Science and Pollution Research* 24 (2017): 12455–61.

Shivanna, B. K., Gangadhara Naik, B., Nagaraja, R., Basavaraja, M. K., Kalleswara, C. M., and Karegowda, C. "Bio Efficiency of New Insecticides against Sucking Insect Pests of Transgenic Cotton." *International Journal of Science and Nature* 2 (2011): 79–83.

Stechert, Christin, Kolb, Marit, Bahadir, Müfit, Djossa, Bruno A., and Fahr, Jakob. "Insecticide Residues in Bats along a Land-use Gradient Dominated by Cotton Cultivation in Northern Benin, West Africa." *Environmental Science and Pollution Research* 21 (2014): 8812–21.

Stokstad, Erik. "Can the Bald Eagle Still Soar After It Is Delisted?" *Science* 316, no. 5832 (2007): 1689–90.

Sundar, V. J., Raghava Rao, J., and Muralidharan, C. "Cleaner Chrome Tanning— Emerging Options." *Journal of Cleaner Production* 10 (2002): 69–74.

Taddese, Girma. "Land Degradation: A Challenge to Ethiopia." *Environmental Management* 27 (2001): 815–24.

Textile Exchange. "Preferred Fibres Market Report." 2016. http://textileexchange.org/wp-content/uploads/2017/02/TE-Preferred-Fibres-Market-Report-Oct2016-1.pdf

Textile World. "Man-Made Fibres Continue to Grow." 2015. http://www.textileworld.com/textile-world/fibres-world/2015/02/man-made-fibres-continue-to-grow/

United Nations Industrial Development Organization, "Future Trends in the World Leather and Leather Products Industry and Trade." 2010. https://leatherpanel.org/sites/default/files/publications-attachments/future_trends_in_the_world_leather_and_leather_products_industry_and_trade.pdf.

Weaver, Timothy B., Ghadiri, Hossein, Hulugalle, Nilantha R., and Harden, Stephen. "Organochlorine Pesticides in Soil under Irrigated Cotton Farming Systems in Vertisols of the Namoi Valley, North-western New South Wales, Australia." *Chemosphere* 88 (2012): 336–43.

Weber, Jan, Halsall, Crispin J., Muir, Derek, Teixeira, Camilla, Small, Jeff, Solomon, Keith, Hermanson, Mark, Hung, Hayley, and Bidleman, Terry. "Endosulfan, a Global Pesticide: A Review of Its Fate in the Environment and Occurrence in the Arctic." *Science of the Total Environment* 408 (2010): 2966–84.

Wiedemann, S. G., Yan, M.-J., Henry, B. K., and Murphy, C. M. "Resource Use and Greenhouse Gas Emissions from Three Wool Production Regions in Australia." *Journal of Cleaner Production* 122 (2016): 121–32.

Woodings, C. R. "The Development of Advanced Cellulosic Fibers." *International Journal of Biological Macromolecules* 17 (1995): 305–9.

Wright, Stephanie L., Thompson, Richard C., and Galloway, Tamara S. "The Physical Impacts of Microplastics on Marine Organisms: A Review." *Environmental Pollution* 178 (2013): 483–92.

5

Fashion: An Unrecognized Contributor to Climate Change

Kim Y. Hiller Connell and Melody L. A. LeHew

Taylor aspires to become a fashion vlogger and recently posted a clothing haul from her favorite fast fashion shops, H&M and Forever 21, to YouTube. She is excited to share with others her passion for shopping and styling upcoming season finds. When checking the number of views, likes, and reading comments for her video later in the week, she was confused by one particular comment: "Aren't you concerned about the environmental harm your fashion addiction is causing?" This made her indignant but curious. She began wondering: How does fashion negatively impact the environment?

Introduction

Many consumers are unaware of the negative environmental impacts caused by the fashion industry, and even less clear about the contributions of the industry to climate change. Each stage of fashion manufacturing and distribution requires inputs (e.g., raw materials, energy, chemicals) and creates outputs (e.g., pollution, waste). The purpose of this chapter is to provide an overview of some of the complex environmental consequences associated with increased fiber, textile, and clothing manufacturing. Specifically, this chapter highlights the fashion industry's contribution to climate change. Climate impacts are predominantly hidden in the minds of designers, manufacturers, retailers, and consumers. Therefore, this chapter's objective is to underline the connection between clothing and climate change, with the goal of helping present and future fashion industry professionals to recognize the climate change consequences of fashion, and their role and responsibility in addressing these consequences.

Climate change and the increasing average global temperature is one of the most urgent challenges facing humanity. According to independent reports by both NASA and the National Oceanic and Atmospheric Association, average global surface temperatures made 2016 the hottest year on record—the third year in a row to break records (NASA, 2017). Since the late 1800s, the earth's average global surface temperature has increased by 1.1^C (1.98^F) and the international scientific community asserts that this change is primarily attributable to increases in atmospheric greenhouse gases. Additionally, there is overwhelming agreement amongst scientists that human activities are the main cause of current global warming and that the impacts of climate change (including, but not limited to, increased droughts in some regions, heavier rainfall in others, melting glaciers, rising sea levels, coastal flooding, and acidification of oceans) will drastically disrupt and alter the earth's ecosystems and natural resources (IPCC, 2014). Therefore, altering human activities that are driving climate change and limiting emissions of greenhouse gases into the atmosphere has become a priority for many individuals, companies, cities, and countries around the world.

The fashion industry, because of its size and global scope, is one of the biggest emitters of greenhouse gases, and in particular, carbon dioxide, on the planet. Many processes and materials necessary for making fashion products require substantial quantities of fossil fuels inputted into the system. First, the fashion industry is energy intensive. The manufacturing of fibers, fabric, and clothing requires massive energy inputs into the system; and a primary output of energy production (if generated through fossil fuels) is carbon dioxide. Second, the fashion industry is global, requiring products to be transported around the world via trucks, ships, and planes—all of which are major contributors to carbon dioxide emissions. Because of these factors, the fashion industry accounts for approximately 10 percent of total carbon emissions (Conca, 2015).

The chapter begins with an overview of greenhouse gases and carbon emissions—where they come from and their significance in climate change. The second part of the chapter is a review of the fashion industry—outlining the activities occurring in the production stages of the industry. This information is followed by an explanation of the carbon footprint of the fashion industry—examining it from the perspective of both natural and man-made fibers. After detailing how the production stages of the fashion industry are contributing to climate change, the conclusion discusses current actions by the industry and recommends further initiatives for the future to evolve into a carbon neutral and more sustainable industry. Finally, the chapter ends with a case study illustrating one fashion brand's attempt to reduce its carbon footprint.

The basics of carbon emissions

Greenhouse gases, including carbon dioxide, methane, water vapor, nitrous oxide, and ozone, are natural components of the earth's atmosphere. They are necessary for maintaining global temperatures, and when in balance, greenhouse gases are what make earth livable—not too hot and not too cold. However, because of human behavior, atmospheric greenhouse gases are increasing and warming global surface and ocean temperatures to dangerous levels.

Although all greenhouse gases play a role in global temperatures, carbon dioxide is the primary driver of climate change because the other greenhouse gases do not trap heat as effectively and are not being added to the atmosphere as rapidly (IPCC, 2014). Therefore, most conversations surrounding climate change focus on reducing carbon emissions.

So where do carbon emissions originate? What human behaviors are responsible for releasing carbon dioxide into the atmosphere? By far the largest human source of carbon dioxide emissions is the burning of fossil fuels, including coal, oil/petroleum, and natural gas, for activities such as generating electricity and heat, as well as fueling transportation (EPA, 2017). Electricity and heat production generate approximately 31 percent of greenhouse gas emissions—most of which are carbon dioxide (EPA, 2017). This is because the globe is still predominately reliant on the burning of fossil fuels to generate electricity. In the United States, most of our electricity (64 percent) comes from burning coal and natural gas (EIA 2017); and this is also the case in many other countries such as China and India, where fiber, fabric, and clothing manufacturing industries dominate. Transportation activities (the movement of people and products around the globe through cars, trucks, ships, trains, and airplanes) accounts for 15 percent of global greenhouse gas emissions (World Resources Institute, 2017) and the predominant fuel utilized in transportation is petroleum (including gasoline and diesel) (IPCC, 2014). As shown in Figure 5.1, other sources of greenhouse gas emissions include the industrial and agricultural sectors, residential and commercial activities, and land use and forestry (EPA, 2017).

Fossil fuels contain *stored carbon*—which is carbon that millions of years ago, through photosynthesis and the food chain, was removed from the atmosphere by the plants and animals that eventually geologically transformed into oil, coal, and natural gas. Therefore, every time we burn fossil fuels, we release the stored carbon back into the atmosphere in the form of carbon dioxide gas—setting the carbon cycle out of balance and resulting in more and more carbon dioxide building up in the atmosphere. The extra carbon dioxide then traps more of the sun's

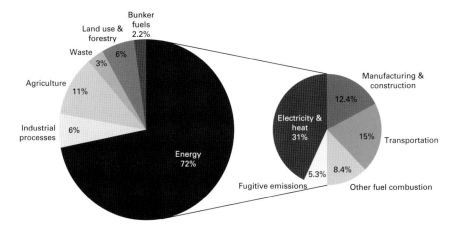

Figure 5.1 Global human-made greenhouse gas emissions by sector.

thermal radiation (i.e. heat) within the atmosphere than is necessary, resulting in the global warming of our planet and changes in our climate. The relationships between carbon emissions, climate change, and the fashion industry is what is explored in this chapter.

The basics of the fashion industry

The fashion industry is truly a global industry spanning every country and touching the lives of every individual. It includes everything from fiber, yarn, fabric, and clothing manufacturing, the wholesalers and retailers who distribute fashion products, and the consumers who purchase, wear, and care for the fashion items. It is an industry that is worth $1.2 trillion (Joint Economic Committee, 2015) and employs millions of individuals.

This chapter focuses on the climate change impacts of the pre-consumer stages of the fashion industry, which (as detailed in Figure 5.2) includes fiber, yarn, fabric, and apparel manufacturing. Other elements of the fashion industry (such as retailing and consumer use) also result in carbon emissions and contribute towards climate change. However, due to its scope, in this chapter the examination of climate change and the fashion industry remains within the boundaries of the production stages.

Fiber manufacturing includes the production of both natural and man-made fibers. In terms of natural fibers, cotton dominates the industry, and the activities

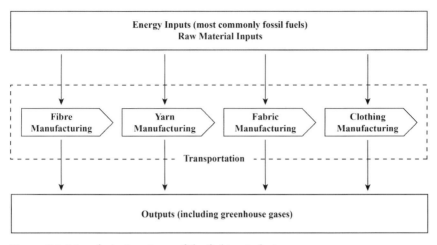

Figure 5.2 Manufacturing stages of the fashion industry.

related to cotton fiber production that are included at this stage cover all the agricultural practices included in cultivating and harvesting cotton. The top cotton producing countries in the world are China, India, and the United States (Statista, 2017). Similarly, polyester, a synthetic fiber manufactured from petrochemicals, is the most prevalent man-made fiber in the industry—with China making 69 percent of it, followed by India, and a variety of other Southeast Asian countries (Textile World, 2015).

Yarn manufacturing for both natural and man-made fibers involves a multitude of steps and processes to prepare the yarns for fabric production. Fibers must be cleaned, carded, combed, drawn, roved, blended, and spun. After the yarns are produced, they will be either woven or knitted into fabrics of varying properties, weights, textures, and so on. Additionally, if it has not already occurred at an earlier stage, this is also the step where color is added—either through dyeing, printing, or a combination of both. Yarn and fabric production, coloring, and finishing are mechanized processes that utilize large industrial equipment in modern factories around the world. Globally, China, the European Union, and India are the top three exporters of fabric (WTO, 2016).

The pre-consumer stages of the fashion industry conclude with clothing manufacturing. At this stage fabric is cut and sewn into garments that consumers will purchase and wear. This stage is labor-intensive, utilizing industrial sewing and other machinery, and employs millions of garment workers throughout the globe—with China and Bangladesh among the largest producers, with Vietnam, Hong Kong, and India also significant exporters (WTO, 2016).

Carbon footprint of the fashion industry

A carbon footprint represents the amount of "carbon dioxide emitted by something during a given period" (Carbon Footprint, para. 1), with "something," in this case, being the manufacture and transport of fashion products. According to the International Organization for Standardization (ISO), understanding the carbon footprint of a product reveals the "cost of a product in grams of CO_2 . . . [giving] us an idea of how our actions . . . affect the amount of greenhouse gases in the atmosphere" (Bird, 2013, para. 2). A growing concern for industry-related environmental impacts have spurred a variety of carbon footprint assessments from several perspectives: comparing the impact of different fibers (e.g., cotton versus polyester), highlighting the impact of a specific fashion product (e.g., cotton T-shirt), or evaluating the overall impact of the supply chain. These carbon footprint studies provide a valuable insight into the fashion industry's contribution to greenhouse gas emissions and climate change. Unfortunately, the lack of uniformity in setting the scope and boundaries of the studies limits the ability to compare results and determine a consistent and agreed upon level of impact for each stage of production.

Early carbon footprint studies focusing on greenhouse gas emissions from the fashion supply chain pinpointed the primary hotspot as being consumer use (BSR, 2009; Steinberger et al., 2009). Laundering (i.e., washing, drying, and ironing) over time represents 39 percent of total emissions in the supply chain (BSR, 2009). However, a more recent study suggests there is too much variability in consumer clothing use and care, which is based on individual habits and cultural norms, to determine a general level of impact (van der Velden, Patel, and Vogtlander, 2014). In fact, some carbon footprint assessments have found the consumer-use phase to emit less carbon dioxide and other greenhouse gases than textile manufacturing processes (van der Velden, Patel, and Vogtlander, 2014; Wang et al., 2015). While consumer fashion consumption is an important area of climate change concern, this section is focused on identifying and discussing key emission concerns within the production stages identified above (see Figure 5.1): fiber, yarn, fabric, and clothing manufacturing, as well as impacts from transporting materials throughout the production process.

Fiber and yarn manufacturing

Fiber production is responsible for approximately 18 percent of GHG emissions in the total supply chain, from fiber production to consumer use; and yarn manufacturing (spinning and blending) accounts for 21 percent (BSR, 2009). The source of carbon emissions from fashion differs dramatically between natural and synthetic fibers. Natural fibers (e.g., silk, cotton, linen, wool) are agriculturally cultivated materials, whereas synthetic fibers (e.g., polyester, nylon, acrylic) are chemically derived from fossil fuel products (i.e. petroleum and coal). Therefore, it is important to differentiate between the two in this section. Cotton will be used to represent natural fiber classification and polyester will represent the synthetic category as these two are the most commonly used fibers for fashion products. In fact, "cotton provides 30–40 percent of all global fibre requirements" (Cherrett et al., 2005, p. 3), and since 2007, when it surpassed cotton, polyester has been the world's most dominant fiber. Annually, 53.3 million tonnes of polyester are produced, with clothing accounting for the end use of approximately half of all polyester manufactured (Bain, 2015).

Cotton

Cotton fiber and yarn production contributes to climate change primarily through agricultural and industrial activities. Fossil fuels are burned by diesel and gas-powered tillers and harvesters used to prepare the land, plant seeds, apply pesticides, insecticides, and other agrochemicals, and harvest the crop. Other emissions are generated by electric-powered ginning machinery used to dry the cotton before separating the seeds, cleaning and compressing the raw cotton into bales for shipping to mills where it is spun into yarns. Once the bales of raw cotton are transported to the mill, the fiber is cleaned, carded, combed, and twisted onto bobbins in preparation for spinning into yarn and winding onto cones (Cherrett et al., 2005). Depending upon the end use, dyes and finishes may be added at the yarn stage of production. In a recent study, cotton yarn production impact was determined with an overall carbon footprint impact of 2.81 $kgCO_2e$ emissions, with yarn dyeing representing 44 percent of the footprint (Bevilacqua et al., 2014).

Cultivating raw cotton creates less greenhouse gas emissions than manufacturing a synthetic fiber such as polyester (BSR, 2009). However, other environmental impacts such as water usage, water pollution, and soil depletion must be weighed in the overall environmental evaluation as well.

Polyester

Synthetic fibers start with the creation of polymers which includes multiple steps: cracking, separation, oxidation, esterification, melt polymerization, solid-state polymerization, and spinning preparation (Cherrett et al., 2005). Once the polymers have been prepared they are spun into filament and then texturized to create the desired yarn characteristics. Polyester production uses more than double the amount of energy that it takes to produce cotton (BSR, 2009), with greenhouse gas emissions being generated primarily from electricity production. It is estimated that "706 billion kilograms of greenhouse gas can be attributed to polyester production for use in textiles in 2015 . . . [equivalent to] 64 million American homes' supply of electricity for 1 year" (Kirchain et al., 2015, p. 17). The level of contribution to climate change varies depending upon whether the energy source used to power these activities comes from non-renewable fossil fuels or renewable energy sources, such as wind, solar, or nuclear power. However, as discussed earlier, coal and gas continue to be the dominant source of energy. There is also additional variation in the carbon footprint based on the size of the filament yarn. Thinner yarns create a higher energy demand than thicker yarns (van der Velden, Patel, and Vogtlander, 2014).

After yarn production, the carbon footprint of the remaining phases in the supply chain is not impacted much by fiber type. Therefore, the remaining sections do not distinguish between cotton or polyester and consider the carbon emissions more holistically.

Fabric manufacturing

The fabrication phase of the fashion supply chain includes several stages, such as texturizing, knitting or weaving, pre-colorization treatments, dyeing or printing, and finishing processes. This stage relies upon fossil fuels to create electricity to power machinery as well as boilers to heat water and create steam to dye and finish fabrics (O EcoTextiles, 2011). Knitting uses less energy than weaving fabric, creating a smaller carbon footprint (van der Velden, Patel, and Vogtlander, 2014).

Dyeing and finishing processes may occur either during yarn or fabric manufacturing. According to a report from Business for Social Responsibility (BSR, 2009), even though there has been little carbon footprint data available specifically targeting dyeing and finishing, these processes require substantial amounts of hot water; and therefore greenhouse gas emissions result due to the energy required to heat dye baths. One study indicated a link between emission levels and several fabric characteristics—fiber, dyestuff, dyeing technique, the number of finishes, and so on—and the carbon footprint is therefore case dependent (van der Velden, Patel, and Vogtlander, 2014). For example, dyeing polyester fiber requires higher temperatures for the fabric to accept disperse dyestuff, requiring more energy and creating greater greenhouse gas emissions (BSR, 2009).

Apparel manufacturing

Fabric is transformed into fashion products through a series of steps dependent upon the particular product specifications. Steps include layout, cutting, sewing, cleaning, and ironing (Palamutcu, 2010). Garment manufacturing is the most labor-intensive phase in the supply chain, but still requires machinery in order to complete each step, with resulting CO_2 emissions coming from the electricity and heat energy needed to power these machines. However, in terms of the supply chain, apparel manufacturing consumes the least amount of electricity and therefore contributes a smaller carbon footprint than other stages (Sule, 2012; Palamutcu, 2010). In fact, some researchers leave out the cutting and sewing processes when assessing carbon footprint for textile products because these account for less than 1 percent of GHG emissions (van der Velden, Patel, and Vogtlander, 2014; BSR, 2009).

Transportation

Due to the highly globalized nature of the fashion industry and the supply chain, raw materials, fibers, yarns, textiles, and garments are transported between and within countries multiple times before ending up on a display rack in a retail store. To facilitate this movement of production materials and final products throughout the globe, the fashion industry utilizes multiple modes of transportation, including planes, trucks, ships, and trains.

The mode of transportation used to distribute raw materials, fabric, and finished products to the next phase of production or distribution creates variability in the carbon impact for a particular product or fashion company. It is the primary direct contributor to the industry's carbon footprint, with most of the other phases in the supply chain indirectly (through electricity generation) contributing to climate change (Wang et al., 2015). The level of impact depends upon the mode of transportation used to ship materials and products, the distance travelled, the number of transports between production phases, the magnitude of the distribution network for a particular company, as well as how often new products are produced and shipped. For example, a vertically integrated fashion company may purchase raw cotton grown in the United States, contract a yarn and fabric manufacturer in China to spin and weave the cotton to be cut and sewn into men's shirts in Bangladesh and then shipped to several European and American retailers to be sold in thousands of geographically dispersed store locations. Fashion products travel around the world before arriving in the stores for consumers to purchase.

Air transportation results in the highest level of greenhouse gas emissions, with trucks contributing the next highest, then ships and trains contributing the least to carbon footprint (Wang et al., 2015; BSR, 2009). With the rapid growth in fast fashion business models, use of air transportation in order to cut the amount of time for products to arrive in stores is growing as well. One of the leaders in fast fashion, Inditex (i.e. Zara's) increasingly utilizes air transportation to ensure their products arrive promptly in distant markets (Orcao and Perez, 2014).

The sheer number of processes that occur during each stage of manufacturing, when coupled with the number of units produced annually for the global fashion market, make the overall footprint of the industry a major concern. Additional carbon footprint studies are needed to get a clearer picture of the industry's contribution to climate change. However, in general terms, when comparing the life cycle greenhouse gas emission impacts, polyester has higher emissions than cotton while woven fabrics have higher emissions than knit (Kirchain et al., 2015).

Strategies for decreasing the industry's carbon footprint

In 2018, recognizing the significant impact that the fashion industry has on climate change, the United Nations Framework Convention on Climate Change, in collaboration with different fashion industry stakeholders, formed the Fashion Industry Charter for Climate Action. The charter recognizes that current patterns of production within the fashion industry are incompatible with meeting the goals of the Paris Agreement on Climate Change and aims, by 2050, for the global fashion industry to be carbon neutral (Fashion Industry Charter for Climate Action). The charter includes the target of reducing GHG emissions in the fashion industry by 30 percent by 2030, and is an indication that leaders within the industry understand the urgency of acting on climate change and are committed to investing resources into developing and implementing solutions.

Broadly speaking, there are two strategies that can be implemented by the fashion industry for initial reduction of greenhouse gas emissions. First, the industry can utilize more energy efficient production processes, equipment, and technology. Closed loop manufacturing, a strategy increasingly used by innovative companies like Patagonia, has the potential to significantly decrease energy demands. Through their Common Threads Garment Recycling Program, customers return unwanted clothing to Patagonia, which are then recycled by the company into new products. This strategy reduces climate change impact because, for example, recycled polyester utilizes less energy than virgin polyester, with some studies finding a reduction in energy requirements of 33–55 percent (O Ecotextiles, 2009), resulting therefore in fewer greenhouse gas emissions. Following the example of Patagonia, other companies within the fashion industry are also exploring closed loop manufacturing processes.

A second initial strategy that companies wanting to reduce their greenhouse gas emissions can pursue is reducing their reliance on fossil fuels for energy production and increasing the use of renewable energy sources such as solar and wind. This strategy has been embraced by companies such as REI. By implementing practices such as using solar power for their retail stores, distribution centers, and headquarters, as well as purchasing renewable energy certificates, REI has reduced its greenhouse gas emissions on an annual basis by an amount equivalent to "removing nearly 8,000 cars from the road or switching more than 990,000 incandescent bulbs to compact fluorescents" (REI, 2014, para. 4). This strategy of utilizing more renewable energy within the fashion industry will hopefully become more mainstream as renewable energy technologies continue to grow and become more accessible and affordable.

Beyond these short-term strategies, the fashion industry must rethink how to more sustainably meet the needs of consumers. Experts agree that a global temperature increase greater than two degrees Celsius will permanently and negatively alter the systems that sustain life on earth. Therefore, the level of decrease in greenhouse gas emissions necessary to avoid these irreversible impacts will require more than becoming energy efficient and using renewable energy. Fundamentally, the overconsumption of fashion, especially fast fashion, cannot continue. While this will require a transformation of the fashion industry, the reality is that the overall supply of fashion products must decrease.

One of the ways the Fashion Industry Charter for Climate Action envisions transforming the fashion industry and achieving climate neutrality by 2050 is by shifting away from a traditional linear economy and towards circular economy principles. A circular economy is

> … an industrial system that is restorative or regenerative by intention and design. It replaces the end-of-life concept with restoration, shifts towards the use of renewable energy, eliminates the use of toxic chemicals, which impair reuse, and aims for the elimination of waste through the superior design of materials, products, systems and business models.
>
> Ellen MacArthur Foundation, 2013, p. 7

A circular economy model of business emphasizes circular supplies (renewable energy, bio-based or fully recyclable materials), resource recovery, product life extension through strategies such as repairing and reselling, sharing platforms to increase utilization rates, and products and services.

In 2017, at the Copenhagen Fashion Summit, the non-profit organization Global Fashion Agenda urged major firms and other stakeholders within the fashion industry to demonstrate their commitment to a circular fashion system by signing the 2020 Circular Fashion System Commitment. Ninety-four major brands (including Eileen Fisher, Esprit, and H&H) and companies, constituting 12.5 percent of the global fashion industry, have signed the commitment (Global Fashion Agenda). Additionally, these strategic partners are sharing resources to spearhead large-scale commercialization of circular business models through initiatives like Nike's *Circularity: Guiding the Future of Design*, which provides

> … designers and product creators across the industry with a framework for circularity that can help inspire more considered design choices. The guide shares 10 key principles for circularity: Materials, cyclability, waste avoidance, disassembly, green chemistry, refurbishment, versatility, durability, packaging and new models.
>
> Global Fashion Agenda, para. 4

Circular economies are vital to meeting the goals of the Paris Agreement on Climate Change and avoiding climate change disaster. Circular economies are regenerative systems that focus on minimizing both resource and energy inputs and waste and emission outputs (Circle Economy, 2019). In the fashion industry, circular economies can be achieved by designing and manufacturing long-lasting products that can be maintained, repaired, reused, reimagined, remanufactured, resold, and eventually, fully recycled. So while developing more energy efficient mechanisms for manufacturing and switching to renewable sources of energy within the industry are positive first steps on the path to decreasing contributions towards climate change, a carbon neutral fashion industry will not be possible without a shift to circularity.

Case study: Puma's InCycle initiative

In March 2013, the active wear fashion brand Puma launched their InCycle collection—a 100 percent closed-loop fashion product line that was intended to have a positive environmental footprint (to actually be good for the earth) by being fully biodegradable and recyclable. The product line consisted of a backpack, shoes, a T-shirt, and a track jacket—all of which at their end-of-life stage could either be safely composted and returned to the earth as nutrients or easily disassembled, recycled, and remanufactured into new products. The T-shirt was made from 100 percent organic cotton and utilized eco-conscious screen printing. The track jacket was made from recycled bottles, and both the jacket and backpack were made from materials that could be fully recycled. The upper of the shoes was manufactured from organic cotton and linen (compostable materials) and the sole was made from an innovative, biodegradable plastic.

InCycle became the first clothing product line to be 100 percent Cradle to Cradle Certified™. To receive this designation, products must meet strict environmental and social standards in terms of the environmental safety of raw materials, the reutilization of raw materials, the use of renewable energy for manufacturing, water stewardship, and social fairness.

The clothing, shoes, and backpack within the InCycle collection were better for the environment in a multitude of ways—the raw materials did not contain dangerous toxic chemicals, the composted garments would become organic nutrients, and all of the products in the collection would also have a smaller carbon footprint (i.e. contribute fewer carbon emissions to the atmosphere) compared to other similar products designed and manufactured through more traditional processes. For example, all the materials in the InCycle backpack were recyclable. Furthermore, the backpack was designed to be easily disassembled. Therefore, after an individual was finished with the backpack, it could be brought back to a Puma retailer through their "Bring Me Back" program. Puma would then disassemble the bags and reuse/recycle all elements of the backpack for manufacturing new products—nothing would end in a landfill. This was also the case with the track jacket and the shoes—and the track jacket had the additional closed loop characteristic of being made from polyester manufactured from recycled plastic bottles.

Making products from recycled materials consumes considerably less electricity compared to making products from brand new materials—and using less electricity means that less electricity must be generated. And, at least when the electricity is generated through the burning of fossil fuels, this means less carbon dioxide is emitted into the atmosphere. Therefore, closed loop manufacturing within the fashion industry such as the InCycle collection by Puma can significantly reduce the contributions the industry makes towards climate change.

Unfortunately, the InCycle collection was ultimately a failure because of a lack of consumer demand. By the fall of 2014 the products were only available to purchase in Puma's own retail environments and by 2015 the company announced that manufacturing of the line was being halted, as was all research and development on future InCycle products.

References

Bain, M. "If Your Clothes are Aren't Already Made Out of Plastic, They Will Be." 2015. https://qz.com/414223/if-your-clothes-arent-already-made-out-of-plastic-they-will-be/.

Bird, K. "Calculating the Carbon Footprint of Products – A Quest for Clarity." 2013. https://www.iso.org/news/2013/11/Ref1801.html.

BSR. "Apparel Industry Life Cycle Carbon Mapping." 2009. https://www.bsr.org/reports/BSR_Apparel_Supply_Chain_Carbon_Report.pdf.

Carbon Footprint. https://www.merriam-webster.com/dictionary/carbon footprint.

Cherrett, N., Barrett, J., Clemett, A., Chadwick, M., and Chadwick, M. J. "Ecological Footprint and Water Analysis of Cotton, Hemp, and Polyester." Stockholm: Stockholm Environmental Institute, 2005. https://www.sei-international.org/mediamanager/documents/Publications/SEI-Report-EcologicalFootprintAndWaterAnalysisOfCottonHempAndPolyester-2005.pdf.

Circle Economy. "The circularity gap report." 2019. https://www.circularity-gap.world/.

Conca, J. "Making Climate Change Fashionable—The Garment Industry Takes on Global Warming." 2015. http://www.forbes.com/sites/jamesconca/2015/12/03/makingclimate-change-fashionable-the-garment-industry-takes-on-global-warming/.

EIA. "Electricity Explained: Electricity in the United States." 2017. https://www.eia.gov/energyexplained/index.cfm?page=electricity_in_the_united_states.

Ellen MacArthur Foundation. "Towards the circular economy: Economic and businessrationale for an accelerated transition." 2013. https://www.ellenmacarthurfoundation.org/assets/downloads/publications/Ellen-MacArthur-Foundation-Towards-the-Circular-Economy-vol.1.pdf.

EPA. "Sources of greenhouse gas emissions." 2017. https://www.epa.gov/ghgemissions/sources-greenhouse-gas-emissions#t1fn3.

Fashion Industry Charter for Climate Action. "Fashion industry charter for climate action." https://unfccc.int/sites/default/files/resource/Industry%20Charter%20%20Fashion%20and%20Climate%20Action%20-%2022102018.pdf (accessed 30 May 2019).

Global Fashion Agenda (a). "2020 Commitment." https://www.globalfashionagenda.com/commitment/# (accessed 30 May 2019).

Global Fashion Agenda (b). "Nikes Circular Design workbook offers sustainable guidelines for designers." https://www.globalfashionagenda.com/nikes-circular-design-workbook-offers-sustainable-guidelines-for-designers/#.

IPCC. "Climate change 2014: Synthesis report." Contribution of Working Groups I, II, and III to the Fifth Assessment Report of the Intergovernmental Panel on Climate Change [Core Writing Team, R. K. Pachauri and L. A. Meyer (eds.)]. IPCC, Geneva, 2014.

Joint Economic Committee. "The Economic Impact of the Fashion Industry." 2015. https://maloney.house.gov/sites/maloney.house.gov/files/documents/The%20 Economic%20Impact%20of%20the%20Fashion%20Industry%20--%20JEC%20 report%20FINAL.pdf.

Kirchain, R., Olivetti, E., Reed Miller, T., and Greene, S. "Sustainable Apparel Materials." 2015. http://msl.mit.edu/publications/SustainableApparelMaterials.pdf.

NASA. "NASA, NOAA Data Show 2016 Warmest Year on Record Globally." 2017. https://www.nasa.gov/press-release/nasa-noaa-data-show-2016-warmest-year-on-record-globally.

O Ecotextiles. "Why is recycled polyester considered a sustainable textile?" 2009. https:// oecotextiles.wordpress.com/2009/07/14/why-is-recycled-polyester-considered-a-sustainable-textile/

O Ecotextiles. "Estimating the carbon footprint of a fabric." 2011. https://oecotextiles. wordpress.com/2011/01/19/estimating-the-carbon-footprint-of-a-fabric/.

Orcao, A. I. E. and Perez, D. R. "Global production chains in the fast fashion sector, transports and logistics: The case of the Spanish retailer Inditex." *Investigaciones Geograficas, Boletin del Instituto de Geograffia, UNAM* 84 (2014): 113–27.

Palamutcu, S. "Electric energy consumption in the cotton textile processing stages" *Energy* 35 (2010): 2945–52.

REI. "REI Now Powered By Renewable Energy." 2014. http://newsroom.rei.com/news/ rei-now-powered-by-renewable-energy.htm.

Statista. "Cotton Production by Country Worldwide in 2015/2016." 2017. https://www. statista.com/statistics/263055/cotton-production-worldwide-by-top-countries/.

Steinberger, J. K., Friot, D., Jolliet, O., and Erkman, S. "A spatially explicit life cycle inventory of the global textile chain." *International Journal of Life Cycle Assessment* 14 (2009): 443–55.

Sule, A. "Life cycle assessment of clothing process." *Research Journal of Chemical Sciences* 2, no. 2 (2012): 87–9.

Textile World. "Man-made Fibers Continue to Grow." 2015. http://www.textileworld. com/textile-world/fiber-world/2015/02/man-made-fibers-continue-to-grow/.

van der Velden, N. M., Patel, M. K., and Vogtlander, J. G. "LCA benchmarking study on textiles made of cotton, polyester, nylon, acryl, or elastane." *International Journal of Life Cycle Assessment* 19 (2014): 331–56.

Wang, C., Wang, L., Liu, X., Du, C., Ding, D., Jia, J., Yan, Y., and Wu, G. "Carbon footprint of textile throughout its life cycle: A case study of Chinese cotton shirts." *Journal of Cleaner Production* 108 (2015): 464–75.

World Resources Institute. "CAIT climate data explorer." 2017. http://cait.wri.org/.

WTO. "World Trade Statistical Review 2016." 2016. https://www.wto.org/english/res_e/ statis_e/wts2016_e/wts16_toc_e.htm.

6

The Dangers in the Fashion Supply Chain: Offshore vs. Domestic Sourcing

Ting Chi and Sheng Lu

The fashion industry plays a vital role in the United States and the global economy. Encompassing apparel, textiles, and footwear, the market value of this industry reached $380 billion in the US and multitrillion in the world in 2015 (US Congress, 2016). The fashion industry employs approximately 2 million people in the US and over 60 million people globally (Stotz and Kane, 2015; US Congress, 2016).

The US fashion industry historically ran on a low-capital and labor-intensive operation, which had been an effective strategy until the early 1990s (Kilduff and Chi, 2006). During the 1990s, US fashion companies faced the growing pressures of rising production costs, a downward spiral of retail prices, and an accelerating movement toward regionalization and globalization as a result of new free trade agreements or trade preference programs (Allwood et al., 2006; Chi and Kilduff, 2010). As production costs rapidly increased with little opportunity to pass these costs on, more fashion companies were forced to reconsider their business strategies and supply chain arrangement. To deliver products in a competitive mix of cost, volume, and lead time, fashion companies looked to source more of their products overseas and to subcontract production to more economically viable locations. Therefore, manufacturing in low-cost labor countries became the norm for fashion companies in the US and other developed countries (Dicken, 2015).

Since the late 1990s, a majority of US fashion companies have adopted the strategy of outsourcing production to low-wage countries and redesigned their supply chains to realize the strategy (Chi and Kilduff, 2010). Jobs in the US fashion manufacturing sector disappeared, and factories closed, while the labels on apparel, textiles, and footwear began to read "Made in Mexico" and then "Made in China," later "Bangladesh" and "Vietnam." Today, approximately 97 percent of apparel sold in the US market is imported, and the number of US apparel manufacturing employees has dropped to around 131,300 people in 2016 from over 1 million in the early 1990s (AAFA, 2017).

The increasingly globalized supply chains and complex subcontracting arrangements have created new challenges for the fashion industry. Environmental degradation and human rights violations are among the top concerns about the negative impacts of fashion brands and apparel retailers' global sourcing practices. Furthermore, while offshore production may help reduce the production cost, fashion companies are under growing pressure from consumers' upgraded demand for speed-to-market, a shortened life cycle of fashion apparel products, and the increasing difficulty of controlling the outsourced manufacturing process (Robinson and Hsieh, 2016). Additionally, China and other leading apparel sourcing destinations in Asia are gradually losing their cost competitiveness in apparel manufacturing because of wage and energy cost increases (Chi, 2011; Chi and Sun, 2013). As the fashion supply chain becomes more agile and responsive, a growing number of fashion brands and apparel retailers are actively exploring the option of domestic sourcing and manufacturing to maintain and protect the value proposition of their products, develop the capacity of offering customized products to consumers, and improve their flexibility in sourcing.

Challenges in the fashion supply chain

The "fashion supply chain" refers to the "chain" linking the source of component parts, the factories where those parts are made into buyable products such as apparel, home textiles, and footwear, and the distribution channels by which the products are delivered to consumers directly or the stores where consumers shop (Chi et al., 2009). Notably, in today's global economy, the fashion supply chain has become vast and super complex, which often spans multiple countries and regions. For example, Lu (2017) found that US fashion brands and apparel retailers adopt truly global supply chains today: of the thirty-four companies the study surveyed between April and May 2017, 58 percent reported sourcing from more than ten different countries or regions and around 54 percent expect their sourcing base would become even more diversified through 2019. The study further finds that apparel products today are typically "Made in the World." It is common to see apparel labeled "Made in Vietnam" actually contain cotton grown in the United States, yarns spun in Japan, and fabrics woven in China.

Despite the cost benefits, the strategy of relying on offshore production has also created challenges for fashion brands and retailers, particularly regarding managing the environmental and social compliance risks with the ever-expanding sourcing destinations. Take the supply chain for one of the most popular fashion products—denim jeans, for example. The global journey of denim jeans typically starts from cotton farms across the world. The raw cotton then will be shipped to countries which have the capacity for spinning yarns and weaving, knitting, and dyeing the fabrics. The cotton fabrics may be further shipped to a third country for cutting and sewing purchases and the finished apparel exported back to the United States and other consumption markets around the world. However, many consumers may not be aware that the carbon emissions from denim jeans' global journey are astronomical (Tseng and Hung, 2014). Furthermore, jeans arrive sealed in plastic bags, which are often simply trashed by consumers. Although cotton decomposes, those plastic bags make their way to landfills, or perhaps end up in the oceans for hundreds of years or even longer.

Similar to the case of denim jeans, virtually every mass-produced fashion item that arrives in America all the way from developing countries requires tens of millions of people and metric tons of water, chemicals, crops, and oil in the process. Our insatiable desire for inexpensive fashion products in an ever-shorter cycle time has resulted in overproduction, overstocking, excessive markdowns, and consequently massive waste and countless environmental damage (see Figure 6.1). Fast fashion that equals disposable fashion is driving businesses in a race to the bottom.

Subcontracting, which refers to manufacturers delegating certain production orders to other factories, without informing the buyer, is a common practice in apparel outsourcing (Gereffi, 1999). Often, limited information is available about the subcontracting factories, which makes it extremely challenging for fashion brands and retailers to control the social and environmental compliance risks involved in their supply chain (Chi, 2015). Firms reliant on overseas suppliers to manufacture their products face potential reputational harm if working conditions in their supplier factories are dangerous, illegal, unsafe, or otherwise problematic. The risk is particularly high when production is outsourced to countries where labor and environmental standards and regulations are so low that suppliers commonly take unwarranted risks in their project execution (Heide, Kumar, and Wathne, 2014). For instance, in the wake of the Rana Plaza building collapse in Bangladesh which killed 1,134 factory workers, the public media, consumer, and activist scrutiny focused on the global fashion brands and retailers that sourced from suppliers using the building. Many of these fashion brands and retailers were under such intense reputational pressure that they agreed to adopt more accountable collaboration with their overseas suppliers,

Figure 6.1 The social and environmental impact of inexpensive fashion products is often ignored. Source: https://upload.wikimedia.org/wikipedia/commons/b/b8/ Kids_apparel_30%25_off_%2826207874555%29.jpg.

which involves strong governance mechanisms, transparency, and a systematic approach across their supply chains (Abnett, 2016).

For most fashion firms, current concerns have gone beyond the "make or buy" dilemma to complex strategic questions about *where to buy and how to buy*, as outsourcing has become a primary means to obtain a majority of apparel, textiles, and footwear to meet the market demand. Choosing suppliers strategically can enhance a firm's value (Chi and Kilduff, 2011) and reduce the risks existing in global sourcing (Alcacer and Oxley, 2014). On the other hand, poor choices can result in a significant financial loss for a firm, including remediation, legal liability, and reputation damage (O'Callaghan, 2007).

Developing a sustainable fashion supply chain

Sustainability as a business strategy

As one of the biggest players in the global economy, the fashion industry has a responsibility to help protect the environment that has been adversely impacted by industrialization and an ever-expanding global economy. Some leading brands have started to take more proactive steps to enhance sustainability in their business operations and reward the firms financially. For example, Kering, an international luxury group which owns brands such as Gucci, Yves Saint Laurent, Balenciaga, Alexander McQueen, and Bottega Veneta, instituted sourcing and waste-reduction reforms company-wide, and established the Material Innovation Lab to encourage its suppliers to use certified sustainable material in manufacturing (Pavione, Pezzetti, and Dall'ava, 2016). Likewise, the sports product giant Nike launched a "Road to Zero" initiative with the goal of reducing water usage and the discharge of toxic chemicals in its supply chain (Paine, Lynn, Nien-he Hsieh, and Lara, 2016). Social responsibility and sustainability have also become more important in fashion brands and apparel retailers' sourcing decisions. According to Lu (2017), nearly 90 percent of surveyed fashion companies said they give more weight to sustainability when choosing where to source in 2017 than five years ago. The study further reveals that approximately 90 percent of respondents map their supply chains (i.e., keeping records of name, location, and function of suppliers). Notably, more than half of respondents track not only Tier 1 suppliers, that is, those they contract with directly, but also Tier 2 suppliers—the supplier's suppliers. Furthermore, the vast majority (93 percent) of respondents said they use third-party certification programs to audit the social responsibility and sustainability practices of their vendors and about half currently use both third-party certification programs and their own compliance teams. Regarding the content of audits, respondents say they usually focus on three primary areas related to social responsibility: treatment of workers (100 percent), the supplier's fire safety provision (91 percent), and supplier's building safety provision (83 percent).

Sustainability and international logistics

International logistics and supply chain activities have a significant economic impact on today's global economy (see Figure 6.2). With over 80 percent of global trade by volume being carried on ships worldwide, the world seaborne trade totaled 10.6 billion tons and 140 million 20-foot equivalent units (TEUs) in 2017 (UNCTAD, 2017). According to Atkearney (2017), logistics activities, including the movement and storage of goods, reached $1.39 trillion in 2016, accounting for around 8 percent of the total US Gross Domestic Product (GDP) that year.

With the increasing emphasis on sustainable shipping as part of the overall supply chain sustainability, significant efforts have been made by leading logistics companies to reduce adverse environmental impacts. Building an effective logistics strategy allows companies to make a positive impact on the environment as transportation has become a major contributor to fashion supply chain sustainability. To find better ways for getting shipments to a location safely with minimal carbon footprint, the industry aims to develop and implement new technologies that would minimize the fuel and resource consumption, generate less waste, reduce greenhouse gas emission, and improve cost control.

For example, the United Parcel Service (UPS) announced its ambitious sustainability goal to add more alternative fuel and advanced technology vehicles to its fleet to reduce its greenhouse gas emissions from global ground operations by 12 percent by 2025. This goal was put forward in the context that rapid development of e-commerce/m-commerce deliveries are driving up energy use in operating its facilities and powering its vehicle fleet. Since 2009, UPS has invested more than $750 million in alternative fuel and advanced technology vehicles and fueling stations globally. The company used more than 97 million gallons of alternative and lower-carbon fuels in its ground fleet in 2016. UPS's *2016 Corporate Sustainability Report* states that the diverse and sustainable energy sources that UPS promotes include on-site solar, off-site wind, renewable natural gas, renewable hydrogen, and renewable diesel delivered via an advanced energy system infrastructure (UPS, 2016).

Likewise, FedEx, an air freight giant, saved more than 153 million gallons of jet fuel in 2016 by continuing to modernize its aircraft fleet and improve operations. In its *2017 Global Citizenship Report*, FedEx states that it reduced over 2 million metric tons of carbon dioxide emissions through fuel and energy saving initiatives which are equivalent to the carbon sequestered by more than 1.9 million acres of US forest in one year. On the ground, in 2015, FedEx Express met its goal of increasing vehicle fuel efficiency by 30 percent by 2020. FedEx Express has set a new goal to increase vehicle fuel efficiency by 50 percent by 2025 from a 2005 baseline (Fedex, 2018).

In another case, CMA CGM Group, a global cargo container giant, which serves over 420 of the world's 521 commercial ports through more than 200 shipping lines, aims to reduce its greenhouse gas emissions per transported container by 30 percent by 2025, after having already improved its performance per transported container per kilometer by 50 percent between 2005 and 2015 (CMA CGM, 2018).

Sustainability in packaging

The efforts made towards green and reusable packaging include abandoning polystyrene foam as a material to package fragile products. Polystyrene foam contains toxic chemicals such as styrene and benzene, which are hazardous to humans and could take thousands of years to decompose in the natural environment. Instead, more eco-friendly, biodegradable, and recyclable materials, like corrugated cardboard, are used for packaging.

An average package generally consists of roughly 40 percent of wasted space. This wasted space means wasting packaging materials unnecessarily and using more filler materials to fill up the wasted space. Most filler materials are petrochemical based and are difficult to reuse or recycle, which will negatively affect the environment. Larger boxes take up more space on freight carriers, which means shipping fewer items in every trip and increasing carbon emissions and fuel usage. The excessive packaging also results in higher insurance costs. When companies use packaging boxes of the right size, they can significantly lessen the environmental impact, minimize carbon emissions, and reduce overall shipping costs. Additionally, they reduce the risk of product damage during transit and free up the warehouse space, too.

Furthermore, to optimize packaging and shipping processes and maximize warehouse productivity, companies can increase the accuracy of shipping and billing with the adoption of new technologies (see Figure 6.2.). Using thermal printers to print labels and automatic identification, like Radio-frequency identification (RFID) tags, for products in the warehouse or distribution center, companies can substantially decrease the time taken to identify products in the warehouse, spot their location and exact quantities, and substantially increase overall productivity and inventory accuracy (Bertolini et al., 2015).

Figure 6.2 International logistics and supply chain activities have a significant economic impact on today's global economy. Source: https://commons.wikimedia. org/wiki/File:Container_ships_President_Truman_(IMO_8616283)_and_President_ Kennedy_(IMO_8616295)_at_San_Francisco.jpg.

Reshoring movement

Since the late 1990s, most US fashion companies have adopted an offshore strategy, outsourcing their manufacturing processes to a global network of suppliers (Pickles et al., 2015). Despite the fact that this trend is likely to continue, the operational challenges and increasing cost in global supply chain management have prompted some companies to reconfigure their supply chain activities, including facility relocation or changing supply bases back to their home countries (Ancarani et al., 2015). The return of production activities back to the home country of the parent company, regardless of ownership of the relocated activities, is commonly referred to as reshoring (Gray et al., 2013). With the advancement of automation technologies in garment manufacturing such as Sewbots, reshoring may become an even more popular phenomenon among Western fashion companies given their comparative advantage in capital and technology-intensive manufacturing (Nayak and Padhye, 2017).

Associated with this reshoring trend, there has been a growing awareness of the importance of combining local and global sourcing and manufacturing activities to meet ever-changing consumer demand and to optimize the trade-off between cost savings and agility in fashion supply chains (Macchion et al., 2015). The revision of firms' supply chain strategy through reshoring is not just about lowering production costs through automation or simply advocating for "Made-in-the USA" products. Rather, the primary objective for a firm's supply chain is about adding value to the competitive strategy of the firm and contributing to meeting its strategic objectives (Holweg and Helo, 2014).

The concept of supply chain strategy has been widely used by academics and practitioners. Most discussions of the concept relate it to the pattern of decisions on supply chain activities, including product development and sourcing, capacity planning, raw material conversion, demand management, communication across the supply chain, and delivery of products and services (Narasimhan et al., 2008). The selection of sourcing destination, sourcing methods, and distribution channels to reach consumers are the key components of a company's competitive strategy.

In general, there are three types of competitive strategy that a company may pursue: speed, cost advantage, and brand equity (Mehrjoo and Pasek, 2015). For example, VF Corporation adopts different sourcing strategies to prioritize speed to market for its fashion-oriented lifestyle brands such as Nautica, but cost advantage for its heritage brands such as Wrangler, which mostly carry basic apparel items (Pisano, 2013).

For those US fashion brands that continue to source products and manufacture domestically or consider reshoring, some critical success factors need to be considered, including style and design excellence, country of origin, and the coherence between brand value/reputation and product uniqueness that conveys appropriate emotional appeal and superior product quality for customer satisfaction (Brun et al., 2008). These factors can affect how a company implements its supply chain strategy.

As a company's business model evolves with a changing global competitive environment, supply chain strategy has to be renewed or adapted to assure it is aligned with the company's competitive strategy. This may sometimes involve changing from outsourcing to reshoring. The decision should be made carefully and supported by a value-driven configuration of domestic and/or global sourcing and production.

Gray et al. (2013) suggest some companies might have followed a herd instinct to outsource production activities, leading to a miscalculation of the overall benefits, costs, and risks of outsourcing. Companies reconsidering the impact of outsourcing production on total costs, benefits, and customer value creation have driven the recent reshoring phenomenon (Ellram et al., 2013). From a total cost perspective, the shrinking labor cost differentiation between offshore countries like China, Mexico, and the US, high transportation and logistics costs, and the higher than expected costs associated with coordination and quality control over supply chain partners in foreign locations, have led some companies like Nike and VF Corporation to return certain production activities, such as the making of high-tech driven or customized products, to the US (Abnett, 2016). The psychic distance (e.g., differences in culture, language, business practices, legal and political systems) between home and host countries may lead to managers underestimating the costs of implementing outsourcing decisions, thus increasing the likelihood of reshoring (Ancarani et al., 2015). The potential for disruption in the chain, delivery delays, and long response times to consumer demand changes have also contributed to the decision made by companies to rethink their location of production (Grappi et al., 2015; Gray et al., 2013).

Some fashion companies reshored their production because they recognized the benefits of co-location of design/product development and manufacturing and its impact on innovation and quick response (Abnett, 2016). Branstetter (2013) argued that design should not be separated from manufacturing in the high-end apparel sector because design/product development innovation and product quality are affected by how fabric is cut and sewn into shape, and fine tuning is always needed for the production of high-end fashion.

Co-location of design/product development and manufacturing offers an effective solution. For example, US sportswear giant Under Armour launched a new state-of-the-art Lighthouse manufacturing innovation facility in 2016 that brings new opportunities in local-for-local manufacturing and customized products. In particular, the local-for-local model is expected to help simplify the existing process of going back and forth with Asia suppliers that means that it currently takes around six months for a company to deliver its end product (Russell, 2016).

Moreover, flexibility is considered to be one of the key advantages of reshoring fashion production, enabling firms to be more responsive to fast-changing consumer needs. This level of responsiveness can only be achieved by greater control of the supply chain and shorter lead times. The ability to react to what sells well, while reducing the production of lines underperforming in selling, can help fashion brands maximize their sales in ever-shorter fashion cycles and mitigate the risk of markdowns. For example, thanks to its near-sourcing strategy, fast fashion retailer Zara was able to offer more fresh products to consumers and sell a much higher proportion of its products at full price than most of its competitors (Mihm, 2010).

Reshoring becomes a sensible and plausible alternative to outsourcing when companies perceive a need for adjustment to protect or reinvent the critical attributes for business success (e.g., innovation, quality, quick response, and country of origin effect) that affect customers' preferences. Reshoring can thus be understood as a revision of supply chain strategy which helps reshape and improve a company's competitiveness in the global economy, enhance its value creation for customers, and substantially minimize the environmental impact from shipping products around the globe.

Conclusion

With global sourcing likely to continue as a major trend for most fashion companies in the foreseeable future, the main challenge now facing the fashion industry is to determine what needs to happen to build sustainable supply chains where adverse environmental impact can be reduced at an industry level, and respect for human rights and the valuing of social responsibility are the norm rather than the exception. Fashion companies must recognize that achieving a balance between economic growth, social wellbeing, and environmental sustainability is no longer optional but an obligation to society.

Case study: A value-creation driven game—"Made in the USA" fashion

AJ Fashion Corporation, the owner of the A&J Apparel brand, celebrated its 30th birthday in 2019. Over the course of three decades, the company has grown retail sales of its stylish and finely constructed women's dresses to an estimated $200 million.

Times are different now in Fall River, South Carolina, and AJ is one of the last of its kind to maintain a local manufacturing presence, as many other apparel companies succumbed to economic pressures and outsourced their manufacturing overseas. AJ certainly felt the same pressures. However, instead of following the outsourcing trend, the company decided to explore the possibility of staying local through redesigning its product development and manufacturing processes and streamlining its distribution methods.

The efforts to remain viable in the market began in the mid-1990s after the North American Free Trade Agreement (NAFTA) was implemented. The AJ leadership was determined to innovate product development and production activities, customer service, and sales. This focus, in turn, improved EBITDA (earnings before interest, depreciation, and amortization), which is a measure of a company's cash flow. To achieve these goals, AJ implemented lean processes throughout its supply chain to free up working capital, reduce costs, and shorten lead times. Consequently, the quality of customer service was improved and the sales continued to grow, even under the price pressure from less expensive imported goods.

The lean strategy is a set of principles that help companies improve product quality, reduce production time and operational costs, and identify and eliminate waste (Dües et al., 2013). The AJ leadership examined the company's existing supply chain and identified the following areas for improvement: a lengthy product development process, fabric sourcing, apparel production, and outsourced distribution using a third-party logistics company (3PL) in Atlanta, Georgia. Three strategies were developed and pursued: 1) integrating the product development process with planning and forecasting; 2) implementing a lean manufacturing process using domestically sourced fabrics; and 3) configuring a lean distribution process that would take advantage of the company's internal assets, physical location, and local culture.

To cater to the retailers' made-to-order request, AJ redesigned its forecasting, planning, and product development processes through adoption of a customized product life cycle management (PLM) system. With timely market feedback, the company was able to update its forecast numbers and adjust its planning and product development activities accordingly. Quick design, in-house small batch production, and an efficient shift between product lines based on demand and sales records were implemented.

AJ created a lean, insourced distribution flow that serves its customers better with lower cost. The company was able to reduce by half the lead time from the moment when apparel left the final inspection area in the factory until the order was ready to ship to the customers. The entire process now takes only one week. The company eliminated several non-value-added processes, such as packing, tracking, processing the goods for shipment, and transporting them to the 3PL first, and then to the customer. By insourcing part of its distribution, AJ adopted a more efficient and sustainable practice as it reduced a significant amount of shipment miles. In the end, the distribution workforce in AJ increased, but the net result was reduced distribution costs and a more efficient supply chain.

The Fall River facility was able to improve efficiency and reduce costs, which allowed the company to stay in its historic hometown. The keys to AJ's success were product value and economic value creation and constant adaptation to the changing business environment. To be able to compete with lower-cost imports, AJ identified the cost-inefficient processes and came up with solutions to adjust or eliminate these processes within its supply chain. The company took advantage of local government support and geographical adjacency to fabric suppliers, adopted a methodical approach to project planning that included periodic adjustments, and relied on the knowledge and expertise of its experienced staff and outside experts.

At a time when fashion companies rely heavily on offshore production, it is refreshing to see some businesses that chose to swim against the tide of outsourcing. The AJ leadership learned that if a company can align its supply chain with its corporate strategy while keeping the customers in mind, its employees will accomplish great things while continually improving its processes and service quality.

References

Abnett, K. "Three Years After Rana Plaza, Has Anything Changed?" July 30, 2016. https://www.businessoffashion.com/community/voices/discussions/can-fashion-industry-become-sustainable/three-years-on-from-rana-plaza-has-anything-changed-sustainability-safety-worker-welfare.

Alcacer, J. and Oxley, J. "Learning by supplying." *Strategic Management Journal* 35, no. 2 (2014): 204–23.

Allwood, J. M., Laursen, S. E., De Rodriguez, C. M., and Bocken, N. M. P. *Well Dressed? The Present and Future Sustainability of Clothing and Textiles in the United Kingdom.* Cambridge: Cambridge University Press, 2006.

American Apparel and Footwear Association (AAFA). "ApparelStats 2017," June 1, 2017. https://www.aafaglobal.org/.

Ancarani, A., Di Mauro, C., Fratocchi, L., Orzes, G., and Sartor, M. "Prior to Reshoring: A Duration Analysis of Foreign Manufacturing Ventures." *International Journal of Production Economics* 169 (2015): 141–55.

Atkearney, 2017. "State of logistics report." https://info.atkearney.com/5/956/uploads/accelerating-into-uncertainty.pdf.

Bertolini, M., Bottani, E., Romagnoli, G., and Vignali, G. "The Impact of RFID Technologies on Inventory Accuracy in the Apparel Retailing: Evidence from the Field." *International Journal of RF Technologies* 6, no. 4 (2015): 225–46.

Branstetter, L. G. "Producing Prosperity: Why America Needs a Manufacturing Renaissance." *Journal of Economic Literature* 51, no. 2 (2013): 562–4.

Brun, A. and Castelli, C. "Supply Chain Strategy in the Fashion Industry: Developing a Portfolio Model Depending on Product, Retail Channel and Brand." *International Journal of Production Economics* 116, no. 2 (2008): 169–81.

Chi, T. "Building a Sustainable Supply Chain: An Analysis of Corporate Social Responsibility (CSR) Practices in the Chinese Textile and Apparel Industry." *Journal of the Textile Institute* 102, no. 10 (2011): 837–48.

Chi, T. "Business contingency, strategy formation, and firm performance: An Empirical study of Chinese apparel SMEs." *Administrative Sciences* 5, no. 2 (2015): 27–45.

Chi, T. and Kilduff, P. P. D. "An Empirical Investigation of the Determinants and Shifting Patterns of US Apparel Imports Using a Gravity Model Framework." *Journal of Fashion Marketing and Management: An International Journal* 14, no. 3 (2010): 501–20.

Chi, T., Kilduff, P. P. D., and Gargeya, V. B. "Alignment Between Business Environment Characteristics, Competitive Priorities, Supply Chain Structures, and Firm Business Performance." *International Journal of Productivity and Performance Management* 58, no. 7 (2009): 645–69.

Chi, T. and Sun, Y. "Development of Firm Export Market Oriented Behavior: Evidence from an Emerging Economy." *International Business Review* 22, no. 1 (2013): 339–50.

CMA CGM. "CMA CGM: a leading worldwide shipping group". 2018. http://www.cma-cgm.com/the-group/about-us/presentation.

Dicken, P. *Global Shift: Mapping the Changing Contours of The World Economy.* London: SAGE Publications Ltd., 2007.

Dickson, M. A. and Chang, R. K. "Apparel Manufacturers and the Business Case for Social Sustainability." *Journal of Corporate Citizenship* 57 (2015): 55–72.

Dües, C. M., Tan, K. H., and Lim, M. "Green as the new Lean: how to use Lean practices as a catalyst to greening your supply chain." *Journal of Cleaner Production* 40 (2013): 93–100.

Ellram, L. M., Tate, W. L., and Petersen, K. J. "Offshoring and Reshoring: An Update on The Manufacturing Location Decision." *Journal of Supply Chain Management* 49, no. 2 (2013): 14–22.

Fedex. *2017 Global Citizenship Report*. http://csr.fedex.com/.

Gereffi, G. "International Trade and Industrial Upgrading in the Apparel Commodity Chain." *Journal of International Economics* 48, no. 1 (1999): 37–70.

Grappi, S., Romani, S., and Bagozzi, R. P. "Consumer Stakeholder Responses to Reshoring Strategies." *Journal of the Academy of Marketing Science* 43, no. 4 (2015): 453–71.

Gray, J. V., Skowronski, K., Esenduran, G., and Rungtusanatham, M. J. "The Reshoring Phenomenon: What Supply Chain Academics Ought to Know and Should Do." *Journal of Supply Chain Management* 49, no. 2 (2013): 27–33.

Heide, J. B., Kumar, A., and Wathne, K. H. "Concurrent Sourcing, Governance Mechanisms, and Performance Outcomes in Industrial Value Chains." *Strategic Management Journal* 35, no. 8 (2014): 1164–85.

Holweg, M. and Helo, P. "Defining Value Chain Architectures: Linking Strategic Value Creation to Operational Supply Chain Design." *International Journal of Production Economics* 147 (2014): 230–8.

Kilduff, P. and Chi, T. "Longitudinal Patterns of Comparative Advantage in The Textile Complex—Part 2: Sectoral Perspectives." *Journal of Fashion Marketing and Management: An International Journal* 10, no. 2 (2006): 150–68.

Lu, S. *U.S. Fashion Industry Benchmarking Study*. Washington, DC: United States Fashion Industry Association, 2017.

Macchion, L., Danese, P., and Vinelli, A. "Redefining Supply Network Strategies to Face Changing Environments: A Study from the Fashion and Luxury Industry." *Operations Management Research* 8, no. 1–2 (2015): 15–31.

Mehrjoo, M. and Pasek, Z. J. "Risk assessment for the supply chain of fast fashion apparel industry: a system dynamics framework." *International Journal of Production Research* 54, no. 1 (2016): 28–48.

Mihm, B. "Fast fashion in a flat world: Global sourcing strategies." *International Business & Economics Research Journal* 9, no. 6 (2010): 55–63.

Narasimhan, R., Kim, S. W., and Tan, K. C. "An Empirical Investigation of Supply Chain Strategy Typologies and Relationships to Performance." *International Journal of Production Research* 46, no. 18 (2008): 5231–59

Nayak, R. and Padhye, R. (eds.). *Automation in Garment Manufacturing*. Duxford, UK: Woodhead Publishing, 2017.

O'Callaghan, T. "Disciplining the Multinational Enterprise: The Regulatory Power of Reputation Risk." *Global Society* 21, no. 1 (2007): 95–117.

Paine, Lynn S., Hsieh, Nien-he, and Adamsons, Lara. "Governance and Sustainability at Nike, no. A)." *Harvard Business School Case* (2016): 313–46.

Pavione, E., Pezzetti, R. and Dall'ava, M. "Emerging competitive strategies in the global luxury industry in the perspective of sustainable development: the case of Kering Group." *Management Dynamics in the Knowledge Economy* 4, no. 2 (2016): 241–61.

Pickles, J., Plank, L., Staritz, C., and Glasmeier, A. "Trade policy and regionalisms in global clothing production networks." *Cambridge Journal of Regions, Economy and Society* 8, no. 3 (2015): 381–402.

Pisano, Gary P. "VF Brands: Global Supply Chain Strategy." *Harvard Business School Teaching Note* 614–009 (2013).

Robinson, P. K. and Hsieh, L. "Reshoring: a strategic renewal of luxury clothing supply chains." *Operations Management Research* 9, no. 3–4 (2016): 89–101.

Russel, M. "How Under Armour's Lighthouse will disrupt production." *just-style*, 2016. https://www.just-style.com/analysis/how-under-armours-lighthouse-will-disrupt-production_id129058.aspx.

Sourcing Journal. "Op-Ed: Five Ways to Create a More Sustainable Shipping Environment." July 25, 2017. https://sourcingjournalonline.com/op-ed-five-ways-create-sustainable-shipping-environment/.

Stotz, L. and Kane, G. "Facts on the Global Garment Industry." August 20, 2015. https://cleanclothes.org/resources/publications/factsheets/general-factsheet-garment-industry-february-2015.pdf.

Tseng, Shih-Chang and Hung, Shiu-Wan. "A strategic decision-making model considering the social costs of carbon dioxide emissions for sustainable supply chain management." *Journal of Environmental Management* 133 (2014): 315–22.

United Nations Comtrade Database. August 15, 2017. https://comtrade.un.org/.

United Nations Conference on Trade and Development, UNCTAD. "Review of maritime transport, 2017." 2017. http://www.unctad.org/en/PublicationsLibrary/rmt2017_en.pdf.

United Parcel Service (UPS). *The Road Ahead: The 2016 UPS Corporate Sustainability Report*. https://sustainability.ups.com/sustainability-reporting/.

United States Congress (US Congress). "The Economic Impact of the Fashion Industry." 2016. https://www.jec.senate.gov/public/_cache/files/66dba6df-e3bd-42b4-a795-436d194ef08a/fashion---september-2016-final-090716.pdf.

Vishnoi, A. and Park, K. "A New Coat of Paint Is Rocking the Global Shipping Industry." *Bloomberg Businessweek*, August 1, 2017. https://www.bloomberg.com/news/features/2017-06-26/an-environmental-push-is-rocking-the-global-shipping-industry.

7

A Look at Labor Issues in the Manufacturing of Fashion through the Perspective of Human Trafficking and Modern-day Slavery

Marsha Dickson and Hayley Warren

Introduction

This chapter explores the issues faced by workers who are trafficked and held in modern-day slavery. Within the context of the fashion industry, slavery has occurred and is an ongoing problem. According to the California Transparency in Supply Chain Act, an estimated 21 million people are victims of forced labor around the globe (Harris, 2015). These violations require action responses by fashion brands and retailers internationally. The characteristics of "Modern-Day slavery" will be examined and contemporary insights on the attempts to abolish such outrages will be reviewed, focusing particularly on the international response to the issue and the passing of recent legislation in the United States and the United Kingdom. The chapter outlines industry best practice and the possible next steps fashion brands can take to identify modern slavery.

What is modern-day slavery?

Slavery was arguably one of the first human rights issues to arouse wide international concern. These concerns led to many international treaties, declarations, and conventions of the nineteenth and twentieth centuries (OHCHR, 1991). Under the 1948 Universal Declaration of Human Rights, slavery is prohibited, specifying that "No one shall be held in slavery or servitude: slavery and the slave trade shall be prohibited in all their forms" (United Nations, 1976).

The terms "modern slavery," "contemporary slavery," "trafficking in persons," and "human trafficking" are often used interchangeably (Scarpa and Cabot, 2018). Definitions of modern-day slavery are mainly taken from the 1956 UN supplementary convention which includes concepts of debt bondage, serfdom, and practices and institutions that are similar to slavery including forced marriage and the transfer of a child to another person for the purposes of labor exploitation (OHCHR, 1956). "Modern-Day slavery" has been defined in many ways and these definitions range from women being forced into prostitution, to child slavery in supply chains or whole families working for nothing to pay off generational debts.

Whilst there is no precise definition, it is accepted that it can involve:

Individuals being forced against their will, to engage in work, this may be through coercion, or mental or physical threat;

Individuals being owned or controlled by an "employer," through mental or physical abuse or the threat of abuse;

Individuals are dehumanized, and treated as a commodity or bought and sold as "property";

Individuals are physically constrained or have restrictions placed on their freedom of movement.

Individuals are transported or traded from one area to another and into conditions of slavery.

Anti-Slavery, 2017

The International Labor Organization (ILO) provides further clarification and notes the involuntariness of modern slavery. The term "offered voluntarily" refers to the free and informed consent of a worker to take a job and his or her freedom to leave at any time. This is not the case when an employer or recruiter makes false promises so that a worker takes a job he or she would not otherwise have accepted (Belser et al., 2005). The understanding of "slavery" covers a variety of human rights violations that have been present within the fashion industry for a number of decades.

Human rights violations and the response of apparel companies

The fashion industry is one of the oldest and largest export industries, and while globalization is not a new phenomenon, the rate at which globalization of the fashion industry occurred during the 1990s changed the way fashion brands and retailers sourced products. Competition between companies to take part in the consumer driven value chain has led companies to source and produce at the lowest cost and to be as cost effective as possible. As such, the manufacturing of fashion was offshored from countries like Europe and North America to those countries which offered lower production costs, such as Bangladesh, India, and China. This in turn led to the development and existence of extensive global sourcing networks and what is often referred to as the "race to the bottom" (see Figure 7.1).

In the early 1990s the "sweatshop" scandals of Nike and Gap profiting from child labor and the suppression of labor rights in the supply chain were well documented (see Carty, 2001; Fisher, 2006; Goldman and Papson, 1998). It was around this time that there was a recognition that these labor issues in fashion production should be addressed by the brands (Dickson, 2013). An array of codes of conduct, social audits, and factory certifications were developed to support the portrayal of brands as "upholders" of human rights (Bartley, 2009). However, some flaws have been noted in this approach, with a failure to identify gross violations of codes of conduct, including a lack of monitoring of the rights of freedom of association and collective bargaining. Workers were excluded from the process because the system was designed to "protect" them rather than

Figure 7.1 A Bangladeshi girl picking up plastics at a wasteyard in Dhaka, Bangladesh, 2013. Photo by Ranak Martin/Anadolu Agency/Getty Images.

empower them to protect themselves by monitoring their own working conditions on a day-to-day basis. Furthermore, there was a lack of follow-up on sanctions to correct such problems (Dickson, 2013).

In the early 2000s, the United Nations (UN) affirmed that businesses could have a negative impact on human rights and in 2005 a mandate was created to tackle the issue. A Special Representative for Business and Human Rights, Professor John Ruggie, was appointed by the UN Secretary General to develop this matter further, and in 2008, he drafted the "Protect, Respect and Remedy" framework. The document framed human rights "in a way that fully reflects the complexities and dynamics of globalization and provides governments and other social actors with effective guidance" (Ruggie, 2008). The framework outlined the duties and responsibilities of states and businesses to address business-related human rights abuses, including those associated with human trafficking and slavery (Ruggie, 2008).

The United Nations Sustainable Development Goals (SDG) also references the problem of slavery, "which locates the problem as one of broad international concern in need of urgent redress" (Landman, 2018, p. 148). SDG target 8.7 calls for the world to "[t]ake immediate and effective measures to eradicate forced labour, end modern slavery and human trafficking and secure the prohibition and elimination of the worst forms of child labour."

A number of international organizations have also developed frameworks and guidance on the issue, notably the Fair Labor Association (FLA), Worldwide Responsible Accredited Production (WRAP), Social Accountability International (SAI), and the Ethical Trading Initiative (ETI). All these organizations have devised standards and support a multitude of brands and retailers to help ensure human rights standards are upheld.

Given the steps taken by brands, retailers, and international organizations such as the UN, there might be an assumption that human rights abuses are no longer present in the fashion industry. However, this is not the case, and within the context of "modern-day-slavery," abuses are still prolific throughout the fashion industry.

Characteristics of modern-day slavery in the fashion industry

In 2016 it was estimated that over 45.8 million people were in some form of modern slavery in 167 countries (Landman, 2018). The Global Slavery Index—which provides a country-by-country ranking of the number of people in modern slavery, as well as an analysis of the actions governments are taking to respond to it, and the factors that make people vulnerable—identifies the countries with the highest absolute numbers of people in modern slavery as India (18.4 million), China (3.4 million), Pakistan (2.1 million), Bangladesh (1.5 million), and Uzbekistan (1.2 million) (cited in Landman, 2018, p. 144). A closer study of these countries reveals the connection to the fashion industry, with the provision of low-cost labor for companies in Western Europe and North America.

In India, the textiles sector is a major foreign exchange earner and is estimated to be the second largest industry, employing significant numbers (Ramachandran, 2015). In 2012, the Clean Clothes Campaign (CCC) reported evidence of systematic human rights abuses of garment workers in India, including inhuman working conditions measures, wage theft, the denial of social security, and suppression of the right to freedom of association (Clean Clothes Campaign, 2012).

Tamil Nadu, one of the major textile production locations in India, has a long record of bonded labor, child labor, long working hours, forced overtime, caste discrimination, unhealthy working conditions, and restricted freedom of movement, for all of which it has been condemned (Fair Labor Association, 2012). Under what is called the "Sumangali Scheme," young female workers have been exploited in the spinning and textile units. The Tamil word "Sumangali" means an unmarried girl becoming a respectable woman by entering into marriage. Under the scheme, the girls' parents, who were often of poor and of lower caste, were persuaded by brokers to sign their daughters up to a scheme which promised a financial return once the girls have completed between one and three years' factory work (Fair Labor Association, 2012).

The textile and clothing sector is by far the most important industry in Bangladesh, accounting for 85.9 percent of all exports, which makes it the second largest garment exporter in the world, with approximately 60 percent of all production going to Europe and 23 percent to the United States (D'Ambrogio, 2014). The collapse of Rana Plaza in 2013, which was considered the worst disaster ever in the fashion industry, brought attention back to the plight and working conditions of clothing workers in the country. It is estimated that over 1,100 people died and that 2,000 more were severely injured, many becoming permanently disabled (Aizama and Tripathi, 2015).

Uzbekistan is the world's sixth largest producer of cotton and it has been widely reported that children are forced to harvest the crop (Bhat, 2013). Monitoring by international organizations has forced the government to take some steps to improve the situation, but reports in 2015 estimate that there were still over 1 million people who were forced to work in this sector (Global Slavery Index, 2016).

In 2016 the Business and Human Rights Resource Centre (BHRRC) estimated that between 250,000 and 400,000 Syrian refugees were working illegally in Turkey. The research focused on twenty-eight major garment brands that were associated with the payment of low wages, child labor, and sexual abuse. BHRRC also found that few garment brands were taking adequate steps to protect vulnerable refugees, with the main issues being the lack of a targeted approach, auditing processes that were not fit for purpose, and limited government engagement (BHRRC, 2016).

It is estimated that there are around 2 million migrant workers in Thailand, in which much of the focus of concern is on Mae Sot, one of the main entry points of migrant workers from Myanmar and where more than 200 textile and garment factories are located (SOMO, 2016). The Clean Clothes Campaign notes that factories in this area have poor working conditions for migrant labor and that pay is well below the minimum wage and working hours often exceeding twelve per day during peak periods. Workers are reported to live in factory dorms and are not permitted to leave due to a lack of legal documentation (Clean Clothes Campaign, 2014).

In 2006 the *New York Times* reported that Jordanian factories that produce garments for Target, Wal-Mart, and other American retailers operated 20-hour days and that workers often went unpaid for several months and were physically abused by their supervisors if they complained (Greenhouse and Barbaro, 2006). Other reported human rights violations from over 100 Bangladeshi and Indian workers, including forced labor, physical and verbal abuse, and inadequate accommodation, forced one particular factory to be closed in February 2017 (Azzeh, 2017).

Modern Slavery is also found in the West. In the United States, the El Monte sweatshop slavery case revealed Thai garment workers to be employed in makeshift and unsuitable factories and exposed to generally atrocious working conditions (Rojas, 2015). Workers were brought to the United States on fake passports and when they arrived, the legal papers were revoked. The Thai people were forced to work 17–20-hour days sewing clothes, cut off from the outside world and often held captive (Ramachandran et al., 2017; Kimitch, 2015). More recently in the United Kingdom in 2015, sports retailer SportsDirect was investigated and found to be employing staff supplied by human traffickers. The workers were subjected to poor working conditions, pay below the minimum wage, and having their passports taken away (Davies, 2017).

What is being done about modern slavery?

The affirmation and protection of human rights has been at the core of a number of international statements and sets of guidelines:

- The UN *Guiding Principles on Business and Human Rights* (UNGP) calls on private companies to respect human rights, including appropriate due diligence and disclosure procedures (OHCHR, 2011).
- The OECD *Guidelines for Multinational Enterprises* (OECD Guidelines) contains a chapter which calls on companies to apply due diligence in relation to human rights (OECD 2011).
- The UN *Sustainable Development Goals* (SDG) include the expectation that companies be accountable for their global supply chains (United Nations, 2016).
- The ILO *Tripartite Declaration of Principles Concerning Multinational Enterprises and Social Policy* was revised to include guidance on due diligence processes for enterprises (ILO, 2017).

Most countries have some form of policy to try to eliminate modern slavery and the issue is very much on the political agenda (Global Slavery Index, 2016). In Germany, for example, Chancellor Angela Merkel put the matter of international retail and supply chain standards on the agenda of the G7 Summit in order to promote debate on international working standards agreements. The German Textile Alliance is a partnership founded in October 2014 in response to the tragic accidents in textile factories in Bangladesh and Pakistan. It was initiated by the German Federal Minister for Economic Cooperation and Development, Dr. Gerd Müller. Today, members of the Textiles Partnership represent about half of the German textile market and are focused on bringing government, non-profit organizations and textile firms together to uphold ethical and environmental standards in their supply chains.

France has a Bill on the Duty of Care of Businesses and Subcontractors, passed by its parliament on March 30, 2016. This law extends the liability of French companies by including both companies and subcontractors in the due diligence requirements. The French Corporate Duty of Vigilance Law requires all companies headquartered in France to establish plans to monitor their supply chains for human rights and environmental protection violations and to implement their vigilance plans.

In the Netherlands the Dutch government, along with a group of trade organizations and NGOs, agreed a textile covenant in March 2016 (SER, 2016).

The aim of the covenant is to prevent child labor, improve poor working conditions, and increase wages in textile producing countries such as Bangladesh, India, Pakistan, and Turkey. The Dutch government expects 80 percent of clothing companies to sign the covenant by 2020. In addition, the Dutch Child Labor Due Diligence Law, adopted in February 2017, requires companies doing business in the Netherlands to examine whether child labor occurs in their production chain and to draw up declarations about their investigations and plans of action.

In August 2017, the Australia government announced plans to produce guidelines on dealing with modern slavery. The federal government stated its intention to make companies with an annual turnover in excess of $100m to publicly file a modern slavery report each year. The aim is to force these larger companies to take measures to ensure that their supply chains are free of exploitation (Tomazin, 2017).

Two of the most important responses to the phenomenon of modern slavery have come from the United States, with its California Transparency in Supply Chains Act 2010 (SB657), and the United Kingdom, with the Modern Slavery Act 2015.

The US response to modern slavery

The California Transparency in Supply Chains Act 2010 (SB657), which came into effect in January 2012, requires retailers and manufacturers who do business in California and earn over $100 million in annual sales worldwide to report the steps they are taking to address and eliminate human trafficking and slavery from their direct supply chains. This Act outlines five key areas in which companies must report the extent of their activities.

1. Verification: Engages in verification of product supply chains to evaluate and address risks of human trafficking and slavery.
2. Auditing: Conducts audits of suppliers to evaluate supplier compliance with company standards for trafficking and slavery in supply chains.
3. Certification: Requires direct suppliers to certify that materials incorporated into the product comply with the laws regarding slavery and human trafficking of the country or countries in which they are doing business.
4. Internal Accountability: Maintains internal accountability standards and procedures for employees or contractors failing to meet company standards regarding slavery and trafficking.

5. Training: Provides company employees and management, who have direct responsibility for supply chain management, training on human trafficking and slavery, particularly with respect to mitigating risks within the supply chains of products. (Harris, 2015)

The Act further requires companies to feature an easily understood link to this information on the homepages of their websites.

The Act has impacted around 120 companies in the fashion industry, all of whom are required to disclose their actions. It has been noted that even prior to this Act, many brands were already addressing the issue in their supply chain and had certain procedures in place to stop labor abuses (Pickles and Zhu, 2013). However, the California Transparency in Supply Chains Act has forced companies to consider human rights, apply due diligence, and report publicly on their actions. Interestingly, the Act does not "regulate a company's labor practices, nor does it require companies to reveal confidential, proprietary and/or trade secret information. Instead, it requires businesses subject to the law to simply disclose their practices in five discrete areas so that interested consumers can make better informed purchasing decisions" (Harris, 2015, p. 3). In April 2015 the Attorney General of California, Kamala Harris, released guidance to help companies understand how to comply with SB 657 requirements. The guidance document recommends model disclosures and best practices to enhance consumers' understanding of its anti-trafficking and anti-slavery efforts.

Content analysis of the disclosures by some eighty-six high-volume apparel companies soon after the law came into effect (January 1, 2012) showed variability in the quality and amount of information provided, though only one-quarter of the companies had not made the required disclosure easily accessible (Dickson and Warren, 2012). In 2014, KnowTheChain, an organization created to promote greater transparency and dialogue around the issue of modern slavery, conducted research on those companies that had not yet provided statements under the SB657 Act. From a small sample of 129 companies, it was found that some fashion brands were still not reporting on the issue. Partners in KnowTheChain include ATEST, CAST, Free the Slaves, Humanity United, the Interfaith Center on Corporate Responsibility, Made in a Free World, Not for Sale, the Responsible Sourcing Network, Sustainalytics, the Tronie Foundation, Verité, Vital Voices, and World Vision.

Adidas, the German sportswear giant, has been commended for their approach, being ranked the top company by KnowTheChain in relation to their Apparel and Footwear benchmark:

Adidas AG demonstrate[s] a strong disclosure of its approach to managing forced labor risks in its supply chain, and discloses a high number of leading practices. Adidas achieves a higher score than any of its peers on the themes of recruitment and worker voice. Adidas provides quantitative data … provides examples of implementing its policies and processes in different countries and of working with different stakeholders. The company also discusses implementation challenges and, most notably, its efforts go beyond its first-tier suppliers. For example, the company provides modern slavery training to its second-tier suppliers.

Know the Chain, 2016

The UK's response to modern slavery

In 2013 the then British Home Secretary, Theresa May, announced the government's intentions to introduce the UK's first Modern Slavery Bill. In 2015 this Bill became law on March 26th after a long process of consultation and amendments.

The UK Modern Slavery Act is designed to tackle slavery in the UK and consolidate previous legislation relating to trafficking and slavery. It includes provisions to increase the maximum sentence for trafficking to life imprisonment and has established an independent Anti-Slavery Commissioner to foster good practice on the prevention of acts of modern slavery and victim identification. The Act also provides mechanisms for the seizure of traffickers' assets, forcing them to contribute to victim compensation payments, and guarantees the provision of an advocate for all trafficked children, who is legally empowered to protect and support them.

The Modern Slavery Act includes a clause on "Transparency in Supply Chains," which requires all eligible companies operating in Britain to report on the measures they have taken to ensure that any goods produced or services provided by workers are free of slavery and trafficking. Company directors now have a legal responsibility to ensure that this is enforced.

In order to comply with the provisions of the Act, businesses need to state the actions they have taken during the financial year to ensure that their operation and supply chains are free of modern slavery. Brands are required to publicly communicate what they are doing to try to prevent, and eliminate, modern slavery, Section 54 of the Act outlining what such a statement should include:

- a brief description of an organization's business model and supply chain relationships;

- a business's policies relating to modern slavery, including due diligence and auditing processes implemented;
- the training provisions available for those in

  1) supply chain management and
  2) the rest of the organization;

- the principal risks related to slavery and human trafficking, including how the organization evaluates and manages those risks in their organization and their supply chain; and
- relevant key performance indicators (KPIs). Statements will be produced annually, so KPIs are useful in demonstrating progress from one year to the next.

The UK government's approach draws on the California Transparency in Supply Chain Act 2012 but goes further in three important ways. The Modern Slavery Act provision covers:

- organizations carrying out any part of their business in the UK;
- all sectors of organizations;
- and both goods and services (whereas the California Act covers only supply chains for goods).

Having only been the law since 2016, it is perhaps still too early to gauge the full impact of the Modern Slavery Act. The UK government has maintained its position that it will not establish a central registry to track adherence to Section 54 of the Act, but a public Modern Slavery Register has been set up. This platform is designed to be a central resource and aims to be independent, accountable to the public interest, robust, credible, free, open, accessible, and sustainable in the long term. This Registry is guided and supported by a governance committee which includes the Freedom Fund, Humanity United, Freedom United, Anti-Slavery International, the Ethical Trading Initiative, the CORE Coalition, UNICEF UK, Focus on Labour Exploitation, the Trades Union Congress, and Oxfam GB.

By October 2016, it was widely considered that although companies had been relatively compliant in providing statements, not all mandatory points in the legislation had been addressed by all companies. This is in contrast to the example set by Marks and Spencer (M&S), one of the UK's leading retailers. As the M&S Group has an annual turnover of £10.4 billion, it was required to comply with the UK Act. The full statement is available online and all of its policies are publicly available. What makes the M&S statement different from others in the industry is the level of detail of their due diligence actions and the disclosure that during financial year 2015/16, ethical audits identified fourteen instances of non-compliance under the heading "employment is freely chosen," with the company confirming that they were actively working towards identifying remedial action. In addition, M&S's CEO has written to suppliers in all areas of its business to raise awareness of the Modern Slavery Act and human rights (Marks and Spencer, 2016).

How can modern slavery be identified?

Modern slavery is something that is often difficult to detect. One of the more common approaches to identification is to carry out social compliance audits. These are often used as the "first line of defense" against modern slavery; however, it is an issue that is not always identified by such traditional audits. Some common shortcomings of traditional factory auditing include:

- weak quality control over auditors;
- multiple audits of the same supplier;
- inconsistent corrective action plans;
- failure to identify serious labor problems;
- the prevalence of fraudulent practices;
- poor auditor skills;
- and lack of local knowledge, language, and understanding.

Despite these flaws, audits still play an important role in trying to uncover cases of modern slavery. However, this should not be the only approach or means of detecting the practice. Modern slavery is not confined to production supply chains, but can be found throughout the value chains in warehouses, among cleaning staff and kitchen workers, and in relation to logistics (see Figure 7.2). It is the responsibility of all employees, stakeholders, and consumers to be aware of the issues and how these can be identified.

There are a number of practical tools to help guide businesses on how to approach this matter. The Ethical Trading Initiative, in partnership with Anti-Slavery, released a guide to help businesses understand the key concepts and legal definition, highlighting their responsibility to tackle modern slavery through a Human Rights Due Diligence (HRDD) process (Ethical Trading Initiative, 2017). The four-step process included in the guide is designed to

Figure 7.2 A photograph of children sorting plastic for recycling in Vietnam.
Photo by Lily FRANEY/Gamma-Rapho/Getty Images.

address any human rights issue and shows how the HRDD framework can be applied to modern slavery. These steps include:

1. Reviewing country and sectoral risks within own business operations and conducting a risk assessment.
2. Identifying leverage, responsibility and actions to increase the capability of business to address the risk of modern slavery.
3. Monitor, review, report and improve by documenting abused and honestly reporting the remedial actions taken by business is an integral part of solving the problem. (Ethical Trading Initiative, 2017)

What are the next steps to eradicate modern slavery?

One step in eradicating modern slavery could be the mandatory requirement by governments that brands and retailers adopt and apply responsible recruitment practices. This would ensure that labor employment practices across the supply chain were carried out in a responsible and ethical manner. The requisite clauses and initiatives could be introduced to safeguard workers and their livelihoods in all countries, especially those characterized by a lack of "red tape" (Neale, 2017).

The Leadership Group for Responsible Recruitment, set up by the UNGC, has called for more emphasis on the creation of responsible recruitment procedures and on raising awareness of the positive benefits of ethical practices. They have also advocated an increase in the supply of ethically sourced labor. The Leadership Group is also noted for championing improved protection for migrant workers by brokering dialogue to promote the effective regulation of the recruitment industry. In order to remedy the current problems it is important to set guidelines for third parties that will help eliminate the use of unscrupulous brokers (Manpower and Verite, 2012).

Although both the UK and US Acts are designed to make it mandatory for companies to disclose elements of their supply chain practice, it can be argued that more needs to be done and that brands have the scope to be more transparent in their operations.

The Fair Labor Association (FLA) is a collaborative effort by universities, civil society organizations, and socially responsible companies to protect workers' rights around the world. The FLA notes that by being more transparent, brands can more effectively identify and address human rights violations, while Human Rights Watch (HRW) has observed, "The need for information about factories involved in production for global brands has become painfully clear in recent years through deadly incidents that have plagued the garment industry" (Clean Clothes Campaign and Human Rights Watch, 2017). According to Carry Somers, founder and global operations director at Fashion Revolution, "The majority of fashion brands have little or no supply chain transparency down to raw material level" (Fashion Revolution 2017). Fashion Revolution believes that the first step towards transparency and transformation starts with one simple question, "Who made my clothes?" The recently launched Transparency Pledge has increased the pressure on brands and retailers to act, emphasizing that the "transparency of a company's manufacturing supply chain better enables a company to collaborate with civil society in identifying, assessing, and avoiding actual or potential adverse human rights impacts. This is a critical step that strengthens a company's human rights due diligence" (Clean Clothes Campaign, 2017).

A prominent topic of discussion in this field is the power that companies have to introduce change. Safia Minney, founder, CEO, and Creative Director of People Tree, notes that companies should "get to know their supply chains and maintain information through good transparency, promote social dialogue, design and plan their orders better, to strengthen local legal systems, challenge corruption and strengthen human rights through laws and codes of practice that work, including paying a living wage and respecting independent trade unions" (Minney, 2017).

Governments can also play a key role. In its 2017 *Trafficking in Persons* report, the US Department of State called for bilateral and multilateral cooperation to address the issue of modern slavery. Traffickers are capitalizing on the lack of cooperation between governments, since the transnational nature of many trafficking crimes can only be tackled by governments cooperating with each other. The report acknowledges that although governments cannot undo the trauma and indignity victims face, they should recognize the injustice of human trafficking and work to ensure that the guilty parties are prosecuted, convicted, and sentenced. Governments everywhere are responsible for taking adequate and appropriate measures to provide justice for victims, create more stable societies to keep the vulnerable safe, and work towards a world free from modern slavery (US Department of State, 2017).

Case study: migrant workers and child labor in Turkey

Since the Syrian war started, the number of migrants coming to Turkey in search of work has increased. The mass movement of Syrian refugees into Turkey began in 2011 and today Turkey hosts approximately 3.2 million such refugees (Sozcu, 2017). This influx, and the restrictions on work permits has meant that thousands of migrant workers had to take up informal work, which is often characterized by exploitative conditions, with reports of instances of child labour and slavery.

In February 2016, two of the United Kingdom's leading high-street fashion giants found Syrian refugee children working in their clothing factories in Turkey, and were forced to examine their own supply chains (Pitel, 2016). Swedish fashion company H&M was one of the brands that admitted to finding child labor in supplier factories. Subsequently it has outlined its approach to human rights due diligence and confirmed its application of an ongoing process to identify, address (prevent, mitigate, and/or remediate), and account for human rights violations (H&M Group, 2017). H&M has developed key processes to try to eliminate the economic exploitation of Syrian refugees and is committed to tracing where such production takes place, setting up a monitoring program that covers 100 percent of its first-tier suppliers. The fashion brand has also committed to a continuous dialogue with suppliers in Turkey ("H&M on Syrian Refugees in Turkey," 2016).

The Turkish government has also taken action on the issue, publishing its *Regulation on Work Permits of Foreigners under Temporary Protection*. This legislation allowed work permits to be granted to refugees under certain conditions and restrictions, including Article 7 which refers to workers who having been "forced to leave their country, cannot return to the country they have left, and have arrived at or crossed the borders of Turkey in a mass influx situation seeking immediate and temporary protection, but cannot be given the individual international protection status" (Turkish Labour Law, 2016). In addition, workers under this temporary protection must also be paid the minimum wage (Göç İdaresi, 2016).

Non-governmental organizations (NGOs), transnational corporations (TNCs), and trade unions have also implemented programs and projects to tackle the varying needs of Syrian refugees (Korkmaz, 2017). Whilst only around 10 percent of textile workers in Turkey is unionized labor (Önday, 2015), union officials have acknowledged that refugees are entitled to basic rights and liberties and have supported policies aimed at improving refugees' working conditions (Korkmaz, 2017).

A transnational response has been facilitated by ETI and its Turkey Program, which includes high-street fashion brands such as Inditex (Zara group), H&M, M&S and Next; the IndustriALL Global Union, and NGOs such as Oxfam and Care. The core focus is on achieving the legal and decent employment of Syrian refugees in the textile-apparel sector (Ethical Trading Initiative, 2018).

Conclusion

This chapter has demonstrated that modern slavery is still a salient issue within the fashion industry. While there are number of voluntary principles which emphasize the need for a sustained and diligent focus on human rights and most countries in the world have some form of policy to try to eliminate the problem, modern slavery still exists. Governments, brands, industry stakeholders, and consumers must all be aware of the impact they can have and work together to eradicate this practice.

References

Aizawa, M. and Tripathi, S. "Beyond Rana Plaza: Next Steps for the Global Garment Industry and Bangladeshi Manufacturers." *Business and Human Rights Journal* 1 (2015): 145–51.

Anti-Slavery International. *What is modern slavery?* 2017. https://www.antislavery.org/slavery-today/modern-slavery/.

Azzeh, L. "Minister orders factory closure after alleged abuse of guest workers." *Jordan Times*, February 25, 2017. http://www.jordantimes.com/news/local/minister-orders-factory-closure-after-alleged-abuse-guest-workers.

Bartley, T. "Standard for Sweatshops: The Power and Limits of the Club Approach to Voluntary Labor Standards." In M. Potoski and A. Prakash (eds.), *Voluntary Programs; A Club Theory Perspective*, pp. 107–32. London; MIT Press, 2009.

Belser, P., de Cock, M., and Mehran, F. "ILO Minimum Estimate of Forced Labour in the World." DigitalCommons@ILR, Cornell University ILR School. 2005. https://digitalcommons.ilr.cornell.edu/cgi/viewcontent.cgi?article=1006&context=nondiscrim.

Bhat, B. A. "Forced Labor of Children in Uzbekistan's Cotton Industry." *International Journal on World Peace* 30, no. 4 (2013): 61–85.

Business and Human Rights Resource Centre (BHRRC). *Syrian refugees in Turkish Garment Supply Chains.* 2016. https://www.business-humanrights.org/sites/default/files/160131%20Syrian%20Refugee%20Briefing%20FINAL.pdf.

Carty, V. T. "The Internet and Grassroots Politics: Nike, the Athletic Apparel Industry and the Anti-sweatshop Campaign." *Journal of Critical Postmodern Organization Science* 1, no. 2 (2001): 34–47.

Clean Clothes Campaign. *Indian Garment Industry to Receive Human Rights Trial.* 2012. https://cleanclothes.org/news/2012/11/20/indian-garment-industry-to-receive-human-rights-trial.

Clean Clothes Campaign. *Migrant Workers in Thailand's Garment Factories: Pay a Living Wage.* 2014. https://cleanclothes.org/resources/publications/migrant-workers-in-thailands-garment-factories.

Clean Clothes Campaign. *The Apparel and Footwear Supply Chain Transparency Pledge.* 2017. https://cleanclothes.org/transparency/transparency-pledge.

Clean Clothes Campaign and Human Rights Watch. *Follow the Thread: The Need for Supply Chain Transparency in the Garment and Footwear industry.* 2017. https://cleanclothes.org/resources/publications/follow-the-thread-the-need-for-supply-chain-transparency-in-the-garment-and-footwear-industry/view.

Davies, R. "Brothers Jailed for Trafficking People from Poland to Work at Sports Direct." *Guardian*, January 23, 2017. https://www.theguardian.com/business/2017/jan/23/brothers-jailed-trafficking-poland-sports-direct-shirebrook.

Dickson, M. A. "Toward an Integrated Human Rights-Based Approach to Corporate Social Responsibility in the Global Apparel Industry." In S. Black et al. (eds.), *The Fashion Studies Handbook*, pp. 523–41. London: Berg, 2013.

Dickson, M. A., and Warren, H. "Slavery and Human Trafficking; Early Lessons from Implementation of the California Transparency in Supply Chains Act." Ethical Sourcing Forum, 2012. http://www.ethicalsourcingforum.com/esf-new-york-2012/.

Ethical Trading Initiative (ETI). *Base Code Guidance: Modern Slavery*. 2017. https://www.ethicaltrade.org/sites/default/files/shared_resources/eti_base_code_guidance_modern_slavery_web.pdf.

Ethical Trading Initiative. *Report on the ETI Turkey Platform Annual Event*. 2018. https://www.ethicaltrade.org/sites/default/files/shared_resources/ETI%20Turkey%20platform%20report%2C%20March%202018_0.pdf.

D'Ambrogio, E. *Workers' Conditions in the Textile and Clothing Sector: Just an Asian Affair? Issues at Stake After the Rana Plaza Tragedy*, European Parliamentary Research Service. 2014. http://www.europarl.europa.eu/EPRS/140841REV1-Workers-conditions-in-the-textile-and-clothing-sector-just-an-Asian-affair-FINAL.pdf.

Fair Labor Association. *Understanding the Characteristics of the Sumangali Scheme in Tamil Nadu Textile & Garment Industry and Supply Chain Linkages*. 2012. http://www.fairlabor.org/sites/default/files/understanding_sumangali_tamil_nadu_0.pdf.

Fashion Revolution. *Fashion Transparency Index*. 2017. https://www.fashionrevolution.org/faqs-fashion-transparency-index-2017/.

Fisher, J. "Free Speech to have Sweatshops? How Kasky v. Nike Might Provide a Useful Tool to Improve Sweatshop Conditions." *Boston College Third World Law Journal* 26, no. 2 (2006): 267–310.

Global Slavery Index. 2016. https://www.globalslaveryindex.org.

Göç İdaresi [Ministry of Interior General Directorate of Migration Management]. *Temporary Protection Regulation, Part One, Objective, Scope, Basis and Definitions*. 2016. http://www.goc.gov.tr/files/_dokuman28.pdf.

Goldman, R and Papson S. *Nike Culture: The Sign of Swoosh*. London: Sage, 1998.

Greenhouse, S. and Barbaro, M. "An Ugly Side of Free Trade: Sweatshops in Jordan." *New York Times*, May 3, 2006. http://www.nytimes.com/2006/05/03/business/worldbusiness/03clothing.html.

H&M Group. *Modern Slavery Act Statement*. 2017. http://sustainability.hm.com/en/sustainability/downloads-resources/about-our-reporting/modern-slavery-statement.html.

"H&M on Syrian Refugees in Turkey." *Business and Human Rights Resource Centre*. 2016. https://www.business-humanrights.org/en/hm-on-syrian-refugee-in-turkey.

Harris, K. D. *The California Transparency in Supply Chains Act—A Resource Guide.* California Department of Justice. 2015. https://oag.ca.gov/sites/all/files/agweb/pdfs/sb657/resource-guide.pdf.

International Labour Organisation (ILO). *Tripartite Declaration of Principles Concerning Multinational Enterprises and Social Policy.* Geneva: International Labour Office, 2017. https://www.ilo.org/wcmsp5/groups/public/---ed_emp/---emp_ent/---multi/documents/publication/wcms_094386.pdf.

Kimitch, R. "Thai Community Remembers Shocking Case of Modern Slavery in El Monte." *San Gabriel Valley Tribune*, 28 July, 2015. http://www.sgvtribune.com/social-affairs/20150728/thai-community-remembers-shocking-case-of-modern-slavery-in-el-monte.

KnowTheChain. *Apparel & Footwear Benchmark Findings Report.* 2016. https://knowthechain.org/benchmarks.

Korkmaz, E. E. "How do Syrian refugee workers challenge supply chain management in the Turkish garment industry?." *International Migration Institute (IMI) Working Papers*, Paper 133, University of Oxford, 2017. https://www.imi-n.org/files/news/wp133-how-do-syrian-refugee-workers-challenge-supply-chain-management-in-the-turkish-garment-industry.pdf.

Landman, T. "Out of the Shadows: Trans-disciplinary Research on Modern Slavery." *Peace Human Rights Governance* 2, no. 2 (2018): 143–62.

Manpower Group and Verite. *An Ethical Framework for Crossborder Labor Recruitment: An Industry/Stakeholder Collaboration to Reduce the Risks of Forced Labor and Human Trafficking.* 2012. https://www.verite.org/wp-content/uploads/2016/12/ethical_framework_paper.pdf.

Marks and Spencer. *M&S Modern Slavery Statement 2015/2016.* 2016. https://corporate.marksandspencer.com/documents/plan-a-our-approach/mns-modern-slavery-statement-june2016.pdf.

Minney, S. "What Do You Know About Modern Slavery in Fashion." Fairtrade Foundation Blog, April 28, 2017. https://www.fairtrade.org.uk/Media-Centre/Blog/2017/April/What-do-you-know-about-modern-slavery-in-fashion.

Neale, E. *Responsible Recruitment and Human Rights: What's the Solution?* Sedex, 2017. https://www.sedexglobal.com/responsible-recruitment-human-rights-whats-solution/.

OECD. *OECD Guidelines for Multinational Enterprises*, OECD Publishing, 2011. http://dx.doi.org/10.1787/9789264115415-en (accessed 3 June 2019).

Office of the High Commissioner for Human Rights (OHCHR). *Supplementary Convention on the Abolition of Slavery, the Slave Trade, and Institutions and Practices Similar to Slavery.* Geneva: United Nations, 1956. https://www.ohchr.org/Documents/ProfessionalInterest/slaverytrade.pdf.

OHCHR. *Fact Sheet No.14: Contemporary Forms of Slavery.* Geneva: United Nations, 1991. https://www.ohchr.org/Documents/Publications/FactSheet14en.pdf.

OHCHR. *Guiding Principles on Business and Human Rights: Implementing the United Nations "Protect, Respect and Remedy" Framework*. Geneva: United Nations, 2011. https://www.ohchr.org/documents/publications/GuidingprinciplesBusinesshr_eN.pdf.

Önday, Ö. "A Trial Research on Turkish Textile Research." *International Journal of Contemporary Applied Sciences* 2, no. 12 (2015).

Pickles, J. and Zhu, S. "The California Transparency in Supply Chains Act." *Capturing the Gains Working Paper 15*. 2013. https://ssrn.com/abstract=2237437.

Pitel, L. "Syrian Refugee Children Found Working in Next and H&M Factories." *Independent Newspaper*, February 1, 2016. https://www.independent.co.uk/news/world/middle-east/syrian-children-found-working-for-uk-clothing-suppliers-including-next-and-hm-a6845431.html.

Ramachandran, Hon. G., Collins, A. B., Su, J., Cummings, S., and Muneer Ahmad, M. "Panel Discussion: The El Monte Sweatshop Slavery Cases." *Southwestern Journal of International Law* 23 (2017): 279–302. http://www.swlaw.edu/sites/default/files/2017-04/SWT115.pdf.

Ramachandran, M. "Recent Trends and Developments in Textile Industry in India." *International Journal on Textile Engineering and Processes* 1, no. 4 (2015): xxx.

Rojas, L. B. *El Monte Sweatshop Slavery Case Still Resonates 20 Years Later*. Southern California Public Radio (SCPR), July 31, 2015. http://www.scpr.org/news/2015/07/31/53458/el-monte-sweatshop-slavery-case-still-resonates-20/.

Ruggie, J. (2008), *Protect, Respect and Remedy: A Framework for Business and Human Rights: Report of the Special Representative of the Secretary-General on the Issue of Human Rights and Transnational Corporations and Other Business Enterprises.* Human Rights Council. https://www.business-humanrights.org/sites/default/files/reports-and-materials/Ruggie-report-7-Apr-2008.pdf.

Scarpa, S. and Cabot J. *Contemporary Forms of Slavery*. Brussels: Policy Department for External Relations Directorate General for External Policies of the Union PE 603.470, European Parliament, 2018. http://www.europarl.europa.eu/RegData/etudes/STUD/2018/603470/EXPO_STU(2018)603470_EN.pdf.

SER. *7t Signatories Endorse Sustainable Garment and Textile Sector Agreement*. Den Haag: SER, 2016. https://www.ser.nl/en/publications/news/20160704-sustainable-garment-textile-scctor.aspx.

SOMO. *Fact Sheet: Migrant Labour in the Textile and Garment Industry: A Focus on The Role of Buying Companies 2016*. 2016. https://www.somo.nl/fact-sheet-migrant-labour-in-the-textile-and-garment-industry/.

Sozcu. *Last Minute: How many million refugees in Turkey? Minister Noble announces* [in Turkish]. 2017. http://www.sozcu.com.tr/2017/gundem/turkiyede-kac-milyon-multeci-var-bakan-soylu-acikladi-1680764/.

Tomazin, F. "Big business will be forced to report annually on slavery in supply chains." *The Age*, 2017. http://www.theage.com.au/national/big-business-will-be-forced-to-report-annually-on-slavery-in-supply-chains-20170815-gxwv20.html.

Turkish Labour Law. *Turkey Grants Work Permit for Syrian Refugees*. 2016. https://turkishlaborlaw.com/news/legal-news/362-turkey-grants-work-permit-for-syrian-refugees - (accessed 20 August 2017).

United Nations. *Sustainable Development Goals*. 2016. https://sustainabledevelopment.un.org/?menu=1300.

United Nations International Convention on Civil and Political Rights, *United Nations Treaty Series*, 999 (14668) (1976): 171–346. https://treaties.un.org/doc/publication/unts/volume%20999/volume-999-i-14668-english.pdf.

US Department of State. *Trafficking in Persons Report 2017*. 2017. https://www.state.gov/trafficking-in-persons-report-2018/.

8

Exodus to Elsewhere: Exploring the Effects of Fashion Industry Globalization on Local Communities

Nancy Hodges

We often consider the negative effects of the fashion industry on those living in countries other than the United States. And typically the effects we are talking about are employment related, such as low wages, dangerous working conditions, and child labor. The 2013 collapse of Rana Plaza in Bangladesh, which caused more than a thousand casualties, is often cited as an example of the devastation that is caused by manufacturing facilities that are not safe to work in. Unfortunately, such dangers have frequently defined what it means to work in the industry. However, they have not been limited to foreign countries. The 1911 Triangle Shirtwaist fire in New York City, which killed nearly 150 workers, offers an example of unsafe factory conditions during the earliest stages of apparel production and manufacturing history in the US. Although such examples of the dangerous nature of apparel industry employment are very real and important, in this chapter we will consider the opposite—that is, the effects of unemployment, and specifically the negative effects experienced by small towns in the United States when the industry is no longer there to support a labor market and provide a solid economic foundation.

As global production has become the industry norm, towns that were built on mills and factories lose more than an economic driver—they lose the opportunity for people to make a living. This is because when the industry leaves a community, the jobs leave with it. In this chapter, we explore the impact of disappearing jobs and the subsequent widespread unemployment that has resulted from the global spread of the fashion industry. It is important to note that the story told here has a bearing on what the future may look like for communities across the globe. Whether the focus is on a small town in the southeastern United States or a city in Bangladesh, China, or Vietnam, jobs move with the industry and the industry is in constant motion.

This chapter presents information collected during a ten-year project that focused on the impact of industry employment dynamics on the people and places that were created by the development of the industry during the late 1800s and early 1900s. The focus of the study was on the southeastern US, and specifically the state of North Carolina. During the ten years of the study, a total of five communities in North Carolina were examined. The goal was to understand the experiences of the people living within each community as they faced a fundamental economic shift when production moved out of their communities to countries in Latin America and Asia. Multiple methods were used to collect data during the course of the project, including in-depth interviews with fifty-seven individuals across the five communities, along with a review of archival information about each community, as well as company records. Observations were conducted within each of the towns at such places as community centers, downtown shops, and at civic events and town meetings. Secondary data were also examined for patterns of change in industry employment and establishments.

The places that constitute the focus of this study are five small North Carolina communities located in what is referred to as the "Piedmont" area, which comprises the central part of the state, from Greensboro to High Point, Winston-Salem, and Charlotte. Each of the five communities was founded in the late nineteenth or early twentieth century by pioneering textile entrepreneurs as well as established industry tycoons. Each community grew in size through the mill village model (discussed in the next section), and each lost its textile industry foundation when the founding companies were either dissolved or went bankrupt in the early 2000s. Populations of the five communities at the time of the study ranged from 1,650 to 33,000, with the average population being 14,000.

The people that serve as the core of the study include a total of fifty-seven residents across the five NC communities. Former textile workers, community leaders, local historians, as well as local business owners and community college administrators were interviewed to provide a broad range of perspectives on the topic at hand.

Findings stemming from the data reveal a three-stage process experienced as a result of industry shifts. The first stage begins with the closure of companies and loss of jobs. The second stage focuses on rebuilding lives and remaking community identity. The third and final stage involves going forward in ways that integrate the community's past into its plans for the future. Each of these stages are explored in this chapter, but first, a look at how the industry came to be located in this part of the country will provide the necessary context.

The evolution of an industry: a brief timeline

Broadly speaking, the textile products industry includes products produced with fabric, such as apparel and fashion, as well as the production of fibers and fabrics that go into textile products. The industry began early in the history of the United States, and at that time was centered in the northeastern part of the country, especially Massachusetts and New York (Carlton and Coclanis, 2005). Lowell, MA, is perhaps one of the better known mill towns that developed during the early stages of industrial development in the US (Glass, 1992). Throughout the nineteenth century, the industry began to migrate south, to states like North Carolina, Georgia, and South Carolina (Simpson, 1948). These locales were attractive to factory and mill owners because of a plethora of natural resources like water (used to power the mills), cotton, and potential labor in the form of rural workers (Potwin, 1927; Zingraff, 1991).

To attract these workers, companies would establish mills as part of villages, much like the Lowell, MA, community (see Figure 8.1). Employee housing was

Figure 8.1 Spinner at the Picket Yarn Mill, *c.* 1941–2. Courtesy of Federal Government Federal Works Agency.

provided by the company, and these houses were built in close proximity to the mill or factory buildings (Hodges and Frank, 2014; Jennings, 1923). Designed to be company-centered communities, mill villages were usually built outside of established towns and cities in order to foster worker dependence (Anderson, 2000; Fink and Reed, 1994; McHugh, 1988). Ultimately, many of these mill villages would grow to become towns in their own right. These early mill villages and textile towns soon became linked through an extensive railway system built to connect North Carolina, South Carolina, Georgia, and Alabama (Simpson, 1948).

The industry flourished in the South during the late 1800s and into the 1900s, so much so that it became the country's largest employer (Glass, 1992). At its peak during the 1950s, the industry included thousands of mills and factories, and employed several hundred thousand people in states across the country (Zingraff, 1991). Most of the jobs were concentrated in the states that offered proximity to raw materials, which remained the Southern states. Indeed, in North Carolina alone there were more than 1,000 mills employing over 250,000 people by the mid-twentieth century (see Figure 8.2) (Glass, 1992). This growth continued until the end of the twentieth century.

Figure 8.2 Spinning—Saco-Lowell machine, *c.* 1941–2. Courtesy of Federal Government Federal Works Agency.

Changes began to happen most noticeably during the 1990s. For example, in 1997 there were 220,000 jobs in the textile products industry in North Carolina. In five years, by 2003, this number had dropped by almost 50 percent to 116,300. By 2015, the numbers were cut by more than half again, dropping to just 60,000 jobs (Bureau of Labor Statistics, 2015). The state's rural areas have been hit the hardest, as those areas tended to be where the mill towns were established. Unemployment rates skyrocketed to 15 percent in some counties within the Piedmont region. Most blamed inexpensive labor in Asian and Latin American countries, but other changes served to bring about the industry's demise, including automation and technology that made the more labor-intensive, low-skills jobs obsolete (Gaventa and Smith, 1991). This was the case not just in textiles, but in all types of manufacturing (Dudley, 1994).

The move offshore began earlier for apparel than textile producers, starting in the 1970s and 1980s with innovations in manufacturing and reduction in the need for people to run the machines (Cooper, 1970). However, many point to the North American Free Trade Agreement (NAFTA), which was ratified in 1994, as the ultimate blow to the industry (ATMI, 2001). The combination of advancements in production technology, globalization, and trade agreements would firmly entrench the new normal of the global supply chain, as the idea that textile products could be made more cheaply outside of the United States achieved a firm grip on companies and consumers (Dudley, 1994; Gereffi, 2000; Hodges and Karpova, 2008). Consumers were demanding lower prices and the industry responded by moving to countries where employees could be paid a fraction of the wage that US employees received (Gaventa and Smith, 1991; Norris, 2003). As one displaced worker participating in the present study explained, "The wages that they are paying people in other countries, I mean it doesn't even come near to what I was making. Why would they want to pay somebody $17 an hour when somebody else is going to do it for $2 or $3?" (Tonya).

In response, most of the large companies were restructured, while many that did not respond quickly enough went bankrupt (Hodges and Karpova, 2008). Displaced workers were faced with the "three Rs" of either relocating to find production work elsewhere, or retraining and re-employment for non-manufacturing type jobs (Hodges and Lentz, 2010). The labor market within many of the towns affected was too small to accommodate the large numbers of individuals who suddenly found themselves without jobs. Likewise, the community colleges were overwhelmed by the number of people seeking retraining and receiving government support for going to school to acquire skills in something other than manufacturing (Hodges, 2013). By the early 2000s, the mills and their villages were largely deserted (Anderson, 2000). Factory equipment was packed up and shipped out to countries in Asia where locations were experiencing growth similar to that of the Southern US in the early twentieth century (Gaventa and Smith, 1991; Suggs, 2002). It was a difficult process to watch, as one participant put it, stating, "So we gave them the jobs and then we're giving them the equipment to do it with" (Charlotte). However, much like when the jobs moved south, and the Southern states thrived, the economies of communities in countries across the developing world would begin to have regular work and engage in the global economy. It remains to be seen whether this will have a positive effect in the long term.

Understanding the experience: five communities, one future

As mentioned earlier, each of the five towns selected for this study was founded by a textile company during the late nineteenth and early twentieth century, a time period that witnessed a booming textile industry. Each town grew through the "mill village" model, with houses provided by the company for workers that were in close proximity to the mills. Several of the communities also had schools run by the company, as well as amenities like access to medical care, a community center, as well as a company store. All of the communities witnessed growth in the service and retail sectors as a result of a robust population earning money to spend. Convenience stores, restaurants, and shops dotted the landscapes around the mill villages and relied on the company and its workers to thrive economically. Even organizations like Little League baseball teams and local YMCAs were supported by the companies. Once core benefactors within their communities, these companies have since either moved away through mergers and acquisitions, or completely disappeared as a result of bankruptcy. Each of the towns now faces an uncertain future, as the companies that founded them are no longer integral parts of the community.

Stage 1: the impact of change

For those who grew up in a mill village, mill work was steady work. Once people started working at the mill, they did not have to worry about having jobs unless they wanted to leave and move on. Patty, an elderly participant who had spent her entire working life at the local mill, explained what it was like during the heyday of domestic textile production in the South:

Well, I went to work in the plant in 1923. I was 14 years old and I weighed 75 pounds. I worked 10 hours a day, five days a week, [for] 10 cents an hour . . . I had a job there . . . until I retired at 65. But now there was times when I was out, when I was raising my family. But I was never hired but one time. When I would be out, say for several times, I would just call and I would ask if I still had a job. And they would say, "You have a job anytime you want it."

By all estimations, mill work was some of the hardest work. And it was not uncommon for minors, like Patty, to go to work in the production facility at fourteen years old and spend their working lives within it. Workers like Patty literally grew up in the mill.

Working in the mill was a family affair (Hall et al., 1987). That is, many generations of families were employed in production jobs at all five of the companies in the study. This was the case until the 1950s and 1960s when it became more common for the younger generations to attend college after high school. As a result, the mill was the community and the community was the mill. As Don explained:

When I was growing up, that is all I knew was textiles. Everywhere you turned around there was a textile building . . . So it was just a part, everybody in the entire neighborhood, worked either one of three shifts and they all worked at [the company]. So everybody looked after everybody's children.

Not only did residents of these communities not have to worry about finding work—they did not have to look for support, such as daycare, as it was already built into the mill village model.

Although it may sound idyllic, there are two problems with the scenario just described. First, each of the towns relied on a single company, representing a single industry, for its economic base. Second, residents came to rely on the company for nearly everything as a consequence of the paternalistic nature of the mill village model. Both represent what happens when a community makes the proverbial mistake of putting all of its eggs in one basket. If something were to go wrong with the company, and in all five cases it went very wrong, there are severe economic implications for all. Linda recalled what happened when the company that owned the mills in her town closed up shop:

Well people didn't have a job and there was a lot of people out looking for jobs. And just, you know, a change in the way people lived. Everyone was used to things, and you know, my husband and my family used to go to the beach on vacation . . . And then when you don't work you don't have the money and then you don't have a chance to go to the beach. I think that was a problem too. No one had any money to go anywhere.

For towns built around a single company, or the industry itself, the loss did not just extend to residents. It meant the community no longer had a tax base to pay for services like water and electricity, or to support the local YMCA. On a more abstract level, it also meant a loss of identity. Helen did not mince words when describing how badly the impact was felt within her community:

> I'm not going to lie to you, it was devastating . . . mentally . . . for a community to lose a company, that this town was built around. I mean it literally was. [The company] did so much for this community, um, in the way of pride. To have a product such as they had that was made here by people that you knew every day and was sold all over the world and cherished.

Thus, the first stage of the process was going from a familiar, comfortable kind of world to a very different kind of one. Ralph talked about how different things were and would be going forward:

> This was very much a textile area, with all the big names. All of them were here. Probably 50% of the population or more was involved in one shape or another with the textile industry. And in the last, um . . . 15 years, that's gone down to be less than 5% of the employment population.

Davis jokingly pointed to what life is like in a mill village in the post-mill era:

> There are no jobs here. There is nothing except for the people that retired, you know. We just wait for the postman, sitting around [laughs].

Stage 2: moving forward

So what does a town do when it loses its economic and social foundation? For the five communities in this study, a future without textiles had been unfathomable. But globalization and the move to offshore production meant that the future had to be reimagined. Interestingly enough, many of the ways the five communities moved forward resembled how they began, including a focus on small business and entrepreneurs seeking to leverage the community to succeed in their enterprises, just as the founding fathers of the textile corporations had done more than one hundred years earlier.

> We have had entrepreneurs now that have been coming in and developed tourism, you know, like all of our wedding venues and canoeing and camping

and things like that. We are starting to become a community of tourism because of entrepreneurs that have the vision to . . . develop something that people want to come here for.

Ellen

As a consequence of the industry leaving the five communities, the mills that once produced the fabrics were usually left vacant. This meant that people were faced with either renovating the buildings, or having them torn down and replaced by something else. Given the central role played by the industry in these communities, such buildings represented not just their histories, but their identities as textile towns (Suggs, 2002), thereby making it difficult for communities to simply demolish them. For this reason, all five of the communities have sought to focus on adaptive reuse of the company mill buildings, many of which had sat in obvious disrepair for some time. Adaptive reuse is the act of finding a new use for an old building (Woodcock, Steward, and Forrester, 1988). In one community in particular, the central mill was turned into a mixed use facility, including apartments, business offices, a general store, and a restaurant. Located in a rural area with a river nearby, the former mill draws residents who are interested in living outside of the city and having quick and easy access to outdoor activities.

Each of the towns had central downtown areas where shops, movie theaters and cafes had emerged to serve the town's residents and company employees. These communities have been focused on revamping the buildings and trying to draw a new kind of clientele, one that is interested in shopping at small, locally-owned stores and eating at independently-owned restaurants. As Helen explained:

> You know, now we are revitalizing our downtowns that were once so vibrant. And some downtowns got left by the wayside and deteriorated a little bit and now the mainstreet push has brought that back again and people are craving downtowns again.

In two cases at least, one building was turned into a museum. These museums are now charged with preserving the important documents, photos, and newspaper stories that tell the story of the founding companies as well as a way to share the history of both communities as textile towns. However, as Melinda pointed out, while such revitalization gives people a reason to come to the town, it does not necessarily reflect the identity of the town or its people:

> It's going to bring people back. [But] it's not going to bring the community back . . . It's going to bring a different type of people. See the people that worked in the

cotton mill, we were just cotton mill people. And this is going to be a different kind of people.

Stage 3: merging the past with the future

Community leaders were faced with an insurmountable task. Not only were they left with very little tax base to support town services, but they had a crisis on their hands when the primary jobs' provider was no longer anchoring the local labor market. What was the solution? For several towns, the first step was to help the people as best as they could. As Helen recounted, in the case of her community:

> [The company] announced they were closing . . . right before school started. And so we kept thinking, you know, all these people are going to have to . . . get their kids calculators, and school supplies and all this and we did a community-wide school supply drive, and backpacks, hundred-dollar calculators you name it. It was amazing what we got and um, we put [the company] kids back to school with everything they needed. And it was so appreciated, and you can't imagine the stories that we heard and the tears we saw from those workers who had worked there for thirty years and were not near retirement age, and you know in their fifties and just didn't know what they were going to do, but so appreciative. It spoke volumes of our citizens and who we are. Everybody stepped up.

The next steps also meant that community leaders needed to develop a plan for recovery, which for all of the communities meant finding an economic replacement for textiles. Several participants talked about the need for their communities to diversify the portfolio instead of relying on one industry or sector, as Mark, a city manager explained:

> I think something that we've learned from what we've seen from closings of large textile mills employing thousands of employees is that when you have all your eggs in one basket, and somebody drops the basket, you break all the eggs.

Alongside the need for a diversified labor and economic base, community leaders realized they also needed to focus on fostering leadership from within the community itself. The industry that had provided the local leadership was gone, in that the textile industry in the Southern US was known perhaps as much for providing jobs and homes for workers, as it was for providing support for the community as a whole. Thus, as Nell pointed out:

When the leadership goes away, a lot of the support goes away as well . . . You see a lot of charitable support in the community that ends up going away when a company closes or moves away.

Economic diversification means developing a broad approach to creating a community's economic foundation. But for each of the five communities, it was important to try to leverage their own particular textile-related heritage as part of their plans for the future. This has happened in a couple of ways. First, some of the areas began looking to the natural resources which drew the founding textile companies to the location in the first place. Textile mills, and particularly cotton mills, required a great deal of water for their power. Hence, many textile companies were founded next to or in close proximity to rivers, which can be an excellent source of power. A river that provides opportunities for recreational activities can still be a reason for people to live in the community. As one community's economic development director put it, it is all in how you look at it:

We have a lot of resources here and if we look at our rivers, if we look at our history, if we look at our natural resources, in my opinion, and start using that as a draw and become a destination, you're going to get the tax base for the sales tax and those types of things.

Donna

Along with recreation, tourism has become an area of focus and can be used by a former textile town to hold onto aspects of the past that are important to keeping the heritage of the community alive, even when it is moving in new and different directions. For some people, this is a very important part of looking to the future. Greg is one of those people:

My dad worked his entire career in this industry and I basically worked my career in it. My children won't do that. But I think it is important for them to understand what kind of stock they came from . . . what their ancestors did.

Conclusion

Textile manufacturing losses in the United States have been intensely painful at the local level. High jobless rates often compounded already record unemployment levels both across the state and nationwide. With the loss of the textile industry came a loss of community identity, and with it, local pride. Vacant buildings and homes meant the potential for severe neighborhood decline. Mill villages no longer had a socio-economic "anchor" and so became too expensive for the displaced workers to continue living in. Although some of the participants in this study expressed a desire to return to the "good old days" of textile manufacturing, they also acknowledged that this is not realistic. Instead, as in the case of Kannapolis, NC, community leaders are considering new types of "community cores," from revamping downtown areas to marketing local natural resources to potential tourists and residents. Regardless of the paths chosen to go forward, each community must draw on its own sense of history and strength of its community members to shape its future.

As small communities, the five places highlighted here are not unique in their struggles to survive. Rural locations throughout the United States often face the difficult challenge of attracting residents and commerce when there are few jobs to be had. However, these five communities are unique in that they share a history of having been created as textile towns. Having evolved alongside the textile industry, each offers an historical perspective on the topic of community building as well as rebuilding. Eventually each of the five towns recovered and most have gone on to thrive, but it takes time and effort. Further study of industry dynamics from the perspective of the community will help to offer a potential model for understanding how small towns can survive fundamental socio-economic change. Similar changes are likely for global communities as industry manufacturing moves from country to country in different regions of the world.

Case study: Kannapolis, NC: focusing on the future

To consider the implications of globalization for local communities, let's look at one of the five communities discussed above: the town of Kannapolis, North Carolina. Named for the industry mogul that founded Cannon Mills, in 1906, James William Cannon bought several farms for the land upon which to build the Cannon Mills Company (Victor, 1930). Under the guidance of James Cannon's son, Charles, by the mid-twentieth century Cannon Mills would become the world's largest producer of household textiles and a household name throughout the country (*Kannapolis: A Pictorial History*, 2008). Kannapolis was built as a mill village consisting of neighborhoods of craftsman-style homes. The mill employees resided in the homes for a low rent payment and enjoyed free maintenance of their homes, low utility expenses, as well as free garbage collection and disposal (Anderson, 2000).

Over time, the company was merged with Fieldcrest, and then bought out by Pillowtex, which was a competitor. Kannapolis remained the center of the company's headquarters, with multiple mill buildings making up the entire complex. Yet it was just a matter of time before, propelled by a challenging economy and US consumers looking for low priced goods, the company finally closed its doors in 2003. When the announcement was made by Pillowtex, Kannapolis became the hub of the biggest lay-off in the history of North Carolina. Out of the total 6,450 company jobs lost that day, over 4,000 were in North Carolina and Kannapolis (Hodges and Frank, 2014; Michels, 2003). This was a tremendous blow to the small community of Kannapolis because jobs were already scarce. As Will, a manager for the company explained, there was support for applying for unemployment benefits provided to the displaced workers, but the sheer number of people who were suddenly out of work made the process nearly impossible to manage, even with support from state and local government:

> You have all of those people and most of them live in [the mill town] or the surrounding area. And, you know, this [company] has been their bread and butter. And so here you pull the rug out from under those people. I think the city government and the County and the State all banded together and said "Look, we have a major issue here." I mean we put 4,500 people on the street and I know we didn't even have to sign up for unemployment. It was done automatically. The State set that up so we did not have to go sign up.
>
> Will

When the company closed its doors for good, state as well as local agencies sought to implement programs based on federal money available as a result of the Trade Readjustment Act (TRA), developed to help those displaced by the loss of US manufacturing ("Focused Industry Support," 2011). The workers that were laid off were given access to counselors who worked for the local community college, which bore much of the burden of retraining the thousands of unemployable workers. For several years the college faced trying to manage the swell of incoming students, many of whom needed remedial courses because they had not been to school in many years (Hodges, 2013). Working in a mill, and particularly the manufacturing-focused jobs, required little more than a high school education. Suddenly these workers were faced with having to learn a new trade. As Jennifer, a college administrator, put it:

> We did a lot of good, but there's still a lot that we didn't do. There's about 1,000 [people] that didn't come in for anything and uh, we wonder about what

happened to that 1,000. Some people retired, a few people died. Some people moved away. But we know that there's still a pocket of people out there that we haven't done anything for.

In the end, of the total number of workers displaced by the company, one newspaper account suggested that only 1,550 had obtained employment by the two-year anniversary of the closing (Nowell, 2005). Now, more than fifteen years later, the buildings that once comprised the headquarters of the company have been demolished and replaced with new buildings that form a research campus affiliated with several North Carolina colleges and universities. Although the campus offers jobs, they are not the kind of jobs that displaced textile workers could fill. Those who have re-entered the job market find themselves working primarily in retail, service, and healthcare positions for less money and fewer benefits than they had received in their manufacturing jobs (Duggan, 2001). Likewise, the mill homes that the workers had lived in for generations were too expensive for them to purchase after the company went bankrupt (Hodges and Lentz, 2010). Many of these homes have since sold for high dollar values as they are in close proximity to the city of Charlotte, NC, and therefore offer a convenient location for commuters.

For generations, the residents of Kannapolis and their families helped to support the town's core economic engine by providing its primary labor market base. Today, Kannapolis is largely a commuter city due to its close proximity to Charlotte. There are also those who live and work there at the research campus. A visit to the city's website suggests that it is focused on the future by emphasizing a family-friendly community that offers amenities akin to small town America, including a restored downtown and the above-mentioned craftsman-style homes along tree-lined streets (www.kannapolisnc.gov). A focus on tourism, as well as entrepreneurship and small business, is also emphasized by the community's leaders, who seek to market Kannapolis as a place for businesses, tourists, and residents alike. While Kannapolis may no longer be defined as a textile town, it is a community that realized it must continue to thrive somehow, and with time and determination, it appears to have been successful thus far.

References

American Textile Manufacturers Institute (ATMI). *Crisis in U.S. Textiles.* Washington, DC: ATMI, 2001.

Anderson, Cynthia D. *The Social Consequences of Economic Restructuring in the Textile Industry: Change in a Southern Mill Village.* New York: Garland, 2000.

Bureau of Labor Statistics. "Current Employment Statistics Survey (1997–2003)." 2003. http://www.bls.gov/ces/home.htm

Bureau of Labor Statistics. "Regional and State Employment and Unemployment Summary." 2015. http://www.bls.gov.

Carlton, David and Coclanis, Peter. "Southern textiles in global context." In Susanna Delfino and Michele Gillespie (eds.), *Global Perspectives on Industrial Transformation in the American South*, pp. 151–74. Columbia: University of Missouri Press, 2005.

Cooper, William. *An Introduction to the US textile Industry of the 70s.* Raleigh: Department of Textiles Extension and Continuing Education, North Carolina State University, 1970.

Delfino, Susanna and Gillespie, Michele. *Global Perspectives on Industrial Transformation in the American South.* Columbia: University of Missouri Press, 2005.

Dudley, Kathryn Marie. *The End of the Line: Lost Jobs, New Lives in Postindustrial America.* Chicago: University of Chicago Press, 1994.

Duggan, Lynn. "Retail on the 'dole': Parasitic employers and women workers." *National Women's Studies Association (NWSA) Journal* 13, no. 3 (2001): 95–115.

Fink, Gary and Reed, Merl. *Race, Class, and Community in Southern History.* Tuscaloosa: University of Alabama Press, 1994.

Focused Industry Support. *North Carolina Department of Commerce.* 2011. www.nccommerce.com.

Gaventa, John and Smith, Barbara Ellen. "The deindustrialization of the textile south: A case study." In Jeffrey Leiter, Michael Shulman, and Rhoda Zingraff (eds.), *Hanging by a Thread: Social Change in Southern Textiles*, pp. 181–98. New York: Cornell University Press, 1991.

Gereffi, Gary. "The transformation of the North American apparel industry: Is NAFTA a curse or a blessing?" *Integration and Trade* 4, no. 11 (2000): 47–95.

Glass, Brent. *The Textile Industry in North Carolina.* Raleigh: Division of Archives and History of the North Carolina Department of Cultural Resources, 1992.

Hall, Jacqueline Dowd, Murphy, Mary, Leloudis, James, Korstad, Robert, Jones, Lu Ann, and Daly, Christopher. *Like a Family: The Making of a Southern Cotton Mill World.* New York: WW Norton & Co., 1987.

Hodges, Nancy. "*What do I do now?* Exploring women's experiences with textile manufacturing job loss and community college retraining." *Community College Journal of Research and Practice* 37, no. 2 (2013): 85–102.

Hodges, Nancy and Frank, Phillip. "The case of the disappearing mill village." *Textile: A Journal of Cloth and Culture* 11, no. 1 (2013): 38–57.

Hodges, Nancy and Frank, Phillip. "Reinventing 'Towel City USA': Textiles, tourism and the future of the Southeastern mill town." *Family and Consumer Sciences Research Journal* 43, no. 2 (2014): 173–87.

Hodges, Nancy and Karpova, Elena "A tale of two industries: An interpretive analysis of media reports on textiles and apparel in North Carolina." *Clothing and Textiles Research Journal* 26, no. 3 (2008): 253–272.

Hodges, Nancy and Lentz, Holly. "U.S. textile sector job loss: Implications for individuals, communities and industry." *Journal of Fashion Marketing and Management* 14, no. 1 (2010): 21–38.

Jennings, Jefferson. *Some Southern Cotton Mill Workers and Their Villages*. Chapel Hill: University of North Carolina Press, 1923.

Kannapolis: A Pictorial History. Kannapolis, NC: City of Kannapolis, 2008.

McHugh, Cathy. *Mill family: The Labor System in the Southern Textile Industry*. New York: Oxford University Press, 1988.

Michels, Susan. "Pillowtex calls it quits; thousands left jobless as 16 plants close." *News & Record*, July 31, 2003, p. A1.

Norris, Lachelle. "The human face of globalization: Plant closings and life transitions." *Journal of Fashion Marketing and Management* 7, no. 2 (2003): 163–81.

Nowell, P. "Hope rises from the ashes of Pillowtex." *News & Record*, December 3, 2005, p. B3.

Potwin, Marjorie Adella. *Cotton Mill People of the Piedmont*. New York: Columbia University Press, 1927.

Simpson, William Hayes. *Southern Textile Communities*. Charlotte, NC: American Cotton Manufacturers Association, 1948.

Suggs, George. *"My world is gone": Memories of Life in a Southern Cotton Mill Town*. Detroit: Wayne State University Press, 2002.

Victor, George. *Kannapolis*. Kannapolis, NC: Charles A. Cannon Memorial Library Archives, 1930.

Woodcock, David, Steward, W. Cecil, and Forrester, R. Alan. *Adaptive Reuse: Issues and Case Studies in Building Preservation*. New York: Van Nostrand Reinhold, 1988.

Zingraff, Rhoda. "Facing extinction?" In Jeffrey Leiter, Michael Shulman, and Rhoda Zingraff (eds.), *Hanging by a Thread: Social Change in Southern Textiles*, pp. 199–216. New York: Cornell University Press, 1991.

Part Three

The Dangers of Consuming Fashion

9

Taking Offense: A Discussion of Fashion, Appropriation, and Cultural Insensitivity

Denise Nicole Green and Susan B. Kaiser

Imagine these scenarios:

1. It is March 14, 1993 and fashion week in Paris. Jean Paul Gaultier's fall/winter collection is about to come down a menorah-lined runway. The collection is titled *Chic Rabbis* and many of the models—both male and female—are coiffed with *payot* (sidecurls) and don *shtraimel*, the fur hats typically worn by married Haredi Jewish men.
2. The "Summer of Love" (1967) is in full force in San Francisco and the emerging "hippie" culture begins using design elements from Native America, India, and other cultural groups across the globe.
3. Abercrombie & Fitch released a series of graphic T-shirts in 2002, including one with the text: "Wong Brothers Laundry Service: Two Wongs can make it white." The text was accompanied by a cartoon caricature of the Wong brothers, each depicted in an Asian conical hat.
4. On July 6, 2017 an article appeared on Vogue.com, intended to provide inspiration for summer wardrobes. The article was titled "In Honor of Frida Kahlo's Birthday, Shop These Colorful Summer Looks."
5. Halloween is a holiday to "dress up" like someone or something else. Imagine you have attended a party, only to find your best friend donned in a Native American headdress and imitation buckskin and another friend dressed as a Geisha girl.
6. It is 2015 and a very cold winter. Ralph Lauren has released the "Cowichan Full Zip" sweater, named for a Coast Salish First Nation from the Northwest coast, but the actual garment is made in China.

In each of these scenarios you are confronted with an experience of fashion that may have offended you, or at the very least, brought up feelings of ambivalence.

Perhaps you asked yourself: Is it disrespectful to use symbols of Judaism in the production of a fashion show and a collection that is to be sold? How would Chinese people feel about being stereotyped as laundrymen and depicted in caricature? Would Frida Kahlo really want her legacy used as inspiration for online shopping? Is another person's culture appropriate for someone's Halloween costume? Did Cowichan knitters profit from the Ralph Lauren sweater?

These scenarios are not anomalies—rather, they are experiences that have become normalized and are characteristic of the complex and pervasive phenomena known as cultural appropriation. You would be hard-pressed to find a fashion item that has not been part of some mechanism of appropriation— from designers taking inspiration from another culture to the appropriation of labor in low-wage regions, appropriation is ubiquitous, and literally woven into the fabric of the fashion system.

Cultural appropriation is also not a new phenomenon: it has a long history in the world of fashion and the arts more generally (Green and Kaiser, 2017). However, only recently has it become highlighted in popular discourse, fostering many of us to reflect upon it and try to understand its meaning and the damage it may do. In this chapter, we begin with working definitions and terminology, followed by a discussion of four different examples and how they help us to think through the potential dangers of cultural appropriation.

Working definitions

In this section we present what we call "working definitions"—in other words, more open-ended interpretations of the array of terminology that surrounds appropriation. Academic and popular media conversations about this topic are complicated and polarized, each using different language and sometimes even different definitions and interpretations of similar terms. While cultural appropriation has long been part of the fashion system, our theoretical, political, and ideological understandings of the term are ever evolving. We often find cultural appropriation entangled with locutions like cultural borrowing, cultural hybridity, cultural exchange, cultural appreciation, cultural inspiration, and strategic anti-essentialism. Disentangling some of these terms, and discussing their key differences, brings about a more nuanced understanding of cultural appropriation. To begin, we will start with a basic definition of cultural appropriation within the context of fashion and follow with working definitions of related terminology (again, using fashion as a reference point). We will then circle back to our initial definition of cultural appropriation and augment it with critiques of the term. The case studies will allow us to thoroughly explore the grey areas.

Cultural appropriation

The most basic definition of cultural appropriation is the taking of aesthetic or material elements from another culture by someone who is not a member of that culture without giving credit or profit. The "taking" is not unlike stealing or plagiarizing—it is often done without permission and/or acknowledgment (like one would use a citation in an academic paper). Typically, those stealing design elements or ideas profit from them, while the culture of origin makes no profit and may be humiliated, disrespected, or harmed through the process. Cultural appropriation is possible because the "taker" is typically in a position of power, whereas those who are taken *from* may not have easy access to legal recourse or enforcement of requital. Appropriation is also dangerous and offensive because it tends to be culturally insensitive and reduces a culture to an aesthetic expression or fashion statement that can be bought and sold.

Cultural exchange

Cultural exchange is often defined as a respectful and mutual interchange—that is, both giving and receiving—between cultures. The line that demarcates cultural exchange from cultural appropriation is a nebulous one because of power. Is it possible to have a truly fair, equitable exchange? Power dynamics make this very challenging. In recent years, the term "collaboration" has stood in for cultural exchange. Examples include the 2015 collaboration between Metis artist Christi Belcourt and Valentino, Phillip Lim's spring 2016 campaign led by Ethiopian model Liya Kebede, and a 2011 sari collection that was a collaboration between Hermes and Sunita Kumar, a Kolkata-based designer. These collaborations are not black and white and have been criticized as examples of "tokenism," like the Belcourt–Valentino collaboration, which was condemned as a way for Valentino to legitimize their appropriation of Native American elements by name-dropping Belcourt (Metcalfe, 2017).

Cultural borrowing

Cultural borrowing is often framed as a more benign, well-intentioned version of cultural appropriation, in which harm to the origin community is not intended; however, the word "borrow" suggests that what was taken will ultimately be returned, and this has rarely, if ever, been the case. Channels through which borrowing occurs are also power-laden; as Olufunmilayo Arewa, Professor of Law at UC Irvine, has argued, "borrowing may become appropriation when it reinforces historically exploitative relationships" and when the borrowing keeps source communities from "opportunities to control or benefit from their cultural material" (2016). In many ways, cultural borrowing is a dangerously euphemistic term for cultural appropriation.

Cultural appreciation

Another tricky term to define is cultural appreciation—once again, the line between appropriation and appreciation is blurry and entangled with power and informed by context (e.g., time, place, and identity politics therein). In many ways, context is crucial. Blogger Dounia Tazi has used the example of wearing henna: when a white person wears henna to Coachella (as a fashion statement) it is a perfect example of appropriation; however, if that same white person is attending a South Asian wedding and is invited to have henna done within the context of this event, Tazi argues it is a form of cultural appreciation and a means of relating to and respecting the cultural event taking place (Tazi, 2015). Cultural appreciation also suggests that the wearer or fashion designer has done their research—that they have educated themselves about the history and significance of the cultural expression. Typically, this kind of research results in an educated decision about when and where the use of a particular mode of dress or design element is appropriate and where and when it is offensive and damaging. Some have argued that cultural appreciation helps to support indigenous arts in the global, capitalist marketplace. The "appreciators" of the first world are a privileged and wealthy market—a source of funding that may support the continuance of traditional arts around the world—but this market also increases prices. For example, Amanda Denham (2017) recently conducted ethnographic fieldwork among Maya weavers in Guatemala and discovered that indigenous women could no longer afford their hand-woven *huipiles* (blouses) and were instead wearing imported, synthetic knock-offs of their own designs in order to sell hand-woven *huipiles* to wealthy tourists. Justification for cultural appropriation is often cloaked behind the guise of cultural appreciation and good intentions—in other words, cultural appreciation runs the risk of becoming a smokescreen that justifies appropriation.

Cultural inspiration

According to the *Oxford English Dictionary*, inspiration is the "process of being mentally stimulated to do or feel something, especially something creative." This stimulation may come from a number of different realms and senses. Cultural inspiration refers to the process of being stimulated and influenced by other cultures, either current or of the past. The language around "inspiration" has evolved since the late nineteenth century alongside the emergence of the named designer—that is, the singular individual who creates, and is inspired, by the world around them.

Cultural hybridity

Hybridity typically refers to a cross between two things—that is, a kind of mixture—but one that does not necessarily result in an amalgamative erasure (e.g., "melting pot"). In the field of cultural studies, the term "cultural hybridity" has sought to subvert the idea of cultures as bounded, separate entities; rather, the concept acknowledges cultural differences and distinctiveness alongside the inevitable influences and cross-fertilization of ideas, aesthetics, and intersectional identities in a global world.

Cultural insensitivity

Understanding the impact and potential dangers of cultural appropriation is tightly bound to the concept of cultural insensitivity. Insensitivity may refer to the creation, promotion, and perpetuation of racial and ethnic stereotypes. The Abercrombie & Fitch "Wong Brothers" T-shirt is a perfect example of cultural insensitivity: the design used cartoon caricature to exaggerate facial features, all the while perpetuating a stereotype of Chinese people as laundrymen (Helmreich, 1983). Cultural insensitivity may also refer to taking and re-presenting culturally sensitive forms—like sacred imagery—in fashion.

Rethinking cultural appropriation

In addition to the laundry list of associated terminology, cultural appropriation itself also works on many levels and has multiple definitions within the context of fashion: from the appropriation of free labor on the part of design interns in the current NYC fashion industry (Ayres, 2017); exploitation of sweatshop labor in low-wage and unregulated places; explicit copying of indigenous and culturally sensitive designs across the world; to the performative costuming of another person's culture, to name a few.

We are faced with appropriation everywhere: in our closets, on and through our bodies, in the media, and the places we shop. It is pervasive and confusing—it can be challenging to determine the difference between cultural appreciation and cultural appropriation. What are the power dynamics at play? As a designer in a global world, is it possible not to be influenced by images and peoples encountered?

Discussions about cultural appropriation are mostly taking place on the internet—in the blogosphere and social media—and the debate is heated and polarized. Journalist Jenni Avins has gone so far as to say, "At my house, getting dressed is a daily act of cultural appropriation, and I'm not the least bit sorry about it," calling criticizers' language "shrill accusations" that are simply part of the "Internet outrage cycle" (Avins, 2015). Avins argues that culture and creativity "work" through the exchange of ideas. But at what point does exchange become exploitation? Blogger Dario Calmese (2017) has argued that "calling out cultural appropriation does not kill creative license, it simply holds those in power accountable to cite their sources." All the while, scholar Minh-Ha T. Pham (2014) has questioned the productivity of the debate when it reaffirms, as Calmese does, "those in power." The debate, according to Pham, is "pointless" and also dangerous because "many critiques of cultural appropriation proceeds [sic] as if there are only two places in the world: 'Western capitalist institution' and 'slum.' Which, of course, reaffirms the very power relations they try to critique." Instead, Pham suggests discussing an "inappropriate" discourse to "challenge the idea of the absolute power and authority of the West to control how the world sees, knows, and talks about fashion." In other words, what is not "appropriate-able"?

Cultural appropriation is theoretically knotted and entangled with issues of power, context (e.g., time, place, manner), identity, and taste. In the remainder of this chapter we discuss four case studies that illuminate (and complicate) our understanding of cultural appropriation and the dangers that arise from it.

Jean-Paul Gaultier: *Chic Rabbis*, fall/winter 1993

By 1993, Jean-Paul Gaultier had earned the byname "enfant terrible" by shocking, provoking, and at times offending the fashion world with his designs and runway spectacles. According to *Vogue Paris*, Gaultier ran ads in *Libération* newspaper in the early 1980s looking for "atypical models, ugly faces welcome" ("Jean Paul Gaultier," 2015); in his 1984 collection, *And God Created Man*, he put men in skirts, and in 1990 outfitted Madonna in the now-iconic cone bra for her *Blond Ambition World Tour*. By the early 1990s, Gaultier had earned a reputation as irreverent and unconventional, a designer who pushed boundaries but simultaneously managed to produce commercial collections. He had the attention of the fashion world and beyond, even touting a second career in television as co-presenter on the late-night program *Eurotrash* for four years (1993–7).

On March 14, 1993, Gaultier premiered his fall/winter collection, *Chic Rabbis*, on the runway at Paris Fashion Week (see Figure 9.1). The staging was described as "campy" by Amy Spindler of the *New York Times*, with invitations in Hebraic script, a runway lined with menorahs, violinists performing klezmer music, and Maneschwitz wine provided to attendees. Each look was accompanied by some kind of Jewish-inspired accoutrement or coiffure – *kippah* (skullcaps), *shtraimel* (wide brimmed fur hats), and *payot* (sidecurls) adorned models, both male and female. The campiness of the show culminated with Gaultier himself, appearing after the final runway piece wearing his signature Breton striped shirt complemented by a matching Breton striped *kippah*. Gaultier, himself a Catholic, claimed to have found inspiration when he encountered a group of rabbis leaving the New York Public Library on one of his trips to New York City (Strubel, 2015). The fashion press wondered if this would be the next great scandal, and yet no serious controversy arose.

While terms like "cultural appreciation" and "cultural appropriation" were not part of the popular media vernacular quite yet, fashion's ongoing history of "inspiration" from other cultures was on the radar of fashion editors and reviewers. Amy Spindler began her review of the collection for the *New York Times* by acknowledging the long history of appropriation: "After decades of buying up ethnically inspired collections, many fashion industry leaders saw their own roots rifled on Sunday. Jean-Paul Gaultier is the first major designer to use Judaism as an inspiration" (Spindler, 1993).

While a few were offended, the general reaction from the fashion industry (as reported by the press) was laudatory and defensive: "You can be inspired by anyone in the world you want to be inspired by," argued Kalman Ruttenstein, fashion director of Bloomingdale's (Spindler, 1993). Perhaps the fashion buyers and the fashion press feared that their critique would become a slippery slope, making "ethnic inspiration" off-limits? Others followed a similar line of

Figure 9.1 A model coiffed with *payot* in Jean-Paul Gaultier's fall/winter 1993 collection *Chic Rabbis*. Photo by Bertrand Rindoff Petroff/Getty Images.

reasoning, not unlike contemporary justifications of cultural appropriation as cultural appreciation. Ruttenstein elaborated: "[Gaultier] did it with taste and charm and dignity. There was no lack of respect whatsoever. In fact, there was a great effort to give respect." Andrew Leon Talley, creative director at *Vogue*, was also adamantly in support: "I think it's so witty and a glorification. I think it's time someone went back to taking ethnic groups and their costumes and glorifying them. It's been done for centuries" he told VH1.

Other reviews claimed that Gaultier's collection was just part of a larger fashion trend of referencing religion. "Everywhere this season designers are giving new meaning to 'religious follower of fashion,'" wrote Julia Szabo for *Harper's Bazaar*.

Gaultier himself claimed the collection was intended to revere Judaism and combat anti-Semitism. In *Vogue* he was quoted as saying the collection was "an homage to the Jewish religion" (Betts, 1993, p. 484). In a VH1 report on the fashion show, Gaultier was queried about his inspiration:

> Interviewer: Tell me where you picked up this idea of playing with the Hasidic imagery?
>
> Gaultier: It was not really playing. Playing in the fact that I did it with pleasure. But it was, why? Because I always find it was a beautiful culture and I wanted to give an homage to them. There are lots of Jewish people in the fashion industry. I wanted to do that but I didn't know when, and I think it was the right time. Why? I think there's coming a lot of racism and anti-Semitism again in Europe and all of the world. So I think it was the right moment to show that and to take position.

Ultimately, the fashion industry—particularly the buyers—were not interested in the debate around the ethics of appropriation, nor whether or not the collection honored Judaism; instead, their concerns were about salability. Media accounts of the show suggested that the only concern about controversy was whether or not the said controversy would impact sales (not whether or not it was damaging or disrespectful to Judaism). "I just cut through all that Judaic stuff and looked at the clothes. Underneath that was a very commercial collection," explained Ellin Salzman, fashion director of Bergdorf Goodman. Barabara Weiser of Charivari concurred: "The clothes were so elegant and beautiful. It was just a vehicle to present the clothes, their way of staging a presentation" (Spindler, 1993).

In the September issue of *Vogue*, Katherine Betts called Gaultier "devoutly irreverent," and pointed out another layer of appropriation—the incorporation of punk subcultural style elements (Betts, 1993). When interviewed about the collection in 2002, Gaultier simply said, "Je ne regrette rien [I do not regret anything]" (Brendan, 2002).

The "Summer of Love" (1967)

The summer of 2017 was the fiftieth anniversary of the "summer of love" in San Francisco. In and around 1967, San Francisco (especially the Haight-Ashbury district) became a highly visual site of the "hippie" social movement. Many of the young people participating in the "be in" and "dropping in, dropping out" happenings (often in the Golden Gate Park near Haight-Ashbury) were from white, middle-class backgrounds, but they were resisting the values of their parents' generation: what the young "baby boomers" (born between 1946 and 1964) saw as conservative, restrictive music, fashion, and gender and sexual norms, for example. The expression "Never trust anyone over 30" captured the generational gap at the time. Rock music and colorful, psychedelic aesthetics (e.g., clothes, posters announcing concerts and happenings, LSD "trips") were interconnected with the idea of "making love, not war," as demonstrated at the De Young Museum's exhibit on the summer of love (D'Allesandro and Terry, 2017).

Especially pertinent to debates on cultural appropriation were the hippies' fascination with Native American culture. The *San Francisco Oracle*, an underground newspaper in Haight-Ashbury, published an "American Indian" issue in 1966. The editors later explained that "the hippies' creation myth centered on the notion that they were reincarnated Indians who returned to earth with the intention of bringing the land and people back to traditional ways" (in D'Allesandro, 2017, p. 62). They looked to Native American culture(s) as a model for an alternative lifestyle that seemed more "natural," "authentic," and "free." To symbolize this philosophical reverence, they dressed in fringed buckskin leather and adorned themselves with beads and feathers.

By the late 1960s, leather shops were taking off in San Francisco. One of the successful ones was North Beach Leather, established by Bill Morgan with his friend Michael Hoban. In addition to designing their own line, the company featured local artists, including Burray Olson, who had studied art in college but had shunned commercial art in favor of Indian-inspired leatherwork. He fashioned outfits for rock musicians such as Jefferson Airplane, the Grateful Dead, and Santana. Olson had been fascinated with Native American culture since he was ten years old, when two Sioux women who worked for his grandmother shared legends and wore beaded buckskin dresses to powwows. Olson and his grandmother learned Sioux beaded embroidery techniques from the two women, and he later visited reservations and trading posts to learn additional sewing techniques and absorb Native American culture (D'Allesandro, 2017, p. 63).

Native American communities did not generally appreciate the hippies' appropriation of their styles and symbols. Singer-songwriter Buffy Sainte-Marie, who is Cree, articulated her concerns and anger in a *New York Times* interview in 1970:

> I just don't know why society women keep wearing those $700 forgeries ... It is most insensitive in the light of Indian poverty to be publicizing those clothes and giving awards to people who design them ... No Indian would wear those things. And look—all of the models are white. Usually they have a few black girls to portray Indians. They never use real Indians. You know, I'm really dismayed by all of the magazines and the fashion industry.

Sainte-Marie continued, that it was not so much that she was opposed to people dressing like Indians, but she had major concerns with the issue of who benefits (and who does not):

> They are probably well meaning, but they cannot save their consciences by wearing Indian dresses. Why don't they stretch their interests to include our problems? Why don't they see to it that the people in the fashion industry who are making money off our thing share it with the poor people of our reservations? ... We're sick of being told that we should feel honored that people want to look like us. They say it's a memorial to our noble race, but that's a lot of bull. We don't want any more memorials. We need things like breakfast programs.
>
> Klemesrud, 1970

Buffy Sainte-Marie herself wore designs created by designer/artist Burray Olson (D'Allesandro, 2017, p. 63). Although she was born on a Cree reserve, she was adopted by working-class parents (who had partial Native American backgrounds themselves) and grew up in Massachusetts. Later, she returned to her place of birth and was adopted by the Cree Nation. She has dedicated approximately fifty years to improving opportunities for Native Americans in the US and Canada through her economic and political support.

Sainte-Marie has used style strategically to highlight her own ethnicity, but carefully and critically, in a way that thoughtfully considers the political, economic, and aesthetic ramifications. In contrast, the vast majority of hippies could not claim any degree of ethnic "authenticity," although some believed that they were "reincarnated Indians" with repressed identities. As Sainte-Marie expressed clearly, the power (including socio-economic) differences between white middle-class hippies and the people they imitated still depended on a kind of "racial disguise" that did not ultimately help anti-racist efforts.

"My culture is not your costume": the importance of context

Forty-five years later, in 2015, Buffy Sainte-Marie was still facing cultural appropriation of Native American cultures. In an interview that year, Sainte-Marie (then seventy-four years old and still actively recording and performing) commented on the trend for scantily clad women (e.g., in leather bikinis or halter tops and cutoffs) wearing Native American headdresses—symbolic of tribal chiefs' prowess and importance—on runways and at concerts (including her own):

> When it comes to things like headdresses, there are some things that are actually, factually, personally, deeply cultural to our heritage ... To some guy who's got models in high heels, bikini bottoms, pasties and a big headdress, and everybody's drunk—I want people to understand why that is painful or disgusting, why that is negative to us ... It'd be like if you really loved your grandmother or your mom and all of a sudden you're watching wrestling on TV and you see your mom's picture on some wrestler's crotch. It's inappropriate. It's not funny. It doesn't help ... You see these people showing up and they have handmade, craftsy, fake headdress-like things, and they somehow think they're paying us a compliment ... I think it's mostly ignorance. I think most people who are doing that probably haven't given it much thought.
>
> Patch, 2015

In the last few years, celebrities such as Jessica Simpson and Gwen Stefani have worn imitation headdresses, and they have become popular accessories at music and arts festivals. In 2013, H&M received criticism from aboriginal groups and activist groups for featuring "faux headdresses" in their Canadian stores. But the trend persisted and there was a cultural dialogue that resulted in a 2015 ban on the garment at music and arts festivals. Teekca Apencer, who runs an aboriginal boutique in Winnipeg, commented that people came in wanting to try on headdresses and "get some pictures." She had to explain that it was "not appropriate. It's a really sacred and restricted item." Manitoba's Grand Chief Derek Nepinak explained that a headdress is not something that can be bought; rather, it is "acquired through sacred and ceremonial processes" (Balca, 2015).

A similar discourse in the US about cultural appropriation has generated considerable debate and media attention. In 2011, the Students Teaching about Racism in Society (STAR) at Ohio University launched a poster campaign called "My culture is not your costume." The campaign aimed to sensitize individuals who were considering (or had been wearing) Halloween costumes that appropriated from cultures other than their own in stereotypical and/or insensitive ways. The posters included images of young white people dressed in "costume-like versions" of Native American attire and headdresses, Mexican sombreros (large-billed hats) and ponchos, and Islamic veils, combined with a student from that culture looking disheartened. As one student in the campaign commented, "We just wanted to say, 'Hey, this is not cool. This is offensive and this shouldn't be taken lightly.'" One poster said, "You wear the costume for one night. I wear the stigma for life." Another read, "This is not who I am, and this is not okay." Within a few years, a number of other universities and colleges had adopted the campaign and posted the copyrighted posters from Ohio University on their campuses (Sand, 2013).

The debate continued, however, because the offensive clothing was still in the marketplace. In 2016, at a store in Winnipeg, outfits with names such as "Reservation Royalty" and "Indian Princess" were on sale for Halloween, and an Aboriginal woman, Alicia BigCanoe, wanted to remind people online that such styles—worn by non-Aboriginal people in a Halloween context—were "hurtful and racist" (Paling, 2016).

Ralph Lauren's native fascination

From subcultural, new-age, and festival-going communities to Mardi Gras tribes, Boy Scouts, sports team mascots, and Halloween-goers, Native American imagery is possibly the most appropriated, appreciated, stolen, exploited, borrowed, essentialized, anti-essentialized, celebrated, revered, reduced, desensitized, and lauded. Philip Deloria has argued that dressing up and "playing Indian" has been an important part of the production of US national identity (Deloria, 1998). From the Boston Tea Party to the hippies, and beyond, "playing Indian" has proven integral to the production of a white US American identity—an identity fraught with tension, insecure and unstable.

Ralph Lauren has created a successful brand empire by designing for this precarious national identity: exploiting ambivalence, appropriating Native American designs, imagining the frontier, and typifying American style. His menswear label began in 1967 with tweeds and ties. As perceptions of masculinity shifted throughout the 1970s, so too did Lauren's design approach. He launched the Polo Western collection in 1979 and the Santa Fe collection in 1981. These collections mixed elements from the American Southwest, including "Navajo-inspired" textile designs, silverwork, and other elements appropriated from Native art from different nations, often paired with "cowboy" elements. Lauren himself was "playing Indian" in his personal styling in the late 1970s, and continues to do so in his personal life on his ranch. Jessica Metcalfe has pointed out the irony of Lauren's ranch, which was featured on a 2011 *Oprah* episode: 17,000 acres of indigenous land, complete with teepees to hold Navajo blankets (a Hogan is a traditional Navajo dwelling, not a teepee), and a mishmash of Native art from different cultures across North America (Metcalfe, 2012). Lauren's ignorance about the differences—aesthetically, culturally, historically—between distinct Native American cultures has resulted in designs with a "generic sense of Indianness," which is reductive and, Metcalfe argues, "reinforces negative stereotypes" (Metcalfe, 2012).

Lauren is a collector, reputed to have an impressive compendium of Pendleton blankets, Native American art, textiles, and ephemera. Part of the collection is preserved as a kind of "inspiration archive" at the New York design headquarters. Over the past thirty years and more, Native American appropriation has been a reoccurring theme for Ralph Lauren, both in collections and advertising campaigns.

The year 2014–15 was particularly challenging for Ralph Lauren. He had used Native designs as inspiration without criticism for decades, and so the brand was not accustomed to giving credit nor to making apologies. The first apology came after a problematic ad campaign, in which historical photographs of unidentified Native American men were used like "dehumanized props," according to Adrienne Keene, "to fulfill a settler imperialist nostalgia fantasy" and to sell a 2014 holiday collection (Keene, 2014).

The second appropriation offense involved the Cowichan, a Coast Salish First Nation, who went to the press to criticize Ralph Lauren's "Cowichan Full-Zip" sweater as a counterfeit (see Figure 9.2; CTV Vancouver, 2015). The sweater featured designs copied from Cowichan knit sweaters, used the Cowichan name, and yet was not a Cowichan-made product (it was manufactured in China). This was not the first time Ralph Lauren had designed a sweater based on Cowichan design work (Figure 9.2), but *it was* the first time he received media attention for doing so. According to a blog called The Fashion Law, the Cowichan did not have a strong legal case: they did not hold an active US federal trademark registration (thus making it impossible to claim counterfeiting) and could not be protected by the Indian Arts and Crafts Board Act of 1990 (the Cowichan are a Canadian First Nation, and therefore are not protected by US federal law) ("Ralph Lauren has Offended a Canadian Tribe with this Sweater," 2015). Ralph Lauren did eventually remove the Cowichan name from the sweater, but the sweaters were still sold, and Lauren profited. As of June 2019, a product called "Cowichan-Inspired Zip Sweater" was available for sale on the Ralph Lauren website. Cowichan knitters—many of whom depend on the sale of knitwear for their livelihood—do not profit from Lauren's sales, and have likely lost business with the prevalence of his knockoff sweaters.

Figure 9.2 In the foreground, a sweater with thunderbird motif, made by a Cowichan First Nation knitter, *c.* 1975. In the background, two thunderbird sweaters that were manufactured in China for Ralph Lauren and sold as Cowichan sweaters. Photo by Grace Anderson.

Conclusion

As the above scenarios and case studies demonstrate, cultural appropriation is a tricky concept that depends on a number of perspectives and situational circumstances to analyse adequately. Overall, attention to context is most helpful to think critically and creatively about cultural appropriation and its conceptual "cousins." In the cases of Ralph Lauren's and the hippies' appropriations of indigenous aesthetics, contextual questions such as the following become relevant: What are the power differences and relations involved? Who profits? Do any of these profits help the life circumstances of indigenous people? Is there thoughtful acknowledgment and citation of cultural innovations and meanings? Such acknowledgment and citation would help to move cultural appropriation toward cultural appreciation, but in these scenarios such processes are absent. It is not clear, either, that Jean Paul Gaultier did his homework to cite Jewish culture, and other than the interview where he articulates his intentions to work against anti-Semitism, how would such intentions be apparent in the context of a fashion show—unless citations, notes, or footnotes were made available to the audience and publicized to the media?

The debate regarding cultural appropriation continues and will probably never be easily resolved, but every style or incident needs to be analysed according to context, intention, implication, citation, power differences, and economic benefit or loss. Like fashion itself, cultural appropriation is fraught with tension, ambivalence, nuance, and even danger. Rarely are there good examples of appropriating scenarios that foster a more equitable, diverse, and inclusive society: one that fights, for example, against racism or poverty. Yet conceptually, at least, it seems possible for there to emerge more aware and thoughtful ways to be inspired by a culture, acknowledge and cite its cultural significance and meaning, and assure an equitable distribution of the resulting resources.

References

Arewa, O. "Cultural Appropriation: When 'Borrowing' Becomes Exploitation." *The Conversation*, June 20, 2016. http://theconversation.com/cultural-appropriation-when-borrowing-becomes-exploitation-57411.

Avins, J. "The Dos and Don'ts of Cultural Appropriation: Borrowing from Other Cultures Isn't Just Inevitable, It's Potentially Positive." *The Atlantic*, October 20, 2015.

https://www.theatlantic.com/entertainment/archive/2015/10/the-dos-and-donts-of-cultural-appropriation/411292/.

Ayres, Jennifer. "Inspiration or Prototype? Appropriation and Exploitation in the Fashion Industry." *Fashion, Style & Popular Culture* 4, no. 2 (2017): 151–65.

Balca, Dario. "Canadian Music Festivals Ban First Nations Headdress over Cultural Insensitivity." *Canadian TV News*, July 26, 2015. http://www.ctvnews.ca/canada/canadian-music-festivals-ban-first-nations-headdress-over-cultural-insensitivity-1.2473299.

Betts, Katherine. "Fashion: Independents' Day." *Vogue*, September 1, 1993.

Calmese, Dario. "Op-Ed: Fashion Does Not Need Cultural Appropriation." *The Business of Fashion*, June 6, 2017. https://www.businessoffashion.com/articles/opinion/op-ed-fashion-does-not-need-cultural-appropriation.

CTV Vancouver. "Cowichan Tribes Take on Ralph Lauren for Selling Knockoff Sweaters." February 7, 2015. http://bc.ctvnews.ca/cowichan-tribes-take-on-ralph-lauren-for-selling-knockoff-sweaters-1.2225614.

D'Allesandro, Jill. "Stitching a New Paradigm: Dress Codes of the Counterculture." In Jill D'Allesandro and Colleen Terry (eds.), *Summer of Love: Art, Fashion and Rock and Roll*, pp. 53–77. Berkeley: Fine Arts Museums of San Francisco, de Young and the University of California Press, 2017.

Deloria, Philip. *Playing Indian*. New Haven, CT: Yale University Press, 1998.

Denham, Amanda. "The Predicament of Maya Textiles in Guatemala: What is Authenticity and Where Can I Buy It?" M.A. diss., Cornell University, 2017.

Gaultier, Jean Paul. *Vogue—Paris*. November 24, 2015. http://en.vogue.fr/vogue-list/thevoguelist/jean-paul-gaultier/1048#zTthQ024Sf1sKUGE.99.

Green, Denise and Kaiser, Susan. "Fashion and Appropriation." *Fashion, Style, and Popular Culture* 4, no. 2 (2017): 145–50.

Helmreich, William B. *The Things They Say Behind Your Back: Stereotypes and the Myths Behind Them*. London: Transaction Publishers, 1983.

Keene, Adrienne. "Dear Ralph Lauren, Our Ancestors are not Your Props!" *Indian Country Today*, December 19, 2014. https://indiancountrymedianetwork.com/culture/arts-entertainment/keene-dear-ralph-lauren-our-ancestors-are-not-your-props/.

Klemesrud, Judy. "Fighting a War in Behalf of Indians." *New York Times*, October 24, 1970. http://www.nytimes.com/1970/10/24/archives/fighting-a-war-in-behalf-of-indians.html.

Lemon, Brendan. "Fresh Prince: A Model Designer." *Out Magazine*, March 2002.

Lipsitz, George. *Dangerous Crossroads: Popular Music, Postmodernism, and the Poetics of Place*. Brooklyn: Verso Publishing, 1994.

Metcalfe, Jessica. "Still on the Fringes of the Fashion World: A Critical Review of Native American-Inspired Fashion (Spring/Summer 2011)." *Beyond Buckskin*, January 8, 2011. http://www.beyondbuckskin.com/search/label/Ralph%20Lauren.

Metcalfe, Jessica. "Ralph Lauren and the American Dream." *Beyond Buckskin*, May 23, 2012. http://www.beyondbuckskin.com/2012/05/ralph-lauren-and-american-dream.html.

Metcalfe, Jessica. "Oh No, Valentino." *Beyond Buckskin*, April 25, 2017. http://www.beyondbuckskin.com/2017/04/oh-no-valentino-appropriation-and-case.html.

Paling, Emma. "'I Am Not a Costume' Reminds People to Choose Halloween Outfits Respectfully." *Huffington Post Canada*, October 16, 2016. http://www.huffingtonpost.ca/2016/10/16/i-am-not-a-costume-aboriginal-halloween_n_12514638.html.

Patch, Nick. "Buffy Sainte-Marie Says Headdresses are 'Painful' as Fashion Trend." *Canadian TV News*, August 6, 2015. http://www.ctvnews.ca/entertainment/buffy-sainte-marie-says-headdresses-are-painful-as-fashion-trend-1.2505054.

Pham, Min-Ha T. "Fashion's Cultural Appropriation Debate: Pointless." *The Atlantic*, May 15, 2014. https://www.theatlantic.com/entertainment/archive/2014/05/cultural-appropriation-in-fashion-stop-talking-about-it/370826/.

"Ralph Lauren has Offended a Canadian Tribe with this Sweater." *The Fashion Law*, February 20, 2015. http://www.thefashionlaw.com/home/ralph-lauren-has-offended-a-canadian-tribe-with-this-sweater.

Sand, Dana. "'We're a Culture, Not a Costume' Campaign Catches On." *USA Today*, October 30, 2013. https://www.usatoday.com/story/news/nation/2013/10/30/halloween-unoffensive-costumes/3312615/.

Spindler, Amy M. "Patterns." *New York Times*, March 16, 1993. http://www.nytimes.com/1993/03/16/news/patterns-082793.html.

Strubel, Jessica. "Shtreimel." in Annette Lynch and Mitchell Strauss (eds.), *Ethnic Dress in the United State: A Cultural Encyclopedia*, pp. 268–70. Lanham, MD: Rowman & Littlefield, 2015.

The Summer of Love Experience: Art, Fashion, and Rock & Roll. San Francisco: de Young Museum, 2017.

Tazi, Dounia. "How to Culturally Appreciate and Not Culturally Appropriate." *Dazed*, December 9, 2015. http://www.dazeddigital.com/artsandculture/article/28767/1/how-to-culturally-appreciate-and-not-culturally-appropriate.

10

Striving to Fit In

Kelly L. Reddy-Best

Culture refers to the characteristics of groups of individuals with shared behaviors, characteristics, values, laws, and customs, such as how they dress, what they eat, and how they interact with one another. The different aspects of each culture are learned over time and are not innate. Those within a culture often define, adhere to, and socialize others on the beauty ideals of their community. These ideals can remain the same, shift gradually, or change dramatically over time. An appearance or beauty ideal refers to the desired or desirable physical characteristics that a culture deems attractive. For many within that culture, the goal then becomes meeting or surpassing that beauty ideal. The ideals related to physical appearance may refer to the actual body, including hair texture and length, body size and shape, or facial arrangement and size; or the aspects of appearance in relationship to objects surrounding or on the body, including fashion, cosmetics, or accessories. Whether the beauty ideals are part of the physical aspects of the body or objects in relation to the body, the ideals are continually shifting as cultures and societies change over time and are impacted by different social, cultural, political, and historical influences. This chapter examines two of these appearance and beauty ideals: *body size and shape* and *skin color*. Included in the discussion are the sources of communication with regards to these ideals and some of the resulting negative (and positive) outcomes for individuals from different communities and cultures. The chapter ends with an examination of a case study on a complex and contentious topic: flight attendant appearance requirements for one particular airline that integrates regulations related to body size and shape.

Body size and shape

Historically and today, individuals have expectations communicated to them on an ongoing basis from media, peers, family members, and numerous other socialization agents related to how their bodies should be shaped in order to reach an ideal. For women in the United States and Europe, the prominent current body ideal is a thin, fit physique (Levine and Murnen, 2009; Poran, 2006). However, this was not always the case; for example, during the 1880s, having a fuller, rounder figure was highly desirable for women. Yet that soon changed by the early twentieth century (Mazur, 1986). In the 1920s, images of tubular, boyish silhouettes permeated the media as the ideal body type for women. Fleshier bodies during the 1920s were often negatively reviewed in editorials and advertisements of fashion magazines such as *Vogue* and *Good Housekeeping* (Keist and Marcketti, 2013). Other popular fashion magazines in the second half of the twentieth century provide evidence that the thin body ideal has continued to permeate the media (Sypeck, Gray, and Ahrens, 2004). In addition to smaller body sizes, fashion magazines including *Seventeen* and *YM* had a significant amount of content on dieting and exercise (Luff and Gray, 2009). While content related to dieting and exercising does promote imagery of the thin ideal, it could also simply be promoting a healthy lifestyle for teenage girls. In more recent mainstream magazine imagery from 2006, there again continued to be very thin models (Jaehee and Lee, 2009). In addition to magazines, the thinness ideal is communicated to women via other media outlets, such as fashion shows, television advertisements, or music videos. Overall, these messages about how women's bodies should appear are around us and influencing us consciously and subconsciously all of the time, and they impact what we perceive as beautiful and how individuals think they should appear (Rudd and Lennon, 1994).

The proliferation of these cultural messages and repeated exposure can result in viewers internalizing the messages, which can lead to moderate or more severe long-lasting negative effects, such as individuals engaging in varying types of risky behavior. For example, when women are repeatedly exposed to and compare each other's bodies with the thin ideal, this exposure and comparison can lead to eating disorders, depression, low self-esteem, and negative body image (Altabe and Thompson, 1996; Stice and Shaw 1994, Stice, Schupak-Neuberg, Shaw, and Stein, 1994; Webster and Tiggemann, 2003). Stice and Shaw (1994) looked at the effects of women viewing magazine pictures with very thin models, average-sized models, and pictures with no models. Individuals who were exposed to the very thin models experienced greater body dissatisfaction and exhibited symptoms that might predict bulimia, or an obsession to lose weight through overeating and then self-induced vomiting. While much of the research on the impact of viewing the thin body ideal in media reports negative outcomes, there is other evidence that this is not always the case. After a careful review of many studies from 1920 to 2002 that examined the impact of media on women's body image, researchers found that being exposed to "depictions of thin women may have little to no effect on viewers" (Holmstrom, 2004, p. 196). The contradictory evidence suggests that more research is needed in this area to understand if and how these messages impact women negatively.

Not all women from different racial or ethnic backgrounds have negative results from viewing the thin body ideal. Black or African American women were more accepting of fuller or more curvaceous bodies as compared to white women, and black women were therefore more shielded from the possible negative effects of unrealistic beauty standards communicated via the media (Molloy and Herzberger, 1998). Black women often consider the ideal body type to be slightly larger than what white women prefer; they feel pressure to achieve a thin waist and curvaceous hourglass body shape with larger breasts and buttocks (Overstreet, Quinn, and Agocha, 2010; Poran, 2009). The desire of black women to achieve curvaceous bodies sometimes stems from their perception of black men's preferences for a shapely female body (Molloy and Herzberger, 1998; Jackson and McGill, 1996; Glasser, Robnett, and Feliciano, 2009). Preferences for a thin yet curvaceous body are not limited to black women, however; Harrison (2003) analysed a group of white women and again found that while thinness was desired, most desirable was a thin body with other curvaceous proportions, including larger breasts and buttocks. Overall, body size ideals are complex and continually changing, and research on the topic can sometimes lead to contradictory evidence due to differences in race, ethnicity, and numerous other cultural characteristics.

Products and industries developed to aid achievement of the desired body size and shape

The different preferences for body size ideals, including larger or smaller body sizes and shapes, have influenced the emergence of entire industries and product lines in order to assist people to achieve these different body ideals. Options available to women include permanent or more invasive treatments such as surgical procedures. In the United States in 2016, there were 1,780,987 cosmetic surgical procedures conducted. Liposuction and breast augmentation were two of the top five procedures, and these two procedures experienced a 6 percent and 4 percent increase from 2015 to 2016, respectively (American Society of Plastic Surgeons, 2016). While tummy tucks were not in the top five procedures, there was a significant increase of 104 percent in the number of procedures completed from 2000 to 2016. There are numerous reasons why people are interested in or more likely to consider invasive cosmetic surgery. Celebrity worship is one reason that motivates young women to be more accepting of or desire cosmetic surgery (Swami, Tayor, and Carvalho, 2009). Women who were more likely to internalize media messages and who "perceive media messages as informative about physical appearance" are also more likely to consider cosmetic surgery (Swami, 2009, p. 317). In the early 2000s, there was a surge in television shows such as *Extreme Makeover*, *The Swan*, *The Doctors*, and currently *Botched*. These reality television shows focused on extreme plastic surgery and manipulation of the body to achieve a more ideal beauty standard, often featuring very drastic changes from multiple surgeries over a series of months. Not surprisingly, when people view cosmetic surgery reality television shows, it can increase acceptance and influence consideration of cosmetic surgery (Sperry, Thompson, Sarwer, and Cash, 2009). Additionally, watching these types of shows can lead to decreased self-esteem and increased pressure to achieve the thin ideal (Mazzeo, Trace, Mitchell, and Gow, 2007).

Other less invasive or permanent options include buying and wearing padded undergarments or various shapewear products from companies such as Spanx or Bubbles Bodywear. Spanx focuses on products meant to slim the body, while Bubbles Bodywear has both slimming and enhancing products, such as buttocks-padded underwear or hip-padded shapewear to give more of a curved silhouette. See Figure 10.1 for an example of a woman wearing a Spanx bodysuit in order to help her achieve a more desirable body silhouette. The company Hourglass Angel currently offers a product called "the transformer firm control body suit," which they state "smoothes your back, cinches your waist and slims your thighs for a bump-free look" and also "helps [the wearer] lose weight through perspiration" as well as "enhances [the] hourglass figure" (Hourglass Angel Corporation, 2017). All of these companies and their products are built around the philosophy that there is an ideal body shape and size, and if you cannot maintain or achieve that ideal through remedies such as diet, exercise, or other physical manipulation procedures, the products can assist you in reaching this goal. The prevalence and acceptance of these types of body shaping garments was illustrated when in 2014, then First Lady Michelle Obama admitted to wearing Spanx during a Fashion Education Workshop, saying, "We all wear them [Spanx] with pride" (Denley, 2014, para. 2). Hearing someone such as the former First Lady acknowledge her usage and admiration of the body slimming garment highlights how prolific and accepted these practices can be within the United States.

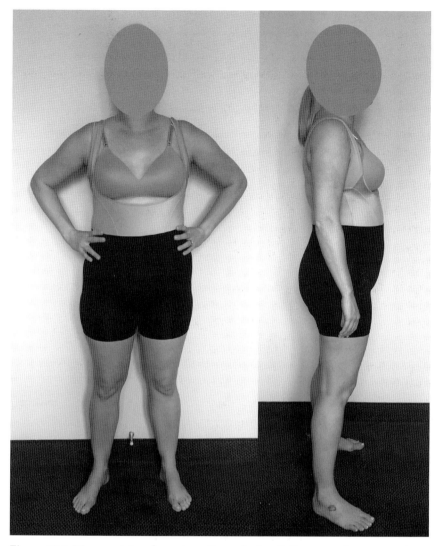

Figure 10.1 Woman pictured wearing a Spanx bodysuit. Courtesy of anonymous photographer.

The previously mentioned work highlights women's interest in trying to achieve a more stereotypically feminine aesthetic; however, that is not always the goal for individuals who are part of the LGBTQ+ (lesbian, gay, bisexual, transgender, and/or queer) community. Hammidi and Kaiser (1999) discussed how lesbians "'complicate' current understandings of beauty" and "negotiate competing and contradictory discourses that operate within and beyond lesbian communities" (pp. 55–6). One example of a contradictory discourse is the use of chest binders by women, transgender, or gender non-conforming individuals in the LGBTQ+ community. Figure 10.2 depicts different colored chest binders designed by FLAVNT STREETWEAR, a company based in Austin, Texas, that recently began producing chest binders for trans masculine or gender non-conforming individuals. Sonny Oram, who writes for *Autostraddle*, one of the most popular blogs for lesbians, defined chest binding as "the practice of using a tight undergarment to flatten your chest," which is the opposite of the previously described ideal for heterosexual women who often want to emphasize their curves and bust (Oram, 2014, para. 2). In Oram's article, they continued to offer advice on brands, care practices, and health-related issues when binding. Peitzmeier, Gardner, Weinand, Corbet, and Acevedo (2017) did a comprehensive analysis of the practice of chest binding, and reported that while binding resulted in numerous negative physical outcomes such as back pain, overheating, or shoulder pain, wearing binders can also have significant psychological effects, included increased self-esteem and confidence. People who bind also explained that they felt a decrease in anxiety, had reduced thoughts of suicide, and less dysphoria after they began binding their chest. While chest binding can have numerous negative physical effects, for a lot of people the positive psychological effects outweighed the negatives and resulted in a more ideal body silhouette and overall positive experience with their body shape.

Men are not excluded from the influence of social messages about how their bodies should appear. Media targeting men often feature them with muscular bodies or focus on strength and bulkiness (Bazzini, Pepper, Swofford, and Cochran, 2015; Daniel and Bridges, 2010). For example, prominent men's magazines such as *GQ*, *Men's Health*, and *Esquire* have almost always represented men's bodies in a singular body type: muscular (Ricciardelli, Clow, and White, 2010).

Like women, men too strive for these body ideals (tall, muscular, increased bulkiness) that they view in the media. While men are interested in different ideals than women, they experience similar negative outcomes to women related to internalizing the media messages and the resulting negative effects on body image (Barlett, Vowels, and Saucier, 2008; Halliwell, Dittmar, and Orsborn, 2007). But not all men have positive responses to media messages. When men are more susceptible to internalizing messages about appearance cues, these messages can result in more body dissatisfaction related to body fat and muscularity (Grammas and Schwartz, 2009). When men are exposed to magazines such as *Muscle & Fitness* and *Men's Health*, which portray these idealized images of body shapes and sizes, they can experience a decrease in their body shape satisfaction (Morry and Staska, 2001). More recently, Barry (2014) interviewed thirty men and found

Figure 10.2 Chest binders produced by FLAVNT STREETWEAR. Courtesy of FLAVNT STREETWEAR.

some of them exhibited anxiety about their bodies when viewing advertisements of men with idealized or muscular bodies.

Skin color

Skin color is another part of one's appearance that is entangled in social hierarchies and beauty ideals. Discussions of skin color are rooted in conversations and dialogues around race. Race typically refers to the physical characteristics of an individual, including facial features, skin color, hair texture, and other visible aspects of a person. While many people think of race as a fixed category, Kaiser (2012) used the term "racial rearticulation" to emphasize that the categories are not fixed, but rather social processes that are continually shifting and evolving depending upon geographic location, time period, and numerous other factors (p. 79). One example of these types of shifts was evident during the apartheid era in South Africa (1948–91), when the government only recognized four race categories: black, white, colored, and Indian; a person was considered black if a pencil could become "stuck" in their hair, associating blackness with hair texture (Reilly, 2012, p. 223). Race becomes complicated when individuals have a multi-ethnic background. For example, an individual who may have a black father and a white mother often identifies as black due to the prevalence of the one-drop rule, a notion with roots in the time of slavery, where if a person had a single drop of blackness they were considered black (Russell, Wilson, and Hall, 1992).

Hierarchies of skin color are intricately interrelated to race and are often referred to as colorism, or the "process of discrimination that privileges light-skinned people of colour over their dark skin counterparts" (Hunter, 2007, p. 237). These preferences for lighter skin colors can be seen in various media throughout the fashion industry. There has been a consistent preference for light-skinned or white models in mainstream fashion magazine, advertisements, and editorial imagery; it is important to note, though, that magazines with these preferences for lighter-skinned people primarily target white people (Baker, 2005; Fowler and Carlson, 2015; Frith, Cheng, and Shaw, 2004; Mayo, Mayo, and Mahdi, 2005). Yet, magazines such as *Essence* and *Black Enterprise*, which target African American or black people, have also had a majority of light- or fair-skinned models pictured within their pages (Keenan, 1996).

Lupita Nyong'o, a dark-skinned actress who is most famous for her performance in *12 Years a Slave*, gave a powerful speech at the ESSENCE Black Women in Hollywood Luncheon in 2014 describing her own experience with colorism and having a dark-skinned complexion. She said:

> I remember a time when I too felt unbeautiful. I put on the TV and only saw pale skin, I got teased and taunted about my night-shaded skin. And my one prayer to God, the miracle worker, was that I would wake up lighter-skinned ... And then Alek Wek came on the international scene. A celebrated model, she was dark as night, she was on all of the runways and in every magazine and everyone was talking about how beautiful she was ... I couldn't believe that people were embracing a women who looked so much like me as beauty. ("In 2014, Black Women in Hollywood Honoree Lupita Nyong'o Delivered a Powerful Speech About Black Beauty," 2014)

At the beginning of her speech, Lupita recited part of a letter she had received from a dark-skinned girl that read, "I think you're really lucky to be *this* Black but yet this successful in Hollywood overnight. I was just about to buy Dencia's Whitenicious cream to lighten my skin when you appeared on the world map and saved me" ("In 2014, Black Women in Hollywood Honouree Lupita Nyong'o Delivered a Powerful Speech About Black Beauty," 2014). The preference for lighter-colored skin has resulted in the desire of some individuals, including this young girl, to bleach their skin in order to achieve this standard of beauty, resulting in an entire segment of the fashion and beauty industry dedicated to developing products to assist in the process (Charles, 2012). Not surprisingly, the imagery and text used to sell these skin-lightening products also reinforces the ideas of colorism. Charles (2011) examined imagery on the labels of skin-bleaching products sold in Harlem, New York, a predominantly black neighborhood, and found 95 percent of the products depicted derogatory images of black people, and perpetuated whiteness or light-colored skin as the ideal. These images then reinforce the point that these products are meant to help dark-skinned individuals achieve the lighter-skin ideal. Such skin-bleaching products may not only be detrimental to an individual's perception of themself, but can also be physically damaging, as the creams may contain harmful products such as mercury and hydroquinone. Products distributed in the United States and Europe are mostly regulated, but other countries do not always have similar regulations, which has led to instances of severe medical problems for those who use the products (Charles, 2012).

While much of the previous discussion on skin-lightening has focused on black or African American individuals, people of color from other races, cultures, and communities, such as Japan, China, Korea, Latin America, the Philippines, and India, also have a preference for lighter-colored skin (Glenn, 2008).

Conclusion

Body size and shape and skin color are just two of the many appearance and beauty ideals that individuals may think about in relation to their own appearance. Other parts of the appearance where individuals negotiate beauty ideals include facial attractiveness, skin tanning, hair texture, or clothing styles and aesthetics. There are some instances where companies directly address some of these previously discussed issues. For example, Dear Kate, Aerie, Modcloth, and Old Navy, companies that are not strictly plus-size, have recently used larger bodies in their advertising campaigns. Additionally, in 2015, Lane Bryant, a plus-size clothing retailer, created a marketing campaign, #PlusIsEqual, to try to normalize different body shapes and sizes. We know that the extent to which imagery impacts individuals varies and has many different positive and negative outcomes. Yet, at least some of the research in this area has highlighted that changing imagery in fashion advertisements could be a good first step to a solution, as some individuals will respond more positively to imagery that is more "normal" or realistic (Barry, 2014). Yet, companies are often profit-driven and are aware that using idealized imagery (thin, white) may sell more products, making this action a hard sell; however, it is one possible solution to offer to issues related to body size and shape and the fashion industry (Aagerup, 2011).

The systemic problem of hierarchies related to skin color has permeated our society for centuries and is not limited to the fashion industry, yet the fashion industry often perpetuates ideals promoting white or light-skinned individuals as the beauty standard. The issue is complex, and offering simple solutions such as including more models of color, particularly dark-skinned individuals, may seem like an easy fix; yet, the problem is rooted deeper than this and in essence may need greater education of privileged individuals to make real change toward progress. However, representation of course could be the first step, as Lupita had mentioned that seeing Alek Wek, a dark-skinned girl like herself, gave her hope that she too could be beautiful.

Case study: flight attendants and body size and shape

Flight attendants, who are part of the cabin crew, are on every passenger flight to ensure safety and to assist with any comfort needs. Their most obvious duties, for anyone who has flown, are to serve beverages and snacks while the plane is in motion. Yet, they are also charged with safety inspections before the flight takes off, keeping passengers calm in the case of turbulence, administering any necessary medical care, and in the event of a major issue or emergency, directing passengers to safety when evacuation is necessary. In essence, flight attendants are responsible for not only increasing comfort, but also maintaining the safety of everyone on board if any trouble arises.

Like many jobs, flight attendants have dress codes regulating numerous parts of their appearance. Most flight crews have matching uniforms with pant, skirt, and dress options. The top portion of the uniform usually includes either a blazer or button-down shirt with vest or another version of a structured top. Other notable elements of the uniform include neckties, stockings, high heels or pumps, and makeup for women.

Recently though, Air India has extended the dress code to include regulation of body size and shape for their flight attendants (Morris, 2015). In 2015, the airline required both male and female flight attendants to be within a certain weight range according to their body mass index (BMI). BMI is one method of measurement to determine a person's body fat by dividing their weight by their height squared. A BMI of below 18.5 is considered to be underweight, 18.5 to

24.9 is considered a normal weight, 25.0 to 29.9 is overweight, and 30 or above is considered obese. The airline measured all of the flight attendants' BMIs and found that about 600 people were categorized as either overweight or obese. The airline declared that women must be within a BMI of 18 to 22, and men must fall within a BMI range of 18 to 25. The airline required those 600 employees to reduce their BMI through lifestyle changes, or diet and exercise, within a specific time period—or they would face dismissal or be assigned to duties on the ground due to failure to meet appearance codes for in-flight employees. After the time period elapsed, employees were measured and about 125 to 130 of them did not meet the new criteria and were deemed unfit for flight attendant duties. The airline claimed that the new appearance code was instituted because individuals who are more fit are able to more quickly respond to unexpected or difficult situations. They argued it was not about weight, but more about fitness and agility. However, this was not the first time that Air India has come under scrutiny for appearance regulations relating to their flight attendants. In previous years, they mandated that flight attendants must have a clear complexion of the face and be free of acne, scars, or other large marks (Makortoff, 2015). The body size and shape appearance regulation is tricky for Air India and could possibly be related to the shifting and changing of beauty ideals. A closer investigation of these types of regulations is warranted in the future.

References

Aagerup, Ulf. "The Influence of Real Women in Advertising on Mass Market Fashion Brand Perception." *Journal of Fashion Marketing and Management: An International Journal* 15, no. 4 (2011): 486–502.

Altabe, Madeline N. and Thompson, J. Kevin. "Body Image: A Cognitive Self-Schema Construct." *Cognitive Therapy and Research* 20, no. 2 (1996): 171–93.

American Society of Plastic Surgeons. "2016 Plastic Surgery Statistics Report." https://www.plasticsurgery.org/documents/News/Statistics/2016/cosmetic-procedure-trends-2016.pdf.

Baker, Christina N. "Images of Women's Sexuality in Advertisements: A Content Analysis of Black- and White-oriented Women's and Men's Magazines." *Sex Roles* 52, no. 1–2 (2005): 13–27.

Barlett, Christopher P., Vowels, Christopher L., and Saucier, Donald A. "Meta-Analyses of the Effects of Media Images on Men's Body-Image Concerns." *Journal of Social and Clinical Psychology* 27, no. 3 (2008): 279–310.

Barry, Ben. "Expanding the Male Ideal: The Need for Diversity in Men's Fashion Advertisements." *Critical Studies in Men's Fashion* 1, no. 3 (2014): 275–93.

Bazzini, Doris G., Pepper, Amanda, Swofford, Rebecca, and Cochran, Karly A. "How Healthy Are Health Magazines? A Comparative Content Analysis of Cover Captions and Images of *Women's* and *Men's Health* Magazine." *Sex Roles* 72, no. 5–6 (2015): 198–210.

Charles, Christopher A. D. "The Derogatory Representations of the Skin Bleaching Products Sold in Harlem." *Journal of Pan African Studies* 4, no. 4 (2011): 117–41.

Charles, Christopher A. D. "Skin Bleaching: The Complexion of Identity, Beauty, and Fashion." In Kimberly A. Miller-Spillman, Andrew Reilly, and Patricia Hunt-Hurst (eds.), *The Meanings of Dress*, pp. 154–60. New York: Bloomsbury, 2012.

Daniel, Samantha and Bridges, Sara K. "The Drive for Muscularity in Men: Media Influences and Objectification Theory." *Body Image: An International Journal of Research* 7, no. 1 (2010): 32–8.

Denley, Susan. "Michelle Obama Wears Spanx, She Reveals at Fashion Workshop." *Los Angeles Times*, October 9, 2014. http://www.latimes.com/fashion/alltherage/la-ar-michelle-obama-wears-spanx-20141008-story.html.

Fowler, Jie G. and Carlson, Les. "The Visual Presentation of Beauty in Transnational Fashion Magazine Advertisements." *Journal of Current Issues and Research in Advertising* 36, no. 2 (2015): 136–56.

Frith, Katherine Toland, Cheng, Hong, and Shaw, Ping. "Race and Beauty: A Comparison of Asian and Western Models in Women's Magazine Advertisements." *Sex Roles* 50, no. 1–2 (2004): 53–61.

Glasser, Carol L., Robnett, Belinda, and Feliciano, Cynthia. "Internet Daters' Body Type Preferences: Race-Ethnic and Gender Differences." *Sex Roles* 61, no. 1 (2009): 14–33.

Glenn, Evelyn Nakano. "Yearning for Lightness: Transnational Circuits in the Marketing and Consumption of Skin Lighteners." *Gender and Society* 22, no. 3 (2008): 281–302.

Grammas, Debbie L. and Schwartz, Jonathan P. "Internalization of Messages from Society and Perfectionism as Predictors of Male Body Image." *Body Image: An International Journal of Research* 6, no. 1 (2009): 31–6.

Halliwell, Emma, Dittmar, Helga, and Orsborn, Amber. "The Effects of Exposure to Muscular Male Models Among Men: Exploring the Moderating Role of Gym Use and Exercise Motivation." *Body Image: An International Journal of Research* 4, no. 3 (2007): 278–87.

Hammidi, Tania N. and Kaiser, Susan B. "Doing Beauty: Negotiating Lesbian Looks in Everyday Life." *Journal of Lesbian Studies* 3, no. 4 (1999): 55–63.

Harrison, Kristen. "Television Viewers' Ideal Body Proportions: The Case of the Curvaceously Thin Woman." *Sex Roles* 48, no. 5–6 (2003): 255–64.

Holmstrom, Amanda J. "The Effects of the Media on Body Image: A Meta-Analysis." *Journal of Broadcasting and Electronic Media* 48, no. 2 (2004): 196–217.

Hourglass Angel Corporation. "The Transformer First Control Bodysuit by Ann Chery 1020." 2017. https://www.hourglassangel.com/the-transformer-firm-control-bodysuit-by-ann-chery-1020/.

Hunter, Margaret. "The Persistent Problem of Colourism: Skin Tones, Status, and Inequality." *Sociology Compass* 1, no. 1 (2007): 237–54.

"In 2014, Black Women in Hollywood Honoree Lupita Nyong'o Delivered a Powerful Speech About Black Beauty." *Essence*, February 27, 2014. http://www.essence.com/2014/02/27/lupita-nyongo-delivers-moving-black-women-hollywood-acceptance-speech.

Jackson, Linda A. and McGill, Olivia D. "Body Type Preferences and Body Characteristics Associated with Attractive and Unattractive Bodies by African Americans and Anglo Americans." *Sex Roles* 35, no. 5–6 (1996): 295–307.

Jung, Jaehee and Lee, Yoon-Jung. "Cross-Cultural Examination of Women's Fashion and Beauty Magazine Advertisements in the United States and South Korea." *Clothing and Textiles Research Journal* 27, no. 4 (2009): 274–86.

Kaiser, Susan B. *Fashion and Cultural Studies.* New York: Bloomsbury, 2012.

Keenan, Kevin L. "Skin Tones and Physical Features of Blacks in Magazines Advertisements." *Journalism and Mass Communication Quarterly* 73, no. 4 (1996): 905–12.

Keist, Carmen N. and Marcketti, Sara B. "'The New Costumes of Odd Sizes': Plus-Sized Women's Fashions, 1920–1929." *Clothing and Textiles Research Journal* 31, no. 4 (2013): 259–74.

Levine, Michael P. and Murnen, Sarah K. "'Everybody Knows That Mass Media Are/Are Not [pick one] A Cause of Eating Disorders': A Critical Review of Evidence for a Causal Link Between Media, Negative Body Image, and Disordered Eating in Females." *Journal of Social and Clinical Psychology* 28, no. 1 (2009): 9–42.

Luff, Gina M. and Gray, James J. "Complex Messages Regarding a Thin Ideal Appearing in Teenage Girls' Magazines from 1956 to 2005." *Body Image: An International Journal of Research* 6, no. 2 (2009): 133–6.

Makortoff, Kalyeena. "Airline grounds 125 staff deemed too fat to fly." CNBC, September 16, 2015. https://www.cnbc.com/2015/09/16/air-india-grounds-125-staff-deemed-too-fat-to-fly.html.

Mayo, Donna T., Mayo, Charles M., and Mahdi, Sharika. "Skin Tones in Magazine Advertising: Does Magazine Type Matter?" *Journal of Promotion Management* 11, no. 2–3 (2005): 49–59.

Mazur, Allan. "U.S. Trends in Feminine Beauty and Overadaptation." *Journal of Sex Research* 22, no. 3 (1986): 281–303.

Mazzeo, Suzanne E., Trace, Sara E., Mitchell, Karen S., and Gow, Rachel W. "Effects of a Reality TV Cosmetic Surgery Makeover Program on Eating Disordered Attitudes and Behaviors." *Eating Behaviors* 8, no. 3 (2007): 390–7.

Morris, Hugh. "Air India's flight attendants 'too fat to fly.'" *Telegraph*, September 14, 2015. https://www.telegraph.co.uk/travel/news/Air-Indias-flight-attendants-too-fat-to-fly/.

Morry, Marian M. and Staska, Sandra L. "Magazine Exposure: Internalization, Self-Objectification, Eating Attitudes, and Body Satisfaction in Male and Female University Students." *Canadian Journal of Behavioural Science* 33, no. 4 (2001): 269–79.

Oram, Sonny. "Binding 101: Brands, Care Tips, and Health." *Autostraddle*, April 3, 2014. https://www.autostraddle.com/binding-101-brands-care-tips-and-health-227942/.

Overstreet, Nicole M., Quinn, Diane M., and Agocha, V. Bede. "Beyond Thinness: The Influence of a Curvaceous Body Ideal on Body Dissatisfaction in Black and White Women." *Sex Roles* 63, no. 1–2 (2010): 91–103.

Peitzmeier, Sarah, Gardner, Ivy, Weinand, Jamie, Corbet, Alexandra, and Acevedo, Kimberlynn. "Health Impact of Chest Binding Among Transgender Adults: A Community-Engaged, Cross-Sectional Study." *Culture, Health and Sexuality* 19, no. 1 (2017): 64–75.

Poran, Maya A. "The Politics of Protection: Body Image, Social Pressures, and the Misrepresentation of Young Black Women." *Sex Roles* 55, no. 11–12 (2006): 739–55.

Reilly, Andrew. "Race and Ethnicity." In Kimberly A. Miller-Spillman, Andrew Reilly, and Patricia Hunt-Hurst (eds.), *The Meanings of Dress*, pp. 223–9. New York: Bloomsbury, 2012.

Ricciardelli, Rosemary, Clow, Kimberley A., and White, Phillip. "Investigating Hegemonic Masculinity: Portrayals of Masculinity in Men's Lifestyle Magazines." *Sex Roles* 63, no. 1–2 (2010): 64–78.

Rudd, Nancy A. and Lennon, Sharron J. "Aesthetics of Body and Social Identity." In Marilyn Revell DeLong and Ann Marie Fiore (eds.), *Aesthetics of Textiles and Clothing: Advancing Multi-Disciplinary Perspectives*, pp. 163–75. Monument, CO: ITAA, 1994.

Russell, Kathy, Wilson, Midge and Hall, Ronald. *The Colour Complex: The Politics of Skin Colour Among African Americans*. New York: Anchor Books, 1992.

Sperry, Stephanie, Thompson, Joel Kevin, Sarwer, David B., and Cash, Thomas F. "Cosmetic Surgery Reality TV Viewership: Relations with Cosmetic Surgery Attitudes, Body Image, and Disordered Eating." *Annals of Plastic Surgery* 62, no. 1 (2009): 7–11.

Stice, Eric, Schupak-Neuberg, Erika, Shaw, Heather E., and Stein, Richard I. "Relation of Media Exposure to Eating Disorder Symptomatology: An Examination of Mediating Mechanisms." *Journal of Abnormal Psychology* 103, no. 4 (1994): 836–840.

Stice, Eric and Shaw, Heather E. "Adverse Effects of the Media Portrayed Thin-Ideal on Women and Linkages to Bulimic Symptomatology." *Journal of Social and Clinical Psychology* 13, no. 3 (1994): 288–308.

Swami, Viren. "Body Appreciation, Media Influence, and Weight Status Predict Consideration of Cosmetic Surgery Among Female Undergraduates." *Body Image: An International Journal of Research* 6, no. 4 (2009): 315–17.

Swami, Viren, Taylor, Rosanne, and Carvalho, Christine. "Acceptance of Cosmetic Surgery and Celebrity Worship: Evidence of Associations Among Female Undergraduates." *Personality and Individual Differences* 47, no. 8 (2009): 869–72.

Sypeck, Mia Foley, Gray, James J., and Ahrens, Anthony H. "No Longer Just a Pretty Face: Fashion Magazines' Depictions of Ideal Female Beauty from 1959 to 1999." *International Journal of Eating Disorders* 36, no. 3 (2004): 342–7.

Webster, Jessica and Tiggemann, Marika. "The Relationship Between Women's Body Satisfaction and Self-Image Cross the Life Span: The Role of Cognitive Control." *Journal of Genetic Psychology* 164, no. 2 (2003): 241–52.

11

Pain from Fashion

Ellen McKinney and Eulanda A. Sanders

Being "fashionable" has not always been good for one's physical or psychological health. In the mid-nineteenth century, women wore long skirts that brushed along the ground. At a time before germ theory was discovered, this meant that families were sickened by germs that hitched a ride along the garments' hems. Additionally, dyes made from unsafe methods sometimes caused rashes, nasal allergies, and even eye damage. At other times in history, women have subjected their bodies to constrictive corsets or unnatural heels that caused short- and long-term damage to their bodies. In our modern era, people are adopting variants to older trends (e.g. corsets have morphed into girdles and now into the "waist training" devices promoted by some celebrities), while there is a resurgence in the popularity of higher heels. While the goal may be to be beautiful and fashionable, the end result often is something else—physical and emotional pain. This chapter will examine the items women have worn (and continue to wear) that can cause pain and try to explain why those items are eagerly sought after and readily worn in the quest to be beautiful and fashionable.

Physical pain

Pain is our body's way of telling us that something is wrong. Perhaps something is too hot or cold. Perhaps there is something poking us or cutting us or even pushing our bodies into forms that are not natural or comfortable. This last case is especially relevant to our look at pain and fashion. When someone is wearing a pair of fashionable shoes that happen to be too small or too tight for the wearer, the nerves in the wearer's foot tell the brain that there is a problem that could harm the feet. For some of us with a low pain threshold, such signals may result in those shoes being removed. For others who have a higher pain tolerance or a strong motivation to wear a pair of fashionable shoes, the warnings may be ignored. Yet, even though the warnings may be ignored, the effects of pain still have an impact on the body, on the ability to focus on everyday tasks, and on the emotional state of the wearer.

Physical pain for fashion

Being "fashionable" is partially about fitting the ideal of what a person should look like and what they should wear. In many eras, especially for women, attaining that ideal look required (and still requires) the assistance of special garments or accessories that physically alters the way a person's body appears or interacts with the environment. In some cases, such as with corsets or high heels, the garments or accessories are worn for purely aesthetic reasons. In other cases, such as with bras or shoes, these garments or accessories also help to support and/or protect their wearer while fitting the fashion of the day.

Additionally, there are other areas of pain for the sake of fashion that impact individuals. These may include aspects of the beauty industry such as cosmetic surgery, tattooing, and piercing. Even dieting to achieve desired ideals may cause pain for the sake of fashion. In this chapter, we focus specifically on garments and accessories. Yet, regardless of whether the purpose is decorative or functional, a poorly fitting or poorly designed item can cause physical pain. Let's now look at some of the most common pain-causing fashion practices.

Corsets and related garments

For centuries, corsets have helped women achieve the desired look particularly in "Western" US and European cultures. Their purpose was to allow women to achieve, through apparel engineering, a smaller waist not often obtainable naturally. It is important to note that historians such as Steele (2001) warn against an oversimplified view of corset wearing in Victorian times. Her historical study revealed that women had a variety of experiences with corsets, wearing different types and laced more or less tightly, depending on the situation. In turn, the negative health effects experienced varied from woman to woman. However, for those women that very tightly laced their corsets, health could be negatively impacted. In the Victorian era of the mid to late nineteenth century, women of the middle to higher classes used corsets and tight lacing to appear as the idealized thin and "fragile" female by tightly lacing their midriff through the aid of corsets. Such "waist training" began around age nine when girls were introduced to the corset by their mothers and the result of such training was that some women reported having a waist as small as the 14 inches—the circumference of her thumb and forefingers (Kunzle, 2006). As a result of this practice, women's health could be negatively impacted. In her research, Steele (2001) found that corsets compressed the ribcage and prevented deep breathing. This, in turn, led to shortness of breath, and occasionally, fainting. Furthermore, the stationary state imposed by corsets did not allow the back muscles to function, as they normally would, leading to their atrophy over time.

Modern corset wearing

Wearing corsets has become popular again among some women. Unlike in the Victorian era when corsets were considered an essential part of a cultured woman's wardrobe to allow her to be the idealized woman, now the wearing of a corset is a more personal choice. These are worn daily by some, but for others worn only for special occasions.

Although there is no research into how the corset is affecting health now, there are those who claim that a properly fitted corset is not a health risk. An example of such advocates is the Tightlacing Society, which is a private Facebook group (2017). According to Andrew Tran, the society administrator, the chart below allows women to use their personal measurements to help them find the best corset for them. The considered factors are reduced waist size, rib spring (the difference between the measurement of the ribs and the waist), upper hip spring (body circumference about 3 inches below the corset waist), and lower hip spring (body circumference about 5 inches below the corset waist). According to Tran's proposed sizing system, the corset wearer selects the amount of compression, based on the measurements they perceive to be comfortable. When new, corsets are worn with a two-inch opening in the centre back, hence the subtraction of two inches from the "comfortable" waist compression measurement. Over time, corset wearers lace the corset tighter and tighter until the corset closes in the back. Then users may purchase a new, smaller corset. This is how the "waist training" occurs.

From the perspective of modern day corset wearers, there are several benefits from wearing such a device. Proponents say that a corset can reduce back pain through increased support, improved posture, and help with a variety of medical issues related to weak bones and joints. In addition, such modern wearers tout psychological benefits such as reduced anxiety, and improved self-confidence

Measurement	Definition
Underbust	Body circumference under the breasts
Desired Reduced Waist	Desired body circumference around the belly button, and generally not at the smallest part of the waist. The proper location to measure is found by pressing the sides of the waist with both hands to find a soft spot between the bottom of the floating ribs, and the top of the pelvis. This is where the corset waist will position itself. To determine how much reduction one's body can handle one should tie a length of ribbon around one's waist as tight as they can comfortably. Measure this waist circumference. Subtract 2″ to determine corset size. e.g. 31″ natural waist. 26″ compressed waist. 24″ corset size.
Upper hip	Body circumference around 3″ below the corset waist.
Lower hip	Body circumference around 5″ below the corset waist.
Rib spring	The difference between measurement of the ribs and the waist. e.g. Underbust (36″) – Waist (24″) = rib spring (12″)
Hip spring	The difference between measurement of the hips and the waist. e.g. Upper Hip (36″) – Waist (24″) = Upper hip spring (12″); Lower Hip (38″) – Waist (24″) = Lower hip spring (14″)

from a more idealized body silhouette. Additionally, it allows women to wear a variety of clothing styles from a wider variety of past eras. Yet, even among such wearers, there are still discussions on various social media sites about such issues as pain, skin marks, and physical discomfort caused by corset wearing. However, the overall theme of such online discussions seems to be more focused on how to enjoy the benefits of corset wearing, while being aware of how to avoid physical pain. In this regard, wearers seem to be more in control of their corset wearing experiences than those is previous eras.

Other waist training devices popularized by celebrities: girdle or faja

Similar to a girdle, the faja is a compression undergarment worn extremely tight on the body to create an exceptionally curvy hourglass figure. The undergarment shifts organs and flesh and has been said to reduce one's appetite (McKinney, 2015). The faja (Spanish for "wrap") originated in Columbia as a post-liposuction surgery medical garment to reduce swelling to make sure that the skin tightens as desired. It was later embraced for daily wear as people desired to pattern their bodies after curvy, idealized celebrities (McKinney, 2015). Celebrities Kim Kardashian, Lindsay Lohan, and Jessica Alba have all promoted so called "waist training" with these devices through social media (Albor, 2015). Kardashian is famous for her waist trainer selfies posted on social media used to market waist training products she sells through various online venues. Women that dress in the style of 1950s' pin-up girls have also adopted the faja to create the hourglass figure that allows them to fit into waist-emphasizing fashions such as capri pants, swing skirts, and halter tops (McKinney, 2015; La Ferla, 2012). Fajas typically extend from under the bust to below hip level and are often made of a material called Powernet, a very firm net-like fabric construction of spandex, nylon, and cotton. Tight belly band versions, similar to a corset, are also seen. These typically close with a center front row of hooks and eyes (McKinney, 2015). There are medical concerns associated with wearing fajas or girdles, including causing the wearer's floating ribs to close, compressing and displacing internal organs; affecting back and thigh nerves; and skin infections (Albor, 2015).

Heels

During the reign of Louis XIV in France, the wearing of high heels became especially popular among ladies of the court (see Figure 11.1). That popularity has continued to varying levels ever since. Yet, wearing high-heeled shoes can harm the body through an increased tendency for foot, ankle, and lower back injuries. They can also lead to curvature of the spine from the unnatural way they change the way a woman walks so that the weight is on her toes. As heel height increases, the wearer's posture become more unstable as the bottom is pushed out and the top of the body is pushed forward. This change essentially makes a wearer "top heavy." As one might expect, over time this leads to increasing levels of back pain. Furthermore, over time, negative physical changes such as shortened Achilles tendons and arthritis in the knees can result.

Skinny jeans

Another fashion development has been the rise in popularity of tight fitting "skinny jeans" with their narrow legs. There have been reports that the confining nature of such jeans can cause swelling and a loss of feeling in the lower legs and feet, which comes from the squeezing of various tendons and nerves in the legs.

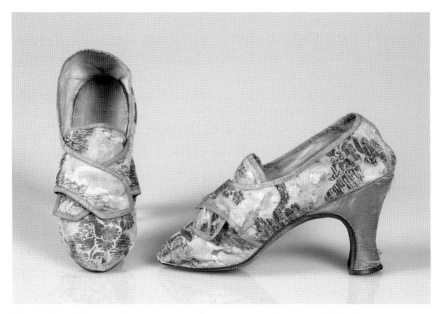

Figure 11.1 Shoes. Silk, metallic. Brooklyn Museum Costume Collection at The Metropolitan Museum of Art, Gift of the Brooklyn Museum, 2009; Gift of Mrs. Clarence R. Hyde, 1928. Accession Number: 2009.300.4130a, b.

Tight jeans can also have a negative impact on the genitals of both men and women. For women, wearing tight jeans can lead to a rise in urinary tract and bladder infections.

Bras

A bra can do many good things for a woman. It offers support that can, if properly fitted, reduce pain. However, if a bra is not properly fitted, it can cause additional pain. Indeed, one study conducted by bra manufacturer Triumph and published in the journal *Chiropractic and Osteopathy* found that the majority of women, 80 percent, were wearing bras that were the wrong size! (Wood, Cameron, and Fitzgerald, 2008). For larger breasted women, an improperly fitted sports bra will not suppress or control the movement and bounding caused by exercising which can lead to muscle tears and discomfort. Additionally, larger breasted women face the issue of too-tight straps digging into their shoulders and causing indentations. Improperly fitted bras can also cause negative impacts for breast-feeding women such as pain and reduced milk production.

Why pain for fashion?

Fashion, clothing, and accessories perform multiple functions for individual wearers or with groups a person belongs to. One important function of fashion is to express and communicate the values of the wearer. Another function is the rational use of clothing, including the utilitarian, protective, and rewarding aspects of fashion (Roach-Higgins and Eicher, 1992). We wear clothes to provide physical comfort, protect us from the climate, and to gain acceptance with our groups of colleagues, friends, and family.

Many fashion items are symbolic, and symbols express shared meanings among a group of individuals (Lauer and Handel, 1977). Wearing high heels can symbolize power in some instances or sexiness in others. Unconsciously, individuals use fashion every day as symbols for communication. As we choose garments or accessories to wear, we send non-verbal messages to those with whom we interact, often unconsciously. In other cases, consciously, fashion, clothing, and accessories are a complex system of communication a wearer uses to present oneself (Damhorst, 1990). For example, if a person decides to wear a waist trainer to improve their posture, they may unconsciously be sending sexual messages due to the modification of their body shape in an hourglass form, which may be perceived as more sexual. However, in another case a person may consciously choose to wear red high heels to visually communicate sex appeal.

The movement of the body, such as walking and running, is an aspect of appearance (Hillestad, 1980) that can be altered by fashion choices. Fashionable, but painful high-heeled shoes may be worn to signal a professional appearance; however, they may also alter the way a person walks. The intended symbolic and shared meaning that high heels communicates may be lost if the wearer walks in a way that communicates pain. Also, a person may make a conscious fashion choice that starts out as painless, long-term wear, but which may result in pain and unintentional messages visually communicated to those the individual encounters.

Solutions to pain

What can be done when your fashion choices cause you pain? There are some common sense solutions to such problems, but there are some innovative ones too. Some solutions are available now while others are on the horizon. Here are a few suggestions for the various garments and accessories we discussed above.

Corset

When it comes to corsets and pain, the old adage "you get what you pay for" definitely applies. Cheap corsets usually have plastic boning, which is not as flexible as the more expensive steel-boned models. According to the FAQ section of the Tightlacing Society's private Facebook group, the secret to comfort is a matter of common sense—pick one that is the right size and fits properly.

Shoes

The higher the heel, the less stable a person is when walking. Such unsure footing can increase the chance of someone stumbling or falling—especially on stairs or uneven ground. To combat this, a wider heel (especially as the wearer ages) can help. Another way to reduce the chance of injury from high heels and reduce the chance of long-term foot damage is to not wear them for long periods each day. One innovative solution to the problems caused by high heels comes from a German company, Mime et Moi (https://mimemoi.com/en/about-mime-et-moi/). These shoes feature a patented "flexheel" mechanism in the shoe's inner sole that allows the shoe to smoothly self-adjust to various heel heights. Each pair of shoes comes with two interchangeable sets of heels—low and high. This way, the wearer can change the heel height of their shoes throughout the day.

Wearing unstable shoes (such as Masai Barefoot Technology (MBT) and Sketchers Shape-ups) has been shown to give relief to those suffering from lower back pain. The built-in instability is thought to help activate, strengthen, and condition some of the less used smaller foot muscles. These shoes may also help to improve posture and the way you walk, which can help reduce the wear and tear on your hips, knees, and ankles. Another possibility is to eliminate shoes entirely while running since, as one researcher noted, "barefoot training can strengthen and condition the smaller neglected muscles of the lower limb, thereby helping to enhance performance and prevent injuries" (Landry, 2011).

Bras

Sports bras

Properly fitted sports bras with additional support in the cup can be helpful in reducing pain that is caused by breast movement during exercise. Sports bra designers can choose stretch fabrics and a compressed cup pad to provide support. The design of bra straps is also important in reducing pain due to wearing a sports bra. Bra straps that are vertically orientated and wide (approximately 2 inches in width) are preferable for women with large breasts during sport and exercise to minimize bra strap pressure and discomfort. The addition of gel pads under bra straps may also decrease discomfort and prevent straps slipping off the shoulders. To maximize their comfort, women with large breasts should seek supportive bras with vertical strap orientation, wider straps, and padded straps.

Fashion communicates who we are consciously and unconsciously. People have made fashions choices historically that have resulted in bodily pain to follow fashion and beauty trends. In other cases, people have made fashion choices based on functional clothing needs that have resulted in pain. Currently, you, as a consumer, have many clothing, fashion, and beauty choices that do not have to result in you tolerating pain.

Case study

Emily is a college student. Here is a story about how she became interested in wearing a corset and her journey to corset wearing today (see Figure 11.2). As you read her story, weigh the pros and cons of her decision. Which outweighs the other? Which factors, if different, would change your opinion of her choices around wearing a corset?

> Ever since I was young I have been intrigued by historical dress. I had a full outfit that I got at renaissance faire when I was in 4th grade with a fake children's corset from the 1800s. It fit snug, but did not actually cinch anything in but I didn't care. I would put the whole costume on any chance I had. When I was fourteen, my interest spiked again when a good friend got a real steel boned corset. She laced me up in it once and it was so painful, it pinched my ribs and I felt like I was going to pass out. I only wore it for about 5 minutes. When I was sixteen, I started taking an AP (Advanced Placement) studio art class and I chose to do costume design for my portfolio. I wanted to produce a historically inspired costume with a corset. I started researching the construction behind corsets on websites and became completely obsessed with the world of corsetry. I made some corsets before I understood how to fit garments properly so they didn't end up that great. Once I understood how to fit garments, the construction was so easy and I finally made my first proper corset in the spring of my sophomore year of college (see Figure 11.2).

The fit is key in finding a corset that suits your body. When I wear my corset it feels quite snug, but not painful, so I try to always wear a tank top underneath because it makes it feel a lot nicer. I started with 2 inches of waist reduction and have gone up to 5 inches reduction. Normally, when I wear it on a daily basis, I do 2–3 inches, sometimes even only 1 inch on days I just want the support of a corset. I was wearing my corset up to four days a week for up to six hours a day. I would almost never wear it at home unless my back was aching, as the corset reduced that pain by providing support. I never wear my corset at night.

For me, [the] advantages of wearing a corset are: it reduces anxiety, improves confidence, reduces menstrual cramps, and reduces back pain by aiding posture. I almost always wear it on days I have a presentation. My corset makes me feel beautiful and reminds me to stand in a confident way. Disadvantages when wearing a corset is that you need to take shorter breaths because you cannot expand your lungs as much as without a corset on, so when doing things like walking upstairs, you can have a shortness of breath. Also you cannot bend at the waist. When I take it off it does leave imprint lines on my skin from where the seam lines are, but they smooth out after a little bit.

Figure 11.2 Emily wearing a corset she made. Courtesy of Emily Kovenock. Photography by Samuel Hogan.

When people find out I wear a corset, some have very negative opinions about it and think it's a shameful thing and harmful to my body. For the most part, people are just intrigued. When people ask specifically about waist training, that can be more bothersome to me; I don't try to waist train and I don't see much point in it, personally. If you want to try [to] wear a corset, do your research. Understand that it is a commitment and takes patience. You need to lace it up slowly and unlacing takes a bit of time as well. It is not like other pieces of clothing that take a few seconds to put on and go.

References

Albor, Laura. "The danger of wearing a belt like that of Kim Kardashian." *Running and Fitness*. http://www.correryfitness.com/fitness/peligros-usar-faja-como-kimkardashi an_2015052657d907a40cf22be35395abbe.html.

Damhorst, Mary Lynn. "In search of a common thread: Classification of information communicated through dress." *Clothing and Textiles Research Journal* 8, no. 2 (1990): 1–12.

Hillestad, Robert. "The underlying structure of appearance." *Dress* 6, no. 1 (1980): 117–25.

Kunzle, David. *Fashion and Fetishism: Corsets, Tight-Lacing and Other Forms of Body-Sculpture*. Cheltenham, UK: History Press, 2006.

La Ferla, Ruth. "A Sly Wink to Pinups of the Past." *New York Times*, May 17, 2012. www. lexisnexis.com/hottopics/lnacademic.

Landry, Scott. "Unstable Shoe Designs: Functional Implications," *Lermagazine*, March 2011. http://lermagazine.com/article/unstable-shoe-designs-functional-implications.

Lauer, Robert H. and Handel, Warren H. *Social Psychology: The Theory and Application of Symbolic Interactionism*. Boston: Houghton Mifflin Harcourt (HMH), 1977, pp. 33–59.

McKinney, Ellen. "Faja." In M. Strauss and A. Lynch (eds.), Ethnic Dress in the United States: A Cultural Encyclopedia, pp. 117–18. Lanham, MD: Rowman & Littlefield, 2015.

Mime et Moi. https://mimemoi.com/en/about-mime-et-moi/.

Roach-Higgins, Mary Ellen and Eicher, Joanne B. "Dress and identity." *Clothing and Textiles Research Journal* 10 (1992): 1–8.

Steele, Valerie. *The Corset: A Cultural History*. New Haven, CT: Yale University Press, 2001.

Tightlacing Society. "FAQ from the Tight Lacing Society FB group." Facebook. https:// www.facebook.com/groups/TightlacingSociety/.

Wood, K., Cameron, M., and Fitzgerald, K. "Breast size, bra fit, and thoracic pain in young women: A correlational study." *Chiropractic and Osteopathy* 16, no. 1 (2008). https://www.ncbi.nlm.nih.gov/pmc/articles/PMC2275741/.

Part Four

The Dangers of Caring for and Disposing of Fashion

12

A Consumer Perspective on Clothing Care: The Economic, Environmental, and Social Costs

Pamela S. Norum and Rachel LoMonaco-Benzing

Clothing consumption and care

Clothing consumption means more than just buying clothes. It also includes 1) acquisition, 2) maintenance, and 3) disposal (Winakor, 1969). Acquisition encompasses the many ways in which we acquire clothing: buying new or used, receiving gifts, hand-me-downs, sewing, or renting. Maintenance involves taking care of clothes, including laundry and repair. Disposal refers to discarding our clothes through means such as donating, giving to friends or family, selling, or throwing away. With the increased focus on sustainability in many areas of our lives, our clothing consumption choices can also affect how sustainably we live (Bras-Klapwijk and Knot, 2001; Clark, 2008). Consumers play an important role in the life cycle of clothing as well as the impact on the environment through clothing care (Fletcher, 2008). We have many choices regarding how to care for clothes. How often do you wash your clothes? How hot is your laundry water? Do you ever hang clothes to dry? Do you mend holes or replace buttons? Answers to questions like these help uncover whether or not a consumer is practicing sustainable clothing consumption. Proper laundering, repair, and less frequent washing can lead to longer garment lives, an important goal of sustainable clothing consumption (Bras-Klapwijk and Knot, 2001; Fisher et al., 2008; Nordic Fashion Association, 2012). While it is clear that some clothing care practices in the past were quite dangerous to people and the environment, harmful aspects still exist. Let's take a look at how far we have come.

The history of clothing care in the US in the twentieth century

Consumption is not only about the individual's daily practices, but also results from the norms and structures of their cultural group (Shove, 2003). For instance, people often do not think about energy as something they consume. They instead consume energy by participating in activities like using a hair dryer or a car which require energy. Friends and family often set the standards for how people take care of their clothes. This also explains how consumption practices differ around the world, across time periods, and between neighboring households. Other factors that impact how a garment is washed include the age or gender of its owner, the level or type of soil on it, and the type of garment. Several broad trends influenced the development of laundry practices in the US over the twentieth century: technological, social, and economic.

Technological impacts

In the late nineteenth and early twentieth century, people generally still washed clothes by hand, using wash basins and boards or hand-crank washers. The overall process was laborious and included washing on the board, rinsing, boiling, rinsing again, then possibly bluing and starching, and finally hanging to dry before ironing (Balderston and Limerick, 1902). Many women still made their own soap, frequently with lye which poisoned children and burned skin and eyes when mishandled (Schaffer, 2011). Clothes irons were heated by coals, or more dangerously by kerosene or gasoline (Wray, 1997). The water available to households was also a hazardous carrier of diseases like typhoid fever and tuberculosis. Also, through the 1930s, many poorer neighborhoods still did not have standard plumbing to run water directly (Hoy, 1995).

While the first automated washers were invented in the early twentieth century, they were not available to most households, which lacked funds or electricity to own and operate them (Hoy, 1995). Even in the 1920s, many women still did washing by hand. Electric irons were also available, but did not become more safely temperature regulated until the 1920s (Wray, 1997). By the 1930s, laundering practice shifted to a focus on automated washers as a wider number of communities throughout the US gained access to electricity. Nonetheless, widespread electrification for rural communities did not happen until after World War II (Hoy, 1995).

The prevalence of automatic washers took hold after the war as women got married and increasingly moved to homes in the suburbs. By this time, automated dryers were also available. Electric washing machines originally attempted to mimic the specialized efforts that handwashing provided resulting in complicated machines with an endless range of settings. Consequently, machines were simplified in the 1970s to a few basic cycles and water temperatures (Shove,

2003). From the 1950s through the 1970s, manufacturers actively worked to convince people that cold water would wash their garments just as effectively as hot water. The simplified machines and decreased emphasis on hot water began to teach people not to worry as much about how the clothing was washed. If it came out of the machine, then it was considered clean. By the late 1980s, many people were no longer separating laundry or using different wash cycles or temperatures; many used the same process for all laundry types (Shove, 2003).

Social and economic impacts

As changes occurred in technology and practice, cleanliness standards also shifted. At the start of the twentieth century, a new push for improved personal hygiene in the US drove a change in societal cleanliness standards. This was due to growing, dirty cities and improved knowledge about how diseases spread. In response, early home economics educators worked to improve hygienic standards, including laundering practices, throughout the early decades of the twentieth century (Hoy, 1995). The cleanliness frenzy peaked at the end of the 1940s and through the 1950s. A rise in advertising, beginning in the 1920s, continued to play a large role in promoting cleanliness around household practices. Ads of the period, targeting women, illustrated the importance of cleanliness for happiness and social acceptance (Hoy, 1995). Women were taught to maintain the household to exacting standards. However, the time dedicated to caring for clothes shifted dramatically over the twentieth century. Time use data shows that the average amount of time women spent taking care of clothes has declined from slightly more than eleven hours per week in the 1920s (Ramey, 2009) to 0.29 hours per week in 2016 (US Bureau of Labor Statistics, 2017). This reflects advances in technology, easy-care fabrics, the increased participation of women in the labor force, purchase of clothing services such as alterations, and simply having less time for activities like mending.

Traditionally, laundry and sewing/mending skills were learned in the home or school. However, as women entered the workforce in greater numbers starting in the 1970s (Toossi, 2012), the role of mothers in passing on these skills to their children began to change. Working mothers simply didn't have as much time to impart knowledge as the stay-at-home moms of earlier decades. Consequently, skills related to mending and sewing have seemingly died out (Clark, 2008). At the same time that women were increasingly entering the labor force, home economics education suffered. This was a primary way in which young people acquired sewing skills that helped them care for their clothes. Over the past forty years, funding for family and consumer sciences programs decreased dramatically (LaRue-Huget, 2010). Gen Y consumers have rated their skills on sewing, mending, and laundering lower than either Gen X or Baby Boomers (Norum, 2013). Yet, prolonging a garment's life is essential to being more sustainable. Clothing that is designed to be discarded, and consumers' current lack of sewing skills makes this a difficult situation. In the next section, we discuss some negative consequences of current care practices.

Contemporary clothing care practices and their dangers

To better understand the negative economic, environmental, and social impacts of clothing care practices today, we look at practices across care stages and around the world. Today, in Europe and the US, the cleanliness standard of a garment is less about how hygienic it is, as in earlier periods, and more about how "fresh" and odor free it is (Shove, 2003). As a result, people wash their clothes more frequently, often after wearing them for very short periods of time. People tend to do more laundry because of the convenience of machines and the interest in wearing a particular garment at any given time. People also tend to change their clothing more often, leading to increases in the number and size of loads. Within US households the amount of laundry done in a year tripled between 1950 and 2000 (Shove, 2003, p. 131). An increase in the amount of laundry negatively impacts the environment through both energy and water use. In fact, in countries where more wash cycles are done per year, per household, such as the United States, Canada, and Japan, these households use significantly more water per year than those in countries with lower numbers of wash cycles (Pakula and Stamminger, 2010). Energy use can be more varied, based on the types of energy and machines prevalent within a country.

Cleaning techniques

The increase in laundry done today does not necessarily mean that environmental and economic costs have increased at the same rate over the same period. The efficiency of washers has improved drastically, with the need for hot water washes, warm water rinses, and the amount of water used per load eliminated or decreased significantly. For example, horizontal axis machines, typically of front-loading design, reduce both energy and water use per load (Hustvedt, 2011). They can also reduce the amount of moisture left in the clothing after the cycle, thereby reducing the amount of energy used for drying. These, and other high efficiency (HE) washers, also reduce the amount of water used during a cycle, in turn calling for less detergent. In Germany, horizontal-axis front-loading machines are the norm. These machines use 25–50 percent less water than the typical US machine with a vertical agitator. Currently, about 30 percent of US households have horizontal-axis machines, and it will probably take decades for these machines to become widespread (Neff, 2010). However, Western Europeans tend to wash their clothes in hotter temperatures (than US consumers) but have begun shifting to cooler temperatures, while also changing the products they use to accommodate water temperature.

Other differences in cleaning techniques exist around the world. For instance, in Brazil, a type of semi-automatic washing machine called a *tanquinho* agitates clothes to such an extent that it produces an excessive amount of suds that can be used for a second load. However, the machine doesn't have a rinse cycle, resulting in the need for the clothes to be rinsed by hand (Neff, 2010). In many developing countries, handwashing clothes is still typical for vast portions of their populations, especially in rural areas. Variations on this do exist from country to country. In the Philippines, communal water sources are used for washing clothes by hand (Tashian, 2016). In India, the Dhobi caste provides laundry services at facilities where the clothes are washed by hand, beaten on a hard surface, and hung to dry (see Figure 12.1). To the extent that modern machines are adopted by Indian consumers, there could be negative social and economic impacts on the Dhobi caste (Moiseeva, 2015).

An alternative to standard washing practices that has been touted in recent years is freezing garments, such as jeans, to reduce the amount of washing needed. However, it is important to do your research on these new techniques as they appear on social media and blogs. While many report that the process reduces odors, there is little evidence to support the theory that it will "clean" or kill germs (Bennett, 2016). Most bacteria will survive, or become dormant, at very low temperatures and the only way to kill them is by the opposite process: to bring garments to much higher temperatures (Zielenski, 2011).

One environmental impact of washing, recently discovered by a research team at the University of California, Santa Barbara, is that a typical fleece jacket releases, on average, 81,317 microfibers into the water in a single wash (O'Connor, 2016). Those washed in top-loading machines released significantly more fibers than those in front-loading machines. These plastic microfibers have even been found in marine life, which may affect their lifespan and filter into our food supply (Boddy, 2017). Companies in Europe and the US are looking at alternative

Figure 12.1 Outdoor laundry facility in India. Courtesy of Pamela Norum.

fibers, yarns, and finishes that may help reduce this problem going forward. Patagonia is now recommending that consumers wash these microfiber products in filter bags or install a filter on their machine, in addition to simply laundering the items less frequently (Scarano, 2017). Other advocates are also looking at alternative detergents, cycles, and laundering bags that may reduce the amount of fibers washed out.

Laundry detergent

An integral part of the washing process is detergent. Detergents are a complex mixture of ingredients that provide surface wetting, oil removal, whitening, brightening, fragrance, and dye (Leverette, 2017). As a result, there are many ways that they can harm people and the environment. Unfortunately, detergent companies often do not list all ingredients, so it can be hard to evaluate brands. We do know that they have long included phosphates, which cause harmful algae blooms in waterways, though today phosphates are banned from detergents in most of the US and Europe. However, detergents continue to use harsh alkalies which can irritate the skin or poison an individual if ingested (Leverette, 2017). Today, there are plant-based detergents which are more biodegradable and seek to avoid harmful chemicals. Additionally, most major brands offer fragrance-free and dye-free options which limit the chemicals used.

One environmental improvement has been the shift to concentrated liquid versions. Concentrated liquid detergents reduce overall plastic packaging, the amount of water in detergent, and the fuel footprint for shipping the equivalent dosage needed for one load of laundry. Method began this shift in 2004 by introducing a 3x concentrated version, which was quickly adopted by most major detergent brands (Gunther, 2013). Today all brands use at least a 2x concentrated version, while Method has continued innovation with an 8x concentrated version. Another form of detergent, laundry pods, has been singled out for an entirely different danger. Children and adults with dementia have ingested them because they are small and colorful, like candy, causing health problems and even death (Consumer Reports, 2017). The industry is working to make them less attractive and bitter tasting to reduce these risks.

Alternatives to detergent exist, though they may not be as effective. Plastic or ceramic reusable wash balls, which claim to clean effectively without the use of detergent, have been on the market for years. However, testing has shown that these do not clean clothing any better than water washing alone (Kruschwitz et al., 2013). They may clean effectively for the first couple of loads because of residual detergent on clothing or in the machine, but that eventually diminishes.

Drying techniques

As part of the laundering process, machine drying can account for more than half of the energy impact during care (Fletcher, 2008). Clothes dryers are a major user of electricity, accounting for 6 percent of all electricity use in American homes (Oxenreider, 2017). However, dryers in the 1980s also began including sensors that allow the moisture content in clothes to dictate drying time, rather than the user setting the time. More recently, manufacturers have begun equipping dryers with a pump that recirculates the hot air used. Both sensors and pumps help reduce the overall amount of energy used to dry. In Germany, consumers use a centrifuge to dry their clothes while in Nordic countries, consumers use a mangle to extract water from clothes and then hang them to line dry (Moiseeva, 2015). Both methods use less energy than a clothes dryer. Related to drying, scented dryer sheets and detergents can contribute to air pollution when multiple hazardous chemicals escape through dryer vents

(Hickey, 2011). Additionally, dryer sheets are disposable, contributing to landfill waste. On the other hand, reusable dryer balls can reduce static with a much lower impact than dryer sheets.

Ethical concerns in laundering

The need for water during laundering poses environmental, social, and moral consequences. In places like the United States and Europe, where access to water is often taken for granted, flagrant water use can be contentious when considering how many others around the world do not have access to indoor plumbing or clean water, and the limited nature of the resource itself. In some areas of Asia and Africa, people often wash clothes in local streams and rivers, as running water is not available in homes. If there are no waterways nearby, they may have to walk miles to a well or pump and then carry heavy containers of water home.

These concerns are not always remote. Within the US, towns like Flint, Michigan, and East Porterville, California, have had to live for years without access to clean water in their homes. East Porterville relied on wells for water until drought dried them up. For three years, until 2016, residents lived without access to running water and had to rely on emergency bottled drinking water and buckets of wash water hauled from tanks brought in by the state (Stevens, 2016). Without running water, people had to minimize their washing routines and reuse water whenever possible. How would you prioritize your water use if you had no access to it at home? What would change first: laundering your clothes after each wear, or taking a bath every day?

Finally, for those who rely on laundromats, access has become problematic. The number of US laundromats and dry-cleaners has fallen by nearly 20 percent since 2005, largely due to the number of laundromats closing in densely populated urban areas (Vartabedian, 2017). As apartment buildings are upgrading for wealthier clientele in gentrifying areas, they are outfitted with washers and dryers, leaving laundromats without enough customers. However, owners of older apartment buildings that remain low-income housing are less likely to invest in installing washers and dryers. So, where will people without machines be able to do their laundry in these densely populated areas? How will they be able to achieve the societal norms of cleanliness without sacrificing more time or money than they already do? Often, laundromats were not particularly affordable (Vartabedian, 2017), but at least they were somewhat convenient.

This brings us to what can be done, right now, by consumers who wish to practice more sustainable clothing care.

Best practices in clothing care

There are a number of ways in which you can take care of your clothing in more sustainable ways. This section discusses some options regarding clothing care, and then it will be up to you to decide which ones are best suited to you.

General tips

When it comes to laundry, an alternative is simply to do less (Fisher et. al., 2008; Nordic Fashion Association, 2012). Another option is to wear your clothes longer before laundering (Laitala, Boks, and Klepp, 2011). Extending the time between washings (and dryings) will not only reduce your impact on the environment, and save you money; it can also help your clothes last longer. To make better decisions about care practices, get to know your textile fibers. Read your clothing labels. All garments sold in the US have to include fiber content and care labels. Knowing about fibers, and how to care for each, can be helpful in making more sustainable care decisions. Do you need to wash in warm water? Do you always need to iron? Do you even need to dry-clean a garment? This is where knowing your fibers can help you!

Laundry

There are several aspects to washing your clothes: your machine, water, laundry additives, and electricity. There are also decisions to be made about drying, ironing, and dry-cleaning. Each one of these can have an impact on caring for your clothes in a sustainable way.

With respect to washing machines, one option to consider is a high efficiency machine that uses less water and electricity relative to other choices. Regarding water, you can choose the amount and temperature of the water. It is important to check the care label when it is time to care for your clothes. Following the manufacturer's instructions can help prolong the life of the garment, and avoid costly mistakes (like shrinking a garment). However, the tendency among apparel manufacturers is to take the most cautious approach in making a recommendation. In some cases, a consumer can choose to do things differently, especially if they are trying to use sustainable practices. For example, a common care recommendation is to wash an item in warm water. However, to be more sustainable, it is recommended to wash garments at a lower temperature (Fisher et. al., 2008; Laitala et al., 2011; Nordic Fashion Association, 2012) without a noticeable difference in the cleanliness of the clothes, especially colorful clothes. White clothes may stay white better in warm water, thereby increasing their life. Certain items that come into more intense contact with perspiration, like workout clothes or sheets, may benefit from a warm wash to reduce odor build-up, increasing the item's life. Nevertheless, reducing the water temperature is something you should explore for everyday washing. Additionally, washing full loads instead of a few items (Nordic Fashion Association, 2012), or at least using the appropriate load setting, is recommended.

One way to limit the impact of your detergent is to consider how much you use. When laundering, the amount of detergent is actually quite important, not only in reducing pollution, but also in maintaining your clothes and washing machine. Using more detergent will not necessarily result in cleaner clothing, if the soil has already bonded with the detergent or all the clothing is fully soaked. Using too much detergent can also cause excess soap to stay in your clothing, causing skin irritation or odor. It can even prevent soap from breaking down and rinsing out fully in high efficiency machines that use less water, leading to problems with the machine. In the case of washers that keep rinsing until the amount of suds reduces, it can actually prolong the rinse cycle, increasing water and energy use (Consumer Reports, 2012). Switching to a low-impact detergent is another option. One tip in evaluating detergents is to look for the Safer Detergents Stewardship Initiative (SDSI) label (EPA). Washers with automatic dispensers can also help reduce errors in measurement. Nevertheless, check to make sure what type of detergent you are using: liquid or powder, concentrated or not? Essentially, consider a combination of what's best for your machine and what's best for the type of detergent you use to maximize performance and reduce excess detergent in waste water.

One of the fastest ways to ruin your clothes is staining. It is important to deal with a stain as soon as possible after it happens. The simplest approach, for most stains, would be to put water on the stain and try to spot wash it as soon as possible. If you are at home, or carry a pre-treat stick, you should try to apply the pre-treatment right away. If you are using a spray treatment, it is best to apply the treatment and let it set prior to washing. Now, one might ask, what is the impact of these treatments? They often include the same types of ingredient as detergents, so they should be approached with the same caution. In fact, you can use your low-impact detergent as a means of pre-treating your stains, instead of alternative sprays. However, if your alternative is not to treat it at all, but rather throw the garment in the trash, then we suggest pre-treating. Another option is to consider common household ingredients that can more naturally help remove stains. For instance, distilled white vinegar can reduce tomato, grass, and coffee stains (Huffstetler, 2017). Finally, don't dry your garment until you remove the stain completely because heat will set it. These steps will help you continue wearing the garment and avoid throwing it out, which is not a sustainable option.

Many advances have been made in drying technology. However, one of the best practices for the environment relies on old technology, a clothes line (Laitala et al., 2011; Nordic Fashion Association, 2012). Since most US households no longer have clothes lines, the dryer still seems like the best option. However, there are mobile drying rack options that can be used inside and outside to still allow for some line drying (see Figure 12.2). And when you use the dryer, you should keep in mind several things. First, dry clothes on a lower heat cycle (Nordic Fashion Association, 2012) and see if your dryer has an "eco" setting available. Also, separate cotton items from synthetics to be more efficient and

Figure 12.2 Vintage drying rack. Courtesy of Pamela Norum.

help save energy costs, or consider hanging synthetics on hangers or an indoor drying rack since they dry faster (Fisher et al., 2008). Also, try to avoid dryer sheets since they include harmful chemicals. Although some items may need to be ironed, eliminate ironing whenever possible (Laitala et al., 2011). This could be done by buying items that don't need to be ironed, taking items out of the dryer and hanging them up before becoming wrinkled, or making the choice not to iron as much.

Dry-cleaning may be the only way to get some clothes clean. How much of your wardrobe do you want to routinely have dry-cleaned? Dry-cleaning not only costs you money, but the solvents used can be hard on the environment. Another alternative is carbon dioxide cleaning, which uses no water and recovers nearly all carbon dioxide used. Carbon dioxide replaces the harmful air pollutant and neurotoxin perchloroethylene (perc), and removes the heating process solvents require (Dos Santos, 2011). However, not all dry-cleaners are eager to make this shift and may even make unclear claims about their eco-friendliness, so you should carefully assess who you use for dry-cleaning.

Repair

In addition to laundry, repairing clothes is critical to maintenance and one way to increase the lifespan of your clothes (Fisher et al., 2008; Nordic Fashion Association, 2012). Unfortunately, clothes that need repairs frequently find their way to the trash. You can keep this from happening by paying someone else to repair it, asking a friend or family member for help, or doing it yourself. There are YouTube videos and Pinterest boards with tips on how to do basic mending, and it is something everyone can learn. One of the best ways to start is by getting a basic sewing kit (which can be any container with a few spools of thread, needles, and scissors).

Another repair option, originally started in Amsterdam in 2009 (McGrane, 2012), is to participate in a Repair Café. These are community venues where people come together to share their repair talents, and provide repair services at the same time. They are springing up in places across the US. If there isn't one near you, consider starting one or asking some friends if they might want to start one.

Finally, you can buy clothes from companies that will repair the clothes for you (Patagonia). This can be an expensive option since the initial investment for clothes may be higher, or they may charge shipping or fees to complete it. It is also one that can be hard to find currently, but it may be a more widely available opportunity in the future.

Below, we present a summary of the best practices for sustainable clothing care.

Summary of best practices:

- Wash clothes only when necessary.
- Check fiber content and care labels.
- Use a high efficiency washer and dryer.
- Use the right amount of water for the load.
- Use the coolest water temperature possible.
- Don't overuse detergent.
- Buy low-impact detergents.
- Look for the Safer Detergents Stewardship Initiative (SDSI) label.
- Take time to pre-treat stains.
- Consider natural stain removers rather than chemicals.
- Hang clothes to dry.
- Reduce use of dryer sheets.
- Dry-clean only as needed.
- Check the practices of your dry-cleaners.
- Learn basic mending techniques.
- Participate in a Repair Café.

Although this list provides specific suggestions, it is important to remember that being informed, making intentional decisions, and learning new skills will help you get to where you want to be in your own sustainable clothing care practices!

Case study

You are looking for a way to get involved in your community and have been exploring options that would fit with your busy schedule, but also allow you to make a meaningful contribution. You are particularly interested in opportunities that fit with the idea of sustainable clothing consumption, more specifically within care and maintenance. The ideal experience would use your skills and knowledge, while also having an impact on the environment and on people's lives. You have come across three opportunities, and you are trying to evaluate each one to determine the best fit for you. They are each looking for volunteers.

You have the following information about each opportunity that will help you decide between the three choices.

1. Repair Café

Repair Cafés started as a way to be more sustainable locally, where people bring broken items for repair. Repair specialists volunteer their time to make repairs for free. The café provides a community gathering spot and an opportunity to interact with others. It also provides a way to keep items out of the landfill. The Repair Café that was recently started in your community is looking for a repair specialist to help with mending clothes.

2. Right to Dry

In communities across the US, clothes lines have been banned by many neighborhood associations, assisted living communities, and other spaces. Although bans have been lifted in some states (Tuttle, 2015), one still exists in your state. A Right to Dry group has been organized locally to advocate for the right to reintroduce line drying to the community. They are looking for volunteers to help staff the office, provide community education, distribute fliers, and otherwise help the organization as needed.

3. Community Sewing Center

The Community Sewing Center (CSC) reflects the trend toward makerspaces that have been springing up across the US (for example, see http://www.citysewingroom.com/). The CSC started two years ago in your community, and their primary purpose is to help people learn to sew. The center is a place where people can learn sewing skills to create, repurpose, alter, or mend clothes, or just come in to use a machine if they already sew. The center is currently looking for volunteers to assist in teaching basic sewing or mending classes, depending on their skills.

References

Balderston, Lydia Ray and Limerick, M. C. *Laundry Manual*. Philadelphia: Avil Printing Co, 1902. http://hearth.library.cornell.edu/cgi/t/text/text-idx?c=hearth;idno=4246998.

Bennett, Alexis. "Should You Put Your Jeans in the Freezer Instead of the Wash?" *Self*, June 12, 2016. https://www.self.com/story/freeze-jeans-bacteria-myth.

Boddy, Jessica. "Are we eating our fleece jackets? Microfibers are migrating into field and food." *NPR*, February 6, 2017. http://www.npr.org/sections/thesalt/2017/02/06/511843443/are-we-eating-our-fleece-jackets-microfibers-are-migrating-into-field-and-food.

Bras-Klapwijk, Remke M. and Knot, J. Marjolijn C. "Strategic Environmental Assessment for Sustainable Households in 2050: Illustrated for Clothing." *Sustainable Development* 9 (2001): 109–18.

"City Sewing Room." http://www.citysewingroom.com/.

Clark, Hazel. "SLOW + FASHION—an oxymoron—or a promise for the future?" *Fashion Theory* 12 (2008): 427–46.

Consumer Reports. "Detergent doses: 'Ultra' confusing." *Consumer Reports*, March 2012. http://www.consumerreports.org/cro/magazine/2012/03/detergent-doses-ultra-confusing/index.htm.

Consumer Reports. "Laundry detergent buying guide." *Consumer Reports*, January 2017. http://www.consumerreports.org/cro/laundry-detergents/buying-guide.htm.

Dos Santos, Alissa. "Dry cleaning or wet cleaning? Liquid CO2 or Green Earth?" *Sylvia's Dry Cleaning*, September 2011. http://sylviasdrycleaning.com/2011/09/dry-cleaning-or-wet-cleaning-liquid-co2-or-greenearth/.

EPA. "What is the Safer Detergents Stewardship Initiative?" Environmental Protection Agency. https://www.epa.gov/saferchoice/design-environment-safer-detergents-stewardship-initiative#recognition

Fisher, Tom, Cooper, Tim, Woodward, Sophie, Hiller, Alex, and Gowork, Helen. *Public Understanding of Sustainable Clothing: A Report to the Department for Environment, Food and Rural Affairs*. London: Defra, 2008.

Fletcher, Kate. *Sustainable Fashion and Textiles: Design Journeys*. London: Earthscan, 2008.

Fletcher, Kate. "Slow fashion: An invitation for systems change." *Journal of Fashion Practice* 2 (2010): 259–66.

Gunther, Marc. "How laundry detergent became a catalyst for green innovation." *YaleEnvironment360*, June 11, 2013. http://e360.yale.edu/features/adam_lowry_how_laundry_detergent_became_green_innovation_catalyst

Hickey, Hannah. "Scented laundry products emit hazardous chemicals through dryer vents." *UW News*, August 24, 2011. http://www.washington.edu/news/2011/08/24/scented-laundry-products-emit-hazardous-chemicals-through-dryer-vents/.

Hoy, Suellen. *Chasing Dirt: The American Pursuit of Cleanliness*. New York: Oxford University Press, 1995.

Huffstetler, Erin. "How to Remove Laundry Stains With Vinegar." *The Balance*, April 30, 2017. https://www.thebalance.com/how-to-remove-laundry-stains-with-vinegar-1387973.

Hustvedt, Gwendolyn. "Review of laundry energy efficiency studies conducted by the US Department of Energy." *International Journal of Consumer Studies* 35 (2011): 228–36.

Kruschwitz, Anke, Augsburg, Aline, and Stamminger, Rainer. "How Effective are Alternative Ways of Laundry Washing?" *Tenside Surfactants Detergents* 50 (2013): 263–9.

Laitala, Kirsi, Boks, Caspar, and Klepp, Ingun Grimstad. "Potential for environmental improvements in laundering." *International Journal of Consumer Studies* 35 (2011): 254–64.

LaRue-Huget, Jennifer. "Bring back Home Ec!" *Washington Post*, May 17, 2010. http://voices.washingtonpost.com/checkup/2010/05/bring_back_home_ec.html.

Leverette, Mary Marlowe. "Laundry detergent ingredients and how they work." *The Spruce*, January 16, 2017. https://www.thespruce.com/how-laundry-detergent-ingredients-work-2146619.

McGrane. Sally. "An Effort to Bury a Throwaway Culture One Repair at a Time." *New York Times*, May 9, 2012. http://www.nytimes.com/2012/05/09/world/europe/amsterdam-tries-to-change-culture-with-repair-cafes.html.

Moiseeva, Liza. "4 Unexpected Ways People Do Laundry Around the World." *People, Planet*, August 11, 2015. https://globein.com/blog/4-ways-people-do-laundry-around-the-world/.

Neff, Jack. "The Dirt on Laundry Trends Around the World." *AdAge*, June 14, 2010. http://adage.com/article/global-news/global-marketing-dirt-laundry-trends-world/144398/.

Nordic Fashion Association. "The NICE Consumer: Framework for sustainable fashion." *BSR*, 2012. http://www.bsr.org/reports/nice-consumer-framework.pdf.

Norum, Pamela S. "An Examination of Consumer Practices and Knowledge Regarding Apparel Maintenance and Care: Implications for Sustainable Clothing Consumption." *Family and Consumer Sciences Research Journal* 42 (2013): 124–37.

O'Connor, Mary Catherine. "Patagonia's new study finds fleece jackets are a serious pollutant." *Outside*, June 20, 2016. https://www.outsideonline.com/2091876/patagonias-new-study-finds-fleece-jackets-are-serious-pollutant.

Oxenreider, Tsh. "5 Reasons to line-dry your Laundry." *Art of Simple*, July 18, 2011. http://theartofsimple.net/5-reasons-to-line-dry-your-laundry/.

Pakula, Christiane and Stamminger, Rainer. "Electricity and water consumption for laundry washing by washing machine worldwide." *Energy Efficiency* 3 (2010): 365–82.

Patagonia. "Patagonia Returns and Repairs." https://www.patagonia.com/returns.html.

Ramey, Valerie A. "Time Spent in Home Production in the Twentieth-Century United States: New Estimates from Old Data." *Journal of Economic History* 69 (2009): 1–47.

Scarano, Genevieve. "Patagonia Urges Consumers to Bag Synthetics for the Environment." *Sourcing Journal*, February 7, 2017. https://sourcingjournalonline.com/patagonia-urges-consumers-bag-synthetics-environment/.

Schaffer, Amanda. "Down the hatch and straight into medical history." *New York Times*, January 10, 2011. http://www.nytimes.com/2011/01/11/health/11swallow.html.

Shove, Elizabeth. *Comfort, Cleanliness, and Convenience: The Social Organization of Normality*. New York: Berg, 2003.

Stevens, Matt. "After years without water, taps are turned on in East Porterville." *Los Angeles Times*, August 19, 2016. http://www.latimes.com/local/lanow/la-me-ln-east-porterville-20160819-snap-story.html.

Tashian, Carl. "Are Americans doing laundry all wrong?" *CityLab*, March 31, 2014. https://www.citylab.com/life/2016/03/are-americans-doing-laundry-all-wrong/475482/.

Toossi, Mitra. "Projections of the labor force to 2050: A visual essay." *Monthly Labor Review*, October 1, 2012. http://www.bls.gov/opub/mlr/2012/10/art1full.pdf.

Tuttle, Brad. "The Nation's Greenest State Will Soon End Bans on This Simple Green Practice." *Time*, September 24, 2015. http://time.com/money/4048660/clothesline-ban-california-green/.

US Bureau of Labor Statistics. "Average Hours Per Day Spent in Selected Household Activities, 2016 Averages." https://www.bls.gov/charts/american-time-use/activity-by-hldh.htm.

Vartabedian, Marc. "The Decline of the American Laundromat." *The Atlantic*, July 31, 2017. https://www.theatlantic.com/business/archive/2017/07/decline-american-laundromat-gentrification/535257/.

Winakor, Geitel. "The Process of Clothing Consumption." *Journal of Home Economics* 61 (1969): 629–34.

Wray, Tina Brewster. "Irons." *White River Journal*, April 1997. http://www.wrvmuseum.org/journal/journal_ftbr_0497.htm.

Zielinski, Sarah. "The myth of the frozen jeans." Smithsonian.com, November 7, 2011. https://www.smithsonianmag.com/science-nature/the-myth-of-the-frozen-jeans-129092730/.

13

Disposing Fashion: From the Ugly . . .

Jana M. Hawley and Elena E. Karpova

If you look under the glitz and glamor of the fashion industry, you might find a very ugly story to be told. "The fashion industry is said to be the second dirtiest industry in the world—second only to big oil" (Lozanova, 2016). The industry contributes an enormous amount of waste to our planet. In fact, more than 150 million tons of clothing are sold around the world each year, with only 15 percent being recycled and the rest either piling up in closets, or headed to the landfills (Wang, 2006).

The ugly: too much stuff

We simply produce and consume too much stuff! We buy a lot of clothing because it helps us express who we are, what is important to us, and communicate this to others—and buying less would feel like we are limiting our means of self-expression, and maybe even our sense of self. Minimalist lifestyle movements are underway, but consumers are drawn to new fashion that keeps us on trend through items that the industry promotes through extremely low pricing. The following list of sixteen facts reveals how much "stuff" we actually own (adapted from Becker, 2017).

1. There are 300,000 items in the average American home.
2. Some reports indicate we consume twice as many material goods today as we did fifty years ago.
3. The average American home has nearly tripled in size over the past fifty years.
4. One out of every ten Americans rent offsite storage—the fastest growing segment of the commercial real estate industry over the past four decades.
5. Twenty-five percent of people with two-car garages don't have room to park cars inside them and 32 percent only have room for one vehicle.

6. British research found that the average ten-year-old owns 238 toys but plays with just twelve daily.
7. Three percent of the world's children live in the United States, but they own 40 percent of the toys consumed globally.
8. The average American woman owns thirty outfits—one for every day of the month. In 1930, that figure was nine.
9. The average American family spends $1,700 on clothes annually.
10. The average American throws away 80 pounds of clothing per year.
11. Americans spend more on shoes, jewelry, and watches ($100 billion) than on higher education.
12. Shopping malls outnumber high schools. And 93 percent of teenage girls rank shopping as their favorite pastime.
13. Women will spend more than eight years of their lives shopping.
14. Over the course of our lifetime, we will spend a total of 3,680 hours or 153 days searching for misplaced items. The research found we lose up to nine items every day—or 198,743 in a lifetime. Phones, keys, sunglasses, and paperwork top the list.
15. Americans spend $1.2 trillion annually on non-essential goods—in other words, items they do not need.
16. The $8 billion home organization industry has more than doubled in size since the early 2000s—growing at a staggering rate of 10 percent each year.

How do these facts make you feel? Don't you feel sorry for yourself that you spend years of acquiring, managing, organizing, and looking for all this stuff? The question then is why does consumption continue to grow at staggering rates? We consume in the pursuit of happiness, with the hope to find ourselves in clothing and other material objects. However, the results are just the opposite.

World fiber production and consumption has steadily increased in the past few decades. In the 1980s, we produced 14 million tons of synthetic fibers such as polyester or nylon. Today we produce 71 million. On top of that, we produce 30 million tons of natural fibers. Most of this growth is in China and India, the top two cotton producers in the world. These two countries also have experienced population explosion and consumers with increased discretionary income. In 2016, the worldwide total fiber market surpassed 100 million tons. That is a lot of fiber!

Annual retail sales of clothing in the United States rose from $120.1 billion in 1992 to $244.5 billion in 2013 (US Census, 2015). Globally, sales in fashion goods have surpassed a trillion dollars and fostered an obsession with fashion, particularly fast fashion. Consumers choose volumes of cheap and trendy fads over well-made classics that last. In Elizabeth Cline's book, *Overdressed*, the author reports that today's average annual clothing budget of $1,700 can buy 485 scoop-neck tops from Forever 21, 240 pairs of sandals from Family Dollar, fifty-six pairs of pants from Target, and forty-seven pairs of platform shoes from Charlotte Russe (Cline, 2013). Fashion has gotten so cheap that very little mindfulness goes into making our fashion purchases. This creates a double-edged sword in that while it stimulates the economy (projected to add ten–twenty new factories each year to meet the world market demand), it also uses enormous amounts of resources and gives rise to the increased problem of disposal.

When we think about the fact that we live in a throw-away society but then realize that natural resources are limited, we can see the problem we have created—too much stuff! In the United States, the average person donates 15 percent of their clothing, but the remaining 10.5 million tons go to our landfills each year.

More than 15 million tons of textile waste are generated annually in the United States alone (LeBlanc, 2017). This alarming number has doubled in the last two decades with each American throwing away approximately 80 pounds of clothing each year. While nearly 100 percent of textiles and apparel are recyclable, most of these clothes are sent to the landfill because consumers do not fully understand the pathways for disposing of their clothes. For more than ten years, Hawley (2006a, 2007) has argued that consumers should always avoid throwing their clothes in the trash and instead donate their clothing to their favorite charity no matter whether the item is still in fashion, torn, or missing a button. However, of all the clothing taken to charities, less than 20 percent is sold and over half is never put on the racks (Cline, 2013). Some of the surplus goes to the landfill, but a lot of it is baled and sold to for-profit companies at pennies on the pound.

The ugly: poor quality

Over the past fifteen years, the global apparel industry has undergone a dramatic transformation as the fashion cycle has become faster and faster. What used to be a stable three-month production cycle has collapsed into an extraordinary two-week cycle that delivers new goods to stores on almost a daily basis. At the same time that the fashion production cycle has gotten faster, clothing prices have dropped dramatically and the quality has taken a nose dive. This astonishing industry transformation is referred to as fast-fashion, sometimes viewed as "disposable fashion." Most of these fashions are made of polyester fibers that have a very slow degradation rate. It might take a hundred years or more to decompose (Li, Frey, and Browning, 2010). Not only do consumers buy more, they keep it about half as long as they did fifteen years ago (Remy, Speelman, and Swartz, 2016). Lewis (2015) pointed out that when consumers perceive the value of clothing as cheap and poor, then they start to see clothing as disposable. In other words, the cheaper the item, the more likely we are to toss it in the trash after wearing it for only a couple of times.

Clothes in today's marketplace are different from those of several decades ago, not only in design and quality, but also in fiber content. After synthetic textiles came onto the market in the second half of the twentieth century, textile recycling became more complex for two distinct reasons: (1) fiber strength increased, making it more difficult to "open" the fibers, and (2) fiber blends made it more difficult to purify the sorting process. Nonetheless, today's recycling industry is working hard to find ways to increase the recycling rate.

Back in 1950, the per capita world consumption of fiber was eight pounds. This is when families built wardrobes over time, children handed their clothing down to younger siblings, clothing was altered and repaired, and high-quality fibers were used to make high-quality fashion. Today, an average person on earth buys more than 24 pounds of textiles (World Apparel Fibre Consumption Survey, 2013). For the United States alone, per year textile consumption rates have skyrocketed upward of 80 pounds per person. While the world's cotton consumption has remained relatively stable over the past twenty-five years (around 7.7 pounds per person a year), consumption of manufactured fibers has risen dramatically to nearly 20 pounds per person. Because synthetic fibers are non-biodegradable, the switch away from natural fibers has made it much more difficult to deal with textile waste.

The fashion recycling industry

The fashion recycling industry touches on social, environmental, economic, and legislative responsibilities. By recycling, companies can realize larger profits, contribute to the goodwill associated with environmentalism, provide employment for over 17,000 people (LeBlanc, 2017), contribute to disaster relief, and transfer clothing to parts of the world where used and inexpensive clothing is needed.

The textile recycling industry is one of the oldest and most established recycling industries in the world. In most countries, used textile and apparel products were salvaged and put to new uses. In China, more than 2,000 years ago, clothing was shredded and hand carded for blending with virgin fibers. During the Napoleonic Wars, military uniforms were made of post-consumer fibers. In the United States, textile recycling is one of the oldest, yet most misunderstood recycling industries (Nousiainen and Talvenmaa-Suusela, 1994).

Textile recycling material can be classified as either pre-consumer or post-consumer waste. Pre-consumer waste is a by-product of manufacturing fashion products. Post-consumer waste is any type of garment or household textile that the owner no longer needs and decides to discard. These garments might be damaged, outgrown, out of style, or they might be in a perfect shape, some still with tags attached.

Clothing that has reached the end of its "first life" often starts as a donation to a favorite charity such as Goodwill Industries or the Salvation Army, where they are inspected for wearability. Better clothing is placed in their retail thrift shops. The Salvation Army has been around since 1865, and Goodwill launched in 1915. It wasn't until the 1950s when these and other charities started resale shops using the used clothing as income to support their charitable activities; yet only about 20 percent of what is taken to charities is actually sold in their retail shops (Hoang, 2015).

The larger charities (again such as Goodwill Industries and the Salvation Army) work strategically as partners to support the textile recycling processes. When charities have more donations than they can manage in their resale shops, they move the excess post-consumer textile waste (PCTW) to textile recycling companies (hereafter referred to as *recyclers*), including both recycling and recovery. Kunz, Karpova, and Garner (2016, p. 93) distinguished between recycling and recovery in that recycling is the process of taking a product at the end of its useful life and using all or part of it to make another product; recovery, on the other hand, is the process of collecting and sorting waste materials for processing into new forms marketed as raw materials for new products.

Charities bale and sell the surplus to recyclers. The price fluctuates based on current market values but often ranges from US\$0.04 – 0.06 per pound. Trucks are dispatched to the charity shops for pick-up and then taken back to the sorting facility to start the sorting process. Nousiainen and Talvenmaa-Kuusela (1994) reported that transportation costs have been a decisive factor in whether or not clothing continues in the recycling pipeline. When fuel costs go up, the problem is further compounded. It should be noted that if clothing is to be recycled, there has to be residual commercial value in the process. As clothing passes through the recycling pipeline, the revenue generated must pay for the infrastructure, transport, sorting, retailing, and other business functions (Durham et al., 2015). In other words, recycling companies must cover all the expenses yet generate some profit.

In the United States alone there are more than 500 recycling companies who divert more than 3.8 billion pounds of PCTW per year. These are typically small family-owned businesses (Council for Textile Recycling, 2017). The Office of Textiles and Apparel (OTEXA, 2017) reports that with the increase in volume, the number of pounds processed has increased dramatically in the past years; however, the quality of the goods is much lower than it used to be because of the poor quality of fast-fashion products.

The volume pyramid

Because textiles are nearly 100 percent recyclable, nothing in the fashion industry should end up in a landfill. Let's see what is actually happening behind the scenes of the recycling industry. Once used clothing arrives at a recycling facility, the clothes are dumped onto a conveyor belt and the sorting begins. Initially, household textiles and heavy items such as coats are pulled from the conveyor. Pants are separated from tops, then women's from men's and from children's. The second sorting process starts to refine the categories based on clothing type, fiber content, quality, condition, and sometimes brand names. In the end, many recyclers have sorted up to 400 categories of used material that is then baled, warehoused, and waits for the next step, which varies from exporting or shipping to industries that process into products for landscaping, housing construction, and automotive industries.

Most sorters have a division of labor whereby the newest employees are trained to do the crude sorts at the beginning of the conveyor belt process. As expertise increases, employees are promoted to more complex sorting and fine grading. For example, Marguerite, a lead sorter and supervisor at a large facility in the United States can "tell cashmere from wool at the touch of a hand." Another sorting facility employs a person with a Masters in Fine Arts who leads the trend division, training workers as to what items to pull from the conveyor belts that meet today's vintage fashion trends.

Once the goods are sorted, it is apparent that the structure of the recycling industry starts to look like a pyramid where the *diamonds* are few and far between but each item has a high relative worth; whereas the landfill and incineration category has many pounds but the value of each pound is very low—in fact worthless. Hawley (2006) explained how the value of used clothing in the United States is inversely proportional to the volume. Sorted categories include used clothing markets, conversion to new products, wipers, landfill and incineration, and diamonds. In other words, the high-value *diamonds* (1–2 percent) are rare and hard to find but have higher value per item. Examples of diamonds include couture clothing, vintage clothes, trend-setters, luxury fibers, and Americana items such as vintage Levis and Jerry Garcia concert T-shirts. Japanese buyers can be seen at recycling companies searching through piles of old clothes looking for such finds as Harley Davidson jackets and branded T-shirts, Grateful Dead concert T-shirts, Ralph Lauren black label, or vintage purses from the 1940s, '50s, or '60s (see Figure 13.1).

The next category is *landfill and incineration*. The volume (less than 7 percent) here reflects only the goods that are put into the recycling pipeline and does not include items that are put in the trash by the consumer. Some goods have no useful after-market path and the only choice is to landfill or incinerate. Recyclers

Figure 13.1 Sorting categories of post-consumer waste based on volume.

work hard to avoid landfill because there is a tipping fee that adds cost to their business. In addition, most recyclers are committed to environmental causes with commitments to find after-market uses for most PCTW.

In the US, testing is underway for the process of incinerating reclaimed textiles for thermal energy production. Although emission tests of incinerated reclaimed fiber are better than satisfactory, the process of feeding the boiler systems in many North American power plants is not feasible (Weide, 2004). The incineration of used textiles as an alternative fuel source is more commonly practiced in Europe (Hawley, 2006) but is still not a preferred method of disposal.

Another category is *wiping and polishing cloths,* which comprises about 17 percent of the used textile volume. Cotton T-shirts are a primary contributor to the wiping cloths category. Containers of used T-shirts are shipped to India where they are processed into rags by cutting off the neck binding, opening the sides, and cutting the front and back into useful wiping cloths. This labor-intensive process results in bags of rags that are sold to furniture, automotive, and other industries where clean-up rags are needed.

The next category in volume (29 percent) is *conversion to new products.* Garments that are not useful to the clothing resale market are often converted to new products. A large number of these products are made from shredded fibers. These value-added products include stuffing for pet beds, non-woven filters for the landscaping or automotive industries, building materials, roofing felt, and low-end blankets for disaster relief. One company shreds 100 percent cotton sweaters into fiber to be mixed with sand for "punching bags." In Prato, Italy, new yarns are produced from sweaters then woven into blankets. In Inman, South Carolina, geotextiles are made from used fiber to help filter water, oil, and debris from construction sites.

A particularly interesting value-added product is Ultra Touch™ by Bonded Logic. Bonded Logic is part of a family of businesses, including United Fibre and Phoenix Fibres, that have a steadfast focus on sustainability. The Ultra Touch™ item is a patented thermal and acoustic product made from recycled blue jeans and denim factory waste. Ultra Touch™ is not only high quality, energy efficient, and acoustically superior, it also meets several of the credits for Leadership in Energy and Environmental Design (LEED) for eco-friendly building materials.

Used blue jeans and factory waste are processed at Phoenix Fibres, a closed-loop textile fiber converter that recycles more than 300 tons of denim monthly into shoddy fiber. The shoddy is then transferred to the Bonded Logic facility where it is further processed into insulation, acoustic sound absorption materials, and stuffing for mattresses. Nothing goes to waste!

Finally, the biggest category of textile recycling is the *used clothing market* (48 percent). The US exported more than $590 million in 2016, down from $613 million the previous year. Yet the weight of clothing that was exported climbed by nearly 4 million kg during the same period (OTEXA, 2017). This is yet another indicator of the increasing volume of poor quality goods that are entering the textile recycling pipeline. Used clothing is exported from the United States to 156 countries (OTEXA, 2017), much of it to developed economies such as Canada, Japan, or Germany (Lee, Zhang, and Karpova, 2016). For example, in 2012, one-third of all US used clothing exports was destined for high-income countries. These are the diamonds of the pyramid as well as raw material for wiping cloths and conversion to new products.

On many street corners throughout the developing world, bales of clothes from developed countries are being sold (see Figure 13.2). Men's neckties and suits go to India as young Indians seek jobs in Western-owned offshore companies. Used sturdy shoes are shipped to Uganda, cotton sleepwear to

Figure 13.2 Bales of used fashion are shipped all over the world. Here a bale is waiting to be opened on the streets of New Delhi. Courtesy of Jana Hawley.

Bolivia, cotton pants and shirts to Haiti. Discarded fashion can be a useful commodity in the world's poorest nations, providing affordable clothing where levels of income are so low that food and clean water take precedence over new clothes. However, some nations are rising up to stop the import of used clothing because it has threatened the traditional dress of many indigenous cultures and thwarts the fledgling textile and apparel industries in their countries (see case below). Moreover, a lot of dated fashion discarded by consumers in prosperous economies has no demand even in the poorest countries. Partly, this might be due to it being unusable due to damage or carrying designs inappropriate for local cultures (e.g., too revealing, flashy, unsuitable colors), and partly because the supply far exceeds the demand. As a result, unwanted fashion ends up in landfills in these low-income countries, where there is no means to recycle it. Not only are we dumping waste in our own countries, but we also send what we do not need to landfills in other nations.

The zero waste pyramid—An inverted pyramid

Europe has long led the way in environmental strategies to reduce waste. The Zero Waste International Alliance (ZWIA) put forth a definition of zero waste:

> Zero Waste is a goal that is both pragmatic and visionary, to guide people to emulate sustainable natural cycles, where all discarded materials are resources for others to use. Zero Waste means designing and managing products and processes to reduce the volume and toxicity of waste and materials, conserve and recover all resources, and not burn or bury them. Implementing Zero Waste will eliminate all discharges to land, water, or air that may be a threat to planetary, human, animal or plant health.
>
> Zero Waste Europe, 2017

In 2013, ZWIA developed the Zero Waste Hierarchy where they adamantly propose that landfill is the last resort. The hierarchy prioritizes actions based on how much they benefit the environment. The goal is to have ethical, economical, efficient, and visionary guides that change human behaviors to effect a sustainable future. Often, when we hear of zero waste movements, the commitment is typically limited to zero waste to landfills—but they are not aiming for zero waste to be produced, just for waste to be managed. If we can't recycle our way to zero waste it raises the fundamental question: Is waste still waste if it gets recycled? In Figure 13.3, we have adapted the Zero Waste Hierarchy to illustrate the categories that we have identified in Chapters 13 and 14.

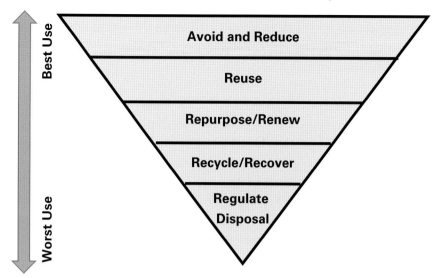

Figure 13.3 Proposed Zero Waste Hierarchy.

The adapted Zero Waste Hierarchy (Figure 13.3) describes a progression of policies and strategies to support the zero waste system. It is designed to be used by everyone, including governments, companies, and consumers. Ultimately, it provides a guide to encourage people to implement systems that contribute to zero waste. The pyramid draws a distinction between waste avoidance and waste management, with recycling fairly low on the hierarchy. Why is recycling accorded this position? Partly because recycling still emits toxins, and requires energy and other resources that cost money. Recycling is also a "down cycling" process where the materials lose quality each time they are recycled, at least in terms of the currently available recycling technology. After several cycles, the materials are degraded and ultimately quality becomes so poor that it still ends up in the landfill.

To reduce the amount of products that need to be recycled, we need to reduce the amount of products consumed and manufactured in the first place. A growing number of advocates have embraced the concept of a circular economy, which aims to achieve greater sustainability by keeping more resources and materials in use for a longer period of time. This can be achieved by better consumer choices, business commitment, smart product design, and improved resource management. Minimizing waste is more important than managing it.

As we transition to a circular economy we should shift to high-value clothing with a much extended life cycle. It may seem as if we are stepping back in time—but why wouldn't that be an excellent idea! Consume better quality. Consume less. Build wardrobes that we can cherish rather than dispose of. There will be more on these strategies in the next chapter.

There is no doubt that consumers across the Western world have too much stuff. Why do we keep buying when we already have far more than enough? We now live in an age of abundance. A century ago, clothing was hard to come by, but today, shirts, shoes, household goods, and toys are cheap and readily available. It is estimated that about two in every three people wish they had less stuff. Wallman (2015) calls this "stuffocation," because we have reached a point of extraordinary clutter and are facing a clutter crisis. It is the material version of the obesity epidemic. Wallman suggests that we should nudge people to spend their money on experiences rather than more stuff. It is a novel idea worth considering and one that would provide people with happy memories and also mean they would be far less likely to be drowning in stuff.

In a move toward a zero waste economy, the Council for Textile Recycling (CTR), a US-based non-profit organization, called for zero waste by 2037 (CTR, 2017). But a fundamental problem arose because US fashion retailers were not willing to embrace this initiative. The ugly part is that only a few retailers committed to this initiative, with little indication that others will step forward. Several reasons can be put forward for not committing to the initiative exist, including associated costs, changes in sourcing strategies, and disruption in the retailing fashion cycle. This means that the initiative will likely sunset in the United States because of lack of interest from retail companies and brands.

Future trends

As landfill space becomes scarce and tipping fees for the landfills continue to rise, so will the relevance of environmentalism. Those in the value-added and upcycling business sectors will continue to make progress in creating new markets for used textiles. At the same time, environmental enthusiasts must be provided with timely information about these markets so that they can make educated choices as to where and how they will dispose of their used textiles. More important, they will make informed and educated choices when shopping and considering new purchases.

Certainly, it is a double-edged challenge. Consumers must be made aware that all of their used clothing should enter the post-consumer pipeline. This is a big task because so many consumers have taken on the notion that "fashion is disposable." At the same time, an attitude shift towards the purchase of garments made from recycled fibers must be embraced in the USA as it has been in Europe. By raising consciousness of environmental issues, channels for disposal, and environmentally conscious business ethics, steps can be made toward a more sustainable—less ugly—situation. To recycle successfully, consumers must embrace the system, not just make occasional charitable donations. Industry has a big role to play in making sure fashion embraces the circular economy and that past seasons' trendy outfits do not end up in landfills. As discussed earlier in this book, fashion design should drive all sustainability efforts to ensure that products can be reused, renewed, and are easier to recycle. In addition, laws and political environments must adapt to make it easy for textiles to be recycled. It will take a commitment from everyone to make it less ugly.

Case study: second-hand clothing to the East African nations

East African countries do not want our used clothing anymore! In March of 2017, Kenya, Uganda, Tanzania, Burundi, and Rwanda proposed banning all imported used clothing and shoes by 2019. The goal is to stop relying on imports so that they can boost their local manufacturing industry and ultimately empower the East African economies. There is also hope that the ban will instill new pride among the people of the region. Clothes that arrive from the wealthy nations to the shores of Africa sell for low prices. A pair of used jeans sells for US$1.50 and a T-shirt with a Coca-Cola logo sells for US$0.25. The average cost of a used garment is about 10 percent of the equivalent new garment produced in the region, meaning that local industries have a hard time competing (Goldberg, 2016).

The global rise of fast-fashion clothing production and consumption has resulted in an overabundance of poor quality clothing. In fact, the issue is now quantity over quality. The more clothing that is produced quickly and cheaply, the more the consumer wants. For example, Forever 21 alone imported more than 100 million pieces of clothing to the US market in 2009, meaning that "trends come in and out faster, clothes are cheaper, and quality is reduced" (Hoang, 2015, p. 1). Yes, fast fashion has created a consumer mindset that sees clothing as out of fashion in a matter of weeks and, therefore, disposable. Seventy percent of the clothing that is taken to charities ends up in Africa (Cline, 2012).

From the 1960s to the early 1980s, clothing and shoe manufacturing in East Africa was thriving, with thousands of people employed in factories and cottage industries. The value chains extended from fiber production to product development and eventually to retail. Over the years, the second-hand market grew significantly and ultimately resulted in a near-collapse of local industries. But used clothing was not the only reason that the local African manufacturing facilities struggled. Other factors have also contributed to the manufacturing demise, including the political climate, import policies, and economic conditions (Brooks, 2013). A comprehensive study conducted by Katende-Magezi (2017) found that second-hand clothing to the value of $151 million was shipped into the East African Community region in 2015

Rwanda has historically imported more than $18 million of used clothes a year. But the government says they will continue with plans to ban imports, pointing out that local production could provide authentic African clothes for the local market (Peralta, 2017). The local leather and textile industries play a critical role in employment creation, poverty reduction, and the advancement of technological capabilities (BBC News, 2016). In contrast, Kenya has backed away from the plans to impose a second-hand clothing ban, conscious that the country's used clothing market employs hundreds of people (*Business Daily Africa*, 2017).

References

BBC News. "Why East Africa wants to ban second-hand clothes." BBC, March 2, 2016. http://www.bbc.com/news/world-africa-35706427.

Becker, J. "21 surprising statistics that reveal how much stuff we actually own." 2017. https://www.becomingminimalist.com/clutter-stats/.

Brooks, A. "Stretching global production networks: The international second-hand clothing trade." *Geoform* 44 (2013): 10–22.

Business Daily Africa. "Kenya rules out banning of second-hand clothes." AGOA, May 18, 2017. https://agoa.info/news/article/15113-kenya-rules-out-banning-of-second-hand-clothes.html.

Cline, E. *Overdressed: The Shockingly High Cost of Cheap Fashion*. New York: Penguin, 2013.

Council for Textile Recycling. 2017. http://www.weardonaterecycle.org/.

Durham, E., Hewitt, A., Bell, R., and Russell, S. "Technical design for recycling of clothing." In R. S. Blackburn (ed.), *Sustainable Apparel: Production, Processing, and Recycling*, Oxford: Woodhead, 2015.

Fair Labor Association. "Local solutions to global problems." 2017. http://www.fairlabor. org/global-issues.

Food and Agriculture Organization of the United Nations and International Cotton Advisory Committee. *World Apparel Fibre Consumption Survey.* Washington, DC: FAO and ICAC, 2013.

Frazer, G. "Used-clothing donations and apparel." *Economic Journal* 118 (2008): 1764–84.

Goldberg, E. "These African countries don't want your used clothing any more." *Huffington Post*, September 19, 2016. http://www.huffingtonpost.com/entry/ these-african-countries-dont-want-your-used-clothing-anymore_us_57cf19bce4b06 a74c9f10dd6.

Hawley, J. M. "Digging for diamonds: A conceptual framework for understanding reclaimed textile products." *Clothing and Textiles Research Journal* 24, no. 3 (2006a.): 262–75.

Hawley, J. M. "Textile recycling: A system perspective." In Y. Wang (ed.), *Recycling in Textiles*. pp. 7–24. Cambridge: Woodhead, 2006b.

Hawley, J. M. "Digging for Diamonds: Building Consumer Awareness of Textile Recycling." Presentation to the Greater Kansas City Family and Consumer Sciences, Olathe, Kansas, November 12, 2007.

Hawley, J. M. and Okun, S. "Textile recycling: the next wave of landfill diversion." White paper presented at the Illinois Recycling and Solid Waste Management Conference and Trade Show, June 13, 2007.

Hoang, N. L. "Clothes minded: An analysis of the effects of donating secondhand clothing to Sub-Saharan Africa. Scripps Senior Thesis." 2015. http://scholarship. claremont.edu/scripps_theses/671/.

Katende-Magezi, E. *The Impact of Second Hand Clothes and Shoes in East Africa.* Geneva: CUTS International Africa, 2017.

Kunz, Grace, Karpova, Elena, and Garner, Myrna. *Going Global: The Textile and Apparel Industry.* 3rd edn. New York: Bloomsbury/Fairchild, 2016.

LeBlanc, R. "Textile recycling facts and figures." 2017. https://www.thebalance.com/ textile-recycling-facts-and-figures-2878122.

Lee, Y., Zhang, L., and Karpova, E. "Examination of two decades in used clothing trade: The case of the United States and other developed economies." *Fashion, Industry and Education* 14, no. 2 (2016): 24–34. http://dx.doi.org/10.7741/fie.2016.14.2.024.

Lewis, T. "Apparel disposal and use." in R. S. Blackburn (ed.), *Sustainable Apparel: Production, Processing, and Recycling*, pp. 233–48. Cambridge: Woodhead, 2015.

Li, L., Frey, M., and Browning, K. "Biodegradability study on cotton and polyester fabrics." *Journal of Engineered Fibers and Fabrics* 5, no. 4 (2010): 42–53.

Lozanova. S. "Textile recycling initiative seeks to save fashion." 2016. http://earth911. com/business-policy/textile-recycling-save-fashion-ico/.

Nousiainen, P., and Talvenmaa-Kuusela, P. "Solid textile waste recycling." Paper presented at the Globalization-Technological, Economic, and Environmental Imperatives 75th World Conference of Textile Institute, Atlanta, GA, September 1994.

OTEXA. "US Total Exports in US Dollars for category 6309 Worn Clothing." 2017. http://otexa.trade.gov/scripts/tqexp_ads.exe/htsdata.

Peralta, E. "Rwanda works to ban sale of secondhand clothes within 2 years." 2017. http://www.npr.org/2017/07/21/538608486/rwanda-works-to-ban-sale-of-second-hand-clothes-within-2-years.

Remy, N. Speelman, E., and Swartz, S. "Style that's sustainable: A new fast-fashion formula." *McKinsey and Company: Sustainability & Resource Productivity* (October 2016). http://www.mckinsey.com/business-functions/sustainability-and-resource-productivity/our-insights/style-thats-sustainable-a-new-fast-fashion-formula.

Vermeer, D. L. ("7 upcycling companies that are transforming the fashion industry." September 8, 2014. http://daniellelvermeer.com/blog/upcycled-fashion-companies.

Wallman, J. "Viewpoint: The hazards of too much stuff." BBC News, January 24, 2017. http://www.bbc.com/news/magazine-30849473.

Wang, Y. "Introduction." in Y. Wang (ed.), *Recycling in Textiles*. Cambridge: Woodhead, 2006.

Zero Waste Europe. *Principles Zero Waste*. 2017. https://www.zerowasteeurope.eu/about/principles-zw-europe/.

14

Disposing Fashion: . . . To the Good

Elena E. Karpova and Jana M. Hawley

This chapter covers preferred, or less harmful, strategies to help divert disposed fashion and other textiles (found in our homes, cars, planes, public spaces) from landfills. In other words, these strategies help keep all these textiles in the economy forever by reusing, repurposing, and recycling them. The prevailing clothing life cycle is linear, which means materials to make fashion are manufactured using renewable and non-renewable resources, fashion styles are designed and produced, then sold, used, and disposed of (see Figure 14.1). The strategies discussed in this chapter can transform this linear clothing life cycle into a circular one.

You might be familiar with some of these strategies—some of them are buzz words: reducing, reusing, recycling, upcycling, repurposing, reprocessing, and so on. Looking at these strategies closely will help better understand the successes and the barriers to their widespread adoption in the fashion industry. After all, with all these wonderful "re-" strategies available, why do we still have so much fashion waste? At the end of the chapter, we will revisit the clothing life cycle to see if it might look a bit more like a circle. To begin, let's agree on what these "re-" strategies mean (see Table 1).

The definitions were developed based on existing literature as well as current industry and consumer practices. These strategies apply to both industry and consumers. The terms in the table are listed from the less preferred in terms of their impact on the environment (i.e., recycling) to the more preferred (i.e., reducing consumption).

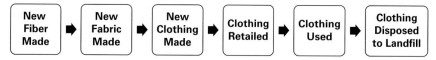

Figure 14.1 Linear clothing lifecycle.

Table 1 Strategies to reduce the environmental impact of fashion

	Strategy	Definition	Examples
Less preferred strategies	**Recycling fashion** (recovering fibers)	Sorting out disposed clothes for processing into new raw materials to make new products.	• Shredding old clothes and other textiles into fibers using mechanical and chemical processing to obtain raw material to be used for new products.
	Repurposing fashion (upcycling)	Taking an otherwise unusable garment and using all or parts of it to make new products.	• Deconstruction of worn clothing to use parts for creating new apparel and non-apparel products (e.g., household items, accessories).
	Reusing fashion	Extending active life of a garment in the hands of the same or different owners, without any substantial physical transformation of the garment.	• Repair and renewal of used clothing. • Resell unwanted garments through different outlets. • Swapping your clothing with other consumers' used clothing.
More preferred strategies	**Reducing fashion consumption**	Minimizing the quantity of new clothes entering the market (being produced) by reducing demand for new products.	• Collaborative consumption • Fashion as an investment • Minimalist fashion.

Recycling fashion

This is the least preferred strategy in terms of environmental impact and represents the last opportunity for fashion products to be diverted from landfills or from being incinerated. Ideally, only non-repairable garments—when fabric cannot be salvaged and repurposed to create new products—should be recycled. At this stage, clothes are shredded into small pieces and converted into fibers that will be manufactured into new yarn, fabric, and, ultimately, new fashion styles.

Repurposing fashion

When a garment is no longer usable as a whole, parts of it can be salvaged to make new products. Old garments can be repurposed into new clothing items, bags, laptop or tablet cases, cushions, rags, and so on. This strategy stretches the useful life of materials from which the product was made, which means reducing the need for making new fibers, yarns, and fabrics, with all the associated environmental impact.

Reusing fashion

Once fashion products are made, many things can be done to keep reusing them "as is" and avoid them going to waste. To extend a product's life, fashion items can be used by the same or different owners. Chapter 13 described the ugly side of disposing of fashion, but in this chapter, we will explore most innovative reuse strategies and see how businesses employ them in the market.

Reducing fashion consumption

The easiest strategy to reduce the waste is not to generate it. With respect to fashion, it means reducing the demand for new clothes, which is minimizing the quantity of new products being produced and purchased. Fashion *is* about new trends and styles, new colors and fabrics. What will fashion become if it loses the excitement of newness? We will look into this contradiction at the end of the chapter to ponder if this strategy is even realistic and viable in contemporary consumption-driven society.

***

The rest of this chapter presents current business and consumer practices for each of the four strategies. We start with the least preferred and gradually move to the most preferred strategies: recycling, repurposing, reusing, and reducing.

Recycling fashion

Recycling, or recovering, is the process of collecting and sorting out discarded clothes to recover fiber and process into new raw materials. These raw materials (e.g., cotton or polyester fibers) can then be made into yarn and fabric, and, finally, new crisp garments and non-fashion products that are made from recycled textile fibers. Many retailers now carry fashion apparel made from recycled fibers such as polyester or nylon. For example, 71 percent of Nike's shoes and clothing contain recycled Nike Grind materials (Nike). Since the beginning of the Nike Grind program, 28 million pairs of used athletic shoes were recycled into new consumer products.

Even though recycled polyester is 25–30 percent more expensive than virgin fiber, the demand for it is high (D'Innocenzio, 2017). A North Carolina-based textile company, Unifi, recycles plastic bottles to manufacture polyester fiber, Repreve™, for 250 apparel companies, including Adidas, Fossil, New Balance, Prana, Quicksilver, Target, and Volcom (Repreve). However, the extra cost typically is not passed on to consumers. Fashion styles containing 20–100 percent recycled polyester do not appear to be sold at higher prices at mass market retailers such as Target or JC Penney (D'Innocenzio, 2017).

It is much easier to recycle clothes made of one type of fiber (e.g., 100 percent cotton or 100 percent nylon) than recycling garments made from a blend of synthetic and natural fibers. It is not only very difficult to separate different fibers woven or knitted together during a recycling process, it also makes it impossible for natural fibers to biodegrade (Schlossberg, 2017). If you check your clothes' fiber content labels, you will see that fiber blends are very common. In fact, today's consumers prefer fiber blends that provide comfort and style.

Even though almost all textiles can be recycled, the majority of them ends up in landfills. One reason for this is that mechanical recycling results in shorter, lower-quality fibers that are not suitable for making new apparel (Remi, Speelman, and Swartz, 2016). These short fibers are used for insulation, furniture stuffing, car seats, and so on. In contrast, chemical recycling produces high-quality fibers, such as Repreve™, which can be used to make new fashion. The problem is that the majority of recycling options today are mechanical. While these lower level recycling practices are beneficial to furniture and construction industries, they are not very helpful to the fashion industry (WRAP, July 2017). Even though recycling is by far a superior option to putting waste in landfills, it is still much better for the environment and all of us to keep our clothes in use for as long as possible before recycling them.

Repurposing fashion

Repurposing, or upcycling, is taking an otherwise unusable garment and using all or parts of it to make new products. This strategy is not yet common in the fashion industry, because it is much easier, faster, and more profitable for fashion brands to make new products rather than repurpose used clothes. Apparel mass production, making many garments of the same style, allows for economy of scale that results in increased productivity and lower manufacturing costs. Repurposing one old garment at a time, each with its unique wear and tear, is time consuming and expensive as it requires individual creative solutions for every item plus a skilled labor force.

Repurposing fashion companies are typically small, boutique-type businesses that emphasize original design, high-quality, and hand-crafted products made locally. There are several different business models within the repurposing, or upcycling, industry. Some companies repurpose their own clothes. For example, Nudie Jeans from Sweden collect old denims brought back by consumers. Each pair is carefully inspected and repurposed when the jeans can no longer be used for wearing. If jeans are still usable, they are cleaned, repaired, and resold (the company provides a free repair service). From each repurposing pair, outer and inner seams are cut out and used to braid cushions for chic folded chairs. The rest of the fabric is repurposed to make stylish rugs. Since the company started the program, almost 3,000 pairs of jeans have been repurposed (Nudie Jeans).

Another business model followed by some companies is not to supply any new products to the market, but only repurpose what has already been produced by other companies and used by consumers. Kallio from Brooklyn, NY, upcycles high-quality men's shirts to handcraft beautiful and comfortable dresses for little girls, retailing at $70–$80 per dress. Like in a typical boutique, quantity and selection are limited. Another example is provided by Freitag in Switzerland, who for more than twenty years have been repurposing tarpaulins—the fabric covering for trucks—into modern and functional messenger bags, backpacks, purses, and other accessories. Freitag has been extremely successful, opening stores throughout Europe and Asia (Kunz, Karpova, and Garner, 2016). Another company from California, Harvey's, has also been making popular handbags from recycled seat belts for years. Other examples of fashion companies incorporating different types of repurposing include Reformation, Looptworks, and Sword & Plough. You can check out all these companies and the products they make on their websites.

What is great about repurposing is that everyone can become an upcycler. The Love Your Clothes organization provides practical tips on how to extend the life of your old outfits. They have partnered with textile artists, fashion designers, and self-taught seamstresses to develop ten- to-fifteen-minute videos and detailed print-out PDF guides on how to creatively repurpose old T-shirts, curtains, jeans, skirts, dresses, and so on (Videos and Guides). These experts demonstrate fun and easy ways to create new bags, tablet sleeves, and memory quilts from baby gowns; halter dresses or sun capes from a man's shirt; and other unique and useful products. Some of the "refashion and upcycle" techniques don't even require a sewing machine or sewing skills. For example, cute cushions and small rugs can be made from old clothes you can find in your closet.

There are thousands of amazing repurposing ideas on Pinterest, some with multiple images and detailed instructions on how to upcycle your old clothes and create unique, one-of-a-kind outfits. Clearly, there is a strong interest from consumers, who might be getting tired of mass market, run-of-the-mill fashion options in stores. Crafty repurposing of fashion helps us to 1) keep our favorite garments longer (albeit with a new function), 2) save money, and 3) reduce our personal environmental footprint. In addition, upcycling provides a not-so-intimidating outlet for our creative expressions. After all, if you were going to throw away these old T-shirts, why not try to make something wonderful from them?

Reusing fashion

Reusing is extending the active life of a product, without any substantial changes, in other words, "as is." This strategy is more sustainable than recycling or repurposing because it keeps the product "alive" and requires fewer additional resources. Reusing has been a part of all societies since people began to wear clothes. Examples include hand-me-downs and mending. Repair, renew, and resell of used fashion are discussed below. Swapping is a fun way to reuse clothes we might be tired of and no longer want to keep in our wardrobe. From informal swapping home parties with friends (preferably, those who wear comparable clothing sizes) to formal community exchanges, these events are becoming increasingly popular, especially for baby, toddler, and children's clothing. Exchanging fashion outfits allows you to (1) acquire new clothes you like for free; (2) clean up your closets guilt-free, without producing waste; and (3) socialize with like-minded people.

Repair

Even though repairing is very important for reusing fashion, few brands offer this service. The reason is quite obvious—companies want to sell more new products instead of repairing old ones, never mind doing it for free. Only businesses truly committed to sustainability embrace this strategy in order to reduce the environmental impact by extending the active life of clothing. Nudie Jeans, referred to earlier, have twenty-five repair shops around the world, and in just one year repaired 21,331 pairs of jeans for free (Nudie Jeans). Another leader in helping consumers keep their favorite outfits longer is Patagonia. In 2016, the company mended 45,000 garments (WRAP, July 2017). To offer its customers greater access to free repair services, Patagonia's repair truck has travelled from the West coast of the United States to East coast in a "Worn Wear Tour," stopping along the way in hundreds of towns and tirelessly fixing garments, both Patagonia products and those made by other companies (Patagonia Works, 2015). Both Nudie Jeans and Patagonia empower customers by providing free repair kits online, along with detailed instructions on how to do it yourself.

Renew

Have you ever wondered what happens with the clothing on clearance racks? Every store has one or several of these full of the latest styles that did not find a home. The Renewal Workshop was created to address the problem of *new* unsellable apparel. These unwanted new styles come from clearance racks, are returned by consumers, or have been damaged during shipping or in stores. In a US-based factory, the company diverts thousands of such garments from being wasted. The renewal process starts with a careful inspection of each garment by a renewal expert. If garments are deemed to be renewable, they are meticulously cleaned using an innovative waterless laundry, custom renewed, and put back to the market, instead of being destined for landfill (Renewal Workshop). The result is one-of-a-kind, high-quality garments.

The Renewal Workshop's goal is to help brands recover maximum value from the fashion products that were manufactured but could not be sold. The company uses a proprietary process where garments are renewed, converted into upcycling material, or recycled. The Renewal Workshop takes care of discarded garments for a dozen of similar environmentally-conscious and socially-dedicated companies that share its values, such as Ibex, Mountain Khakis, Indigenous, Thread, and Toad & Co.

Resell

How many of your clothing items have not been touched for a year? Is it about half of your closet? If yes, then you are close to that "average US woman" who does not wear 60 percent of her closet (ThredUP, 2017). The value of the total "dormant wardrobe" across the country is estimated at $220 billion. Reselling is beneficial for all parties involved by providing some income to the original owner of the clothes and revenue to the businesses that help resell unwanted used fashion. When purchases of pre-loved fashion replace that of new fashion items, "then significant environmental savings are made from avoiding production, processing, and disposal" (WRAP, July 2017, p. 38).

Fashion products (i.e., clothing, shoes, and other accessories) account for almost half of the US resale market (49 percent), with other product categories lagging far behind – books (14 percent), media (11 percent), and electronics (10 percent). In 2017, the US fashion resale industry reached $18 billion (ThredUP, 2017). The industry includes various retail formats, including:

- traditional large and small thrift stores (e.g., Goodwill and the Salvation Army);
- consignment boutiques offering higher quality, branded merchandise;
- peer-to-peer marketplaces (e.g., eBay, Poshmark);
- and augmented marketplaces (e.g., the RealReal, ThredUP);

Within the industry, *resale disruptors*, defined as apparel second-hand retailers that "focus on higher-quality, gently-used, brand-name products and present a more curated product assortment," are growing four times faster than the rest of the second-hand market and twenty times faster than the conventional apparel market (ThredUP, 2017, p. 1).

The majority of fashion resale shoppers are women of sixty and older (32 percent) and millennials (30 percent). Surprisingly, thrifting is more popular with high-income shoppers than low-income consumers. For example, 67 percent of ThredUP customers reported a six-figure income ($100,000+), and only 23 percent had an income of less than $50,000. Consumers are turning to shopping pre-loved fashion because they are bored with traditional retail offerings and, instead, go for the thrill of a treasure hunt when you do not know what gems you might find while shopping used fashion (ThredUP, 2017).

There are many ways to sell your no-longer-wanted fashion items. First, decide how involved you want to be in the process. If selling through an augmented marketer, all you need to do is ship products to a resell company that takes care of photography, listing, and other logistics. Depending on the business model, sellers can get either a flat percentage of every sale, or a percentage determined by a sliding scale from 10 up to 80 percent (Indvik, 2016).

If you want to be highly involved in the process and do all the steps yourself, choose a peer-to-peer platform such as Poshmark that connects people and their closets. It allows each seller to be a fashion stylist and blogger by creating a covertshot for a "magazine-esque" listing (Poshmark). When your item is sold, the company provides pre-paid and pre-addressed labels for easy shipping, and you get to keep 80 percent of the selling price. In 2015, Poshmark grew by 150 percent and added several lines of new clothing from indie brands. The company's success is "attributed to creating a network of influencers who are both good at selling as well as at curating and offering suggestions" (Indvik, 2016, para 10,).

Vestiaire Collective, another successful "re-commerce" disruptor, has created a carefully curated vintage resale hub, focusing on designer fashions (McCall, 2017). The Paris-based company is expanding its market beyond the United States, to Canada and Asia, citing incredible interest and demand. Members of this six-million-member community can interact with each other to ask questions and negotiate prices. The company's unique strategies include editorial content featuring profiles of most prominent members; and a social network with a feel of friends swapping wardrobes (Decker, 2016).

Needless to say, mid-market and high-end fashion has the greatest resell value, encouraging consumers to view fashion as an investment rather than a disposable product. In the near future, consumers might be checking the resell value of fashion items before clicking the "complete order" button, similar to the way they shop for cars. Resell companies have detailed resale value databases, searchable by brand and product category and accessible from any mobile device. With significant investor backup, the size of the fashion resell industry is expected to almost double by 2021 (ThredUP, 2017). Consumers' insatiable demand for luxury, the excitement of the hunt, and a concern for the environment are factors in this incredible growth (Indvik, 2016).

Reducing fashion consumption

Reducing is the most preferred strategy because if lower quantities of fashion items are produced, distributed, sold, consumed, and disposed of, fewer resources are used and less waste and pollution are generated. The best thing consumers and businesses can do for the environment is to limit consumption of new apparel. This is the ultimate goal of any sustainable drive. Let's look at some strategies that can be adopted by both businesses and consumers.

Collaborative consumption

Collaborative consumption, or sharing economy, is a redistribution of used goods that are being passed from someone who does not want them to someone who does want them. In other words, when you need an outfit for an occasion, borrow or rent it instead of buying it. Emerging social lending systems and peer-to-peer platforms are based on the concept of collaborative consumption. Curtsy is an example of peer-to-peer fashion sharing platform that "lets you rent dresses, rompers, and tops from women in your neighbourhood" (Curtsy).

The 2000s saw a fast growth in services leasing fashion apparel and accessories, with the most prominent being Rent the Runway, Wear Today Gone Tomorrow, and Girl Meets Dress. For example, Avelle (former Bag, Borrow or Steal) offers designer accessories with no limit on the amount of renting time. The services are convenient (shipped to your door), affordable (5–10 percent of a product's retail price, or between $50 and $200), and some use organic dry-cleaning only, as part of their environmental commitment.

Rent the Runway's unlimited subscription service unlocks an endless wardrobe. For $139 a month plus tax, customers can swap fashion items as often as they want and have a rotating closet (Willet, 2016). Shipping, dry-cleaning, and insurance are included. The company promotes its rental strategy as a much better alternative to the fast-fashion practice of buying a lot of cheap, low-quality, disposable garments. The service allows fashionistas to try new styles from 450 designers around the world without the guilt of acquiring and discarding more stuff and contributing to the growing textile waste.

Despite some success, renting an outfit for a special occasion (wedding, prom, important business presentation, or job interview) is not as widespread as renting in other industries. For example, the rental car industry reached a record revenue of $27.1 billion in 2015 (Manheim, 2016). Will collaborative fashion consumption become as ubiquitous and easy as streaming a Netflix movie or catching an Uber ride?

Fashion as an investment

Can fashion be an investment (as opposed to disposable consumption)? A 1967 *Vogue* advertisement for a double-knit wool dress and print-lined coat suggests just that: "Can fashion be considered an investment? Don't go overboard with radical new designs. Steer clear of neon colours and fad fabrics. Smooth sailing happens when you wear clothes that weather fashion storms."

Today we keep our clothes about half as long as we did fifteen years ago (Remi et al., 2016). This is true for any type of apparel, whether it be underwear or winter coats. Fashion became fast and disposable. Yet, regardless if clothes are made to last just one season or ten years, they require similar amounts of water, energy, fibers, and other resources to produce and generate the same amount of pollution and waste (Kunz et al., 2016). It makes sense to use renewable and non-renewable resources such as water, petroleum, energy, and so on for making longer-lasting fashion rather than outfits that will be disposed of quickly.

Keeping our outfits in active use longer can help minimize the negative impacts of fiber processing, fabric and garment production, and product distribution and retail–but only if the purchasing of new clothing is avoided (WRAP, July 2017). This is possible if we invest in fashion by buying more high-quality clothes that will last for a long time. One of the most environmentally conscious companies, Patagonia, has emphasized the critical impact of extending the life of our garments:

> At the end of the day, we can tinker with our supply chain, improve sourcing, use all-recycled fabrics and give away millions of dollars to environmental organizations until the cows come in, but nothing is more important and impactful than keeping our clothing in use for as long as possible. In fact, by keeping our clothing in use just nine extra months, we can reduce related carbon, waste and water footprints by 20–30 percent each.
>
> Patagonia Works, 2015

Similar to the repurposing strategy, not many fashion companies promote longer use of apparel, and for the same reason—the goal of businesses is to grow sales and profits by making and selling more new products. Toad & Co. is an example of a company that not only designs clothing to last by using quality materials and advanced manufacturing methods, but has also been encouraging customers to "Wear it out or pass it on" by printing this message on garment labels and educating consumers through their website.

Minimalist fashion

If you are up to the challenge of treating fashion as an investment, some approaches to try are thoughtful consumption, streamlining your wardrobe, moving toward a minimalist fashion, and building a strategic wardrobe over time. Livia Firth (2016), the founder and Creative Director of Eco Age, suggests that any time you are ready to buy a new fashion item, you should pause and ask yourself, "Will I wear it a minimum of 30 times?" If not, then don't buy it. In the light the discussion about fashion as an investment, an even more appropriate question might be, "Will I still wear it in five years?" Stopping to reflect on your future and your values might help you make the "Should I buy it or not?" decision. When selecting new fashion styles, general recommendations include:

- Avoid fly-by-night fads that will be out of fashion next season.
- Turn down cheaply made garments made of low-quality materials.
- Invest in high-quality fabric and high-quality construction, well-made garments.
- Choose versatile styles that are appropriate for different life situations, from professional to casual, and that can be easily dressed up or down.
- Favor classier styles that can be updated with accessories (Kunz, et al., 2016; Nudie Jeans; WRAP, July 2017).

In the 1970s, Susan Faux, a London boutique owner, introduced the term *capsule wardrobe*. A capsule wardrobe consists of a limited number of high-quality apparel and accessory items that look "sharp" and, basically, never go out of style—like the little black dress. The key is that this small fashion collection should be versatile or easily mixed and matched and flatter your body type. The number of pieces in a capsule wardrobe typically ranges between thirty and forty. A more recent version of the same idea is Project 333. The minimalist fashion challenge is to dress using only thirty-three items from your current wardrobe for three months. After carefully choosing the thirty-three items, you pack the rest of your garments in boxes and store them away for ninety days. Since 2010, the project has gained lots of traction. Many participants share via blog that they never went back to their packed boxes!

Conclusion

A circular clothing life cycle (or circular economy) is when each item is used for as long as possible (reused and repurposed) and at the end of its useful life is recycled to make new products (see Figure 14.2). In other words, it describes a process in which no waste is produced and resources are used continuously in a closed-loop system. In the fashion world, with a few exceptions, the circular economy is still a new concept. Patagonia has committed to the circular economy model by aiming to have 100 percent of its garments continuously reused, repaired, or recycled by making new fibers and fabrics from unsalvageable garments (Patagonia Works, 2017). What will it take for the industry and consumers to commit to recycling, repurposing, reusing, and reducing the impact of fashion? Consider the case study of the Renewal Workshop, below.

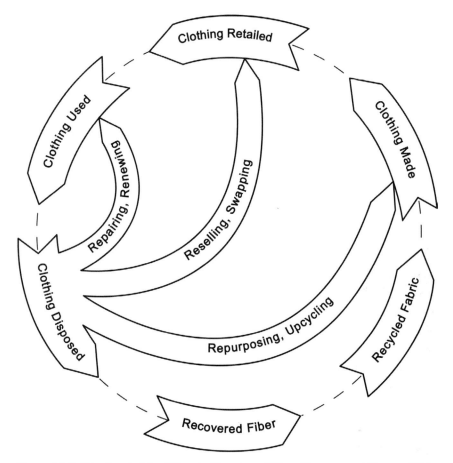

Figure 14.2 Circular clothing lifecycle. Courtesy of Elena Karpova and Bingyue Wei.

To paraphrase *McKinsey on Sustainability & Resource Productivity, Number 4* (2016), how can global consumers be nudged toward a more sustainable fashion consumption? The circular economy goes hand in hand with the creative economy. In this economy, there are no consumers, but instead, everyone becomes an active participant, a contributor to a sustainable lifestyle, and a craftsman of creative solutions. Companies have an enormous opportunity to engage customers beyond the point of selling clothes and offer educational and creative outlets for reselling, repairing, and repurposing fashion items. Co-creating new and repurposed products builds an emotional attachment, which ensures that fashion items are kept and used for a longer period of time.

Can the fashion industry that inherently depends on ever changing trends be sustainable? Without doubt, the answer is yes. With a limited amount of resources and increasing levels of pollution on earth, there is simply no other choice. For consumers, in rethinking fashion consumption and overall lifestyle, it is important to realize that the idea of happiness though material possessions is an illusion, and that our focus should be on the feeling of satisfaction that we can enjoy from making sustainable fashion choices (Brodesser-Akner, 2016; WRAP, July 2017).

Case study: the Renewal Workshop®

This case study was created in collaboration with Nicole Bassett, co-founder of the Renewal Workshop.

***

Refurbishing used products typically includes careful inspection, cleaning, and, if necessary, repair or replacement of some parts. Refurbished products are then certified and put back in the market. This business model has been successful in many industries such as auto, computers, or cell phones. For example, used car sales have been steadily growing, with a record of 38 million units sold in 2016 (Used Vehicle Market Report, 2017). Clearly, consumers see the value of used cars, as the average retail prices are higher than ever—reaching almost $20,000. The used car market is flourishing due to a strong consumer demand as well as dealers' interest in increasing sales. Approximately 30 percent of revenues in the auto industry comes from selling used cars ("Used-Car Demand Going Strong At Dealer Groups," 2017).

Similarly, personal technology companies, such as computers and mobile phones, are establishing refurbishing programs to resell used devices. Several market leaders, such as Apple and Samsung, rolled out sales of certified pre-owned iPhones and smartphones (Spence, 2016; Team, 2016). This strategy allows companies "to capture the budget focused consumers without having to rely on third-party resellers or the second-hand market" (Spence, 2016, para. 4).

What about fashion? Can the industry follow the same path of refurbishing and reselling pre-loved clothing? As discussed in this chapter, online reselling start-ups are booming, but they resell clothing only in good condition, clothing that can be sold "as is"—that is, without repairing and, in some cases, with no cleaning. At present, fashion companies that offer "refurbish and resell" services to consumers or retailers are virtually non-existent. No wonder that the Renewal Workshop claims to be a "new kind of apparel company" (Renewal Workshop, para. 1).

At the outset, the company partnered with five brands to renew their unsellable merchandise and put it back in the market. A year later, Renewal Workshop was able to grow the number of partner apparel businesses to nine brands. According to Nicole Bassett, a co-founder of the Renewal Workshop, one of the major challenges for the young company proved to be getting more partner brands that were committed to diverting unsellable merchandise from landfills. Not many companies are committed to repurposing and reusing fashion because these practices, while sustainable, contradict the market pressure to generate sales and profits, which is easier when making and selling new products. Furthermore, if there was a strong consumer demand for reused, renewed, and repurposed (aka sustainable) fashion, companies would be able to address it by establishing the necessary infrastructure. What ideas do you have to make the renewal (refurnishing) business model work for the fashion apparel market?

References

Brodesser-Akner, T. "Marie Kondo and the Ruthless War on Stuff." *New York Times Magazine*, July 6, 2016. https://www.nytimes.com/2016/07/10/magazine/marie-kondo-and-the-ruthless-war-on-stuff.html.

Curtsy. n.d. https://curtsyapp.com/.

Decker, V. "Fanny Moizant's Vestitaeri Collective is a major player in the luxury consignment market." 2016. https://www.forbes.com/sites/viviennedecker/2016/12/26/fanny-moizants-vestiaire-collective-is-a-major-player-in-the-luxury-consignment-market/#1fdbc18735f6.

D'Innocenzio, A. "Retailers, Brands See Green for Back-To-School Shopping." July 17, 2017. https://apnews.com/10eb79d5c70346309475d1a6fe02044c/Retailers,-brands-see-green-for-back-to-school-shopping.

Firth, L. "Livia Firth: Every time you shop, always think, 'Will I wear it a minimum of 30 times?'" *Telegraph*, May 12, 2016. http://www.telegraph.co.uk/fashion/people/livia-firth-every-time-you-shop-always-think-will-i-wear-this-a/?curator=FashionREDEF.

Indvik, L. "Investors continue to pour millions into online resale startups." 2016. https://fashionista.com/2016/05/online-resale-poshmark-the-realreal.

Kunz, G., Karpova, E., and Garner, M. *Going Global: The Textile and Apparel Industry*. New York: Bloomsbury/Fairchild, 2016.

Love Your Clothes. n.d. http://loveyourclothes.org.uk/.

Manheim. *2016 Used Car Market Report*. 2016. https://www.manheim.com/content_pdfs/products/UCMR-2016.pdf?WT.svl=m_prod_consulting_latestupdates_graphic_2016.

McCall, T. "Vestiaire Collective offcially launches vintage with Chloe Sevigny." 2017. https://fashionista.com/2017/05/vestiaire-collective-vintage.

McKinsey & Company. *McKinsey on Sustainability & Resource Productivity, Number 4*. November 2016. http://www.mckinsey.com/business-functions/sustainability-and-resource-productivity/our-insights/mckinsey-on-sustainability-and-resource-productivity/mckinsey-on-sustainability-and-resource-productivity-number-4.

Nike. "Nike Grind." n.d. https://www.nike.com/us/en_us/c/innovation/grind.

Nudie Jeans. "This is Nudie Jeans." n.d. https://www.nudiejeans.com/page/this-is-nudie-jeans.

Patagonia Works. "Patagonia mobile worn wear tour." 2015. http://www.patagoniaworks.com/press/2015/3/31/patagonia-mobile-worn-wear-tour-if-its-broke-fix-it.

Patagonia Works. "Patagonia wins circular economy multinational award." January 17, 2017. http://www.patagoniaworks.com/press/2017/1/17/patagonia-wins-circular-economy-multinational-award-at-world-economic-forum-annual-meeting-in-davos.

Poshmark. "What is Poshmark?" n.d. https://poshmark.com/what_is_poshmark.

Project 333. n.d. https://bemorewithless.com/project-333/.

Remi, N., Speelman, E., and Swartz, S. "Style that's sustainable: A new fast fashion formula." McKinsey & Company, 2016. http://www.mckinsey.com/business-functions/sustainability-and-resource-productivity/our-insights/style-thats-sustainable-a-new-fast-fashion-formula.

Repreve. "Brands." n.d. http://www.repreve.com/brands.

Scarano, G. "Closing the loop: How sharing circular materials fortifies fashion future." *Sourcing Journal*, June 7, 2017.

Schlossberg, T. "Fig leaves are out. What to wear to be kind to the planet." *New York Times*, 2017. https://www.nytimes.com/2017/05/24/climate/eco-friendly-organic-clothing.html?smprod=nytcore-iphone&smid=nytcore-iphone-share&_r=0

ThredUP. *Annual Resale Report 2017*. https://www.thredup.com/resale.

Toad & Co. "Sustainability." n.d. https://www.toadandco.com/about/sustainability.html.

Videos and Guides. "Love Your Clothes." n.d. http://loveyourclothes.org.uk/guides/videos-and-guides-refashioning-and-upcycling.

Willet, M. "I spent $150 a month renting clothes, and now I'm never going back to fast fashion." *Business Insider*, 2016. http://www.businessinsider.com/rent-the-runway-unlimited-subscription-2016-4/#rent-the-runway-is-known-for-its-model-of-renting-out-thousand-dollar-designer-gowns-to-customers-for-under-100-for-four-or-eight-days-1.

WRAP. *Sustainable Clothing: A Practical Guide to Enhancing Clothing Durability and Quality*. June 2017. http://www.wrap.org.uk/sites/files/wrap/Sustainable%20Clothing%20Guide%202017.pdf

WRAP. *Valuing Our Clothes: The Cost of UK Fashion.* July 2017. http://www.wrap.org.
    uk/sites/files/wrap/valuing-our-clothes-the-cost-of-uk-fashion_WRAP.pdf.

Case study references

Renewal Workshop. "About Us." https://renewalworkshop.com/en/general/about-us.
Spence, E. "Apple's Secret iPhone Discounts." 2016. https://www.forbes.com/sites/
    ewanspence/2016/11/08/can-you-buy-refurbished-iphone/#7c69c1a666eb.
Team, T. "Why Samsung Is Planning to Sell Refurbished Smartphones?" August 29,
    2016. https://www.forbes.com/sites/greatspeculations/2016/08/29/why-samsung-is-
    planning-to-sell-refurbished-smartphones/#634a058c3b6f.
"Used-Car Demand Going Strong At Dealer Groups." *Automotive News*, April 24, 2017.
    http://www.autonews.com/article/20170424/RETAIL04/304249985/used-car-
    demand-going-strong-at-dealer-groups.
Used Vehicle Market Report. 2017. https://dealers.edmunds.com/static/assets/
    articles/2017_Feb_Used_Market_Report.pdf.

Conclusion: Creative Solutions to the Dangers of Fashion

Elena E. Karpova and Sara B. Marcketti

Uniqueness of the fashion industry

Fashion is a fascinating and essential part of our lives in many ways. From a historical viewpoint, textile and apparel manufacturing started the Industrial Revolution in the eighteenth century and helped moved our civilization from the agrarian economy to where we are now, a knowledge-based economy. The fashion industry became the second largest in the world, only to agriculture. Today "fashion is a highly sophisticated, multitrillion dollar global industry" (Joint Economic Committee Democrats, 2016).

The fashion industry is also unique because every single country in the world (almost 200 countries in total) has at least some form of fashion industry. This is because clothing is a very basic human need that comes right after food and shelter. People have to wear clothes to protect them from harsh climates (sun, snow, rain, wind, etc.) and to function in society.

Did you know that some of the richest people on the planet made their fortunes in the fashion business? Yes, fashion!—not oil, banking, or high tech, as you might think. Fashion has allowed some people to build incredible business empires and mind-boggling wealth. For example, Sweden's richest person is Stefan Persson, chairman of H&M and a member of the family that owns the fast-fashion brand's business (McGregor, 2016). According to Forbes, his estimated net worth is roughly $20 billion. Similarly, the wealthiest individual in Japan, Tadashi Yanai ($17 billion) is the founder of the Fast Retailing Company that owns multiple fashion brands, including Uniqlo. What about the pioneer of the fast fashion trend Zara? Its founder, Amancio Ortega, is one of the richest people on the planet. His estimated net value is $75 billion (Brain, 2016).

Even though the industry made the wealthiest people in the world and is commonly perceived as a glamorous business, unfortunately it is also known for the lowest wages and poor working conditions, as discussed in Chapter 7, "A Look at Labor Issues in the Manufacturing of Fashion." One of the darkest sides of the industry is the exploitation of docile workers in sweatshop conditions, even in the twenty-first century. This is due to the extremely labor-intensive nature of apparel manufacturing. Because fabrics are highly pliable and unstable materials, as discussed in Chapter 4, "Fibers and Materials," as well as the enormous variation in garment styles and sizes, it has not been possible to mechanize apparel assembly processes, resulting in the highest need for manual labor among any manufacturing industries.

In addition to providing wealth and livelihood to millions of people, clothing is our chosen skin. It surrounds us every day and stays with us every step all the way through our lives. Fashion helps people express to the world who they are, communicate their identity, and is an excellent outlet for one's creativity (see Figure Con.1). As such, our fashion choices impact each of us in many ways,

Figure Con.1 Fashion is an expression of creativity. Courtesy of Elena Karpova.

from physical health (Chapter 11, "Pain from Fashion") and psychological wellbeing (Chapter 10, "Striving to Fit In") to significant impacts on the environment (Chapters 13 and 14, "Disposing Fashion"). In the words of Livia Firth (2016), a film producer and human rights advocate, "fashion—i.e., what we wear every single day, has huge relevance and huge consequences on human, social and environmental capital."

Recognizing fashion dangers

What are your thoughts and feelings after reading this book? It is our hope that you will take some time to reflect on the fashion dangers discussed here. The idea of the book was to help you, the reader, look at fashion from different perspectives and be mindful in your daily choices when you shop, wear, store, care, and dispose of your clothes. Which of the dangers spoke the most to you? *Why* do you think these dangers stood out? Can you think of any other dangers related to the fashion industry that were not discussed in the book? Even though the book covers a wide range of topics—from fashion design, production, and the supply chain to appropriation of fashion, and its economic, environmental, and social costs—fashion is so pervasive that it would not be possible to discuss all its facets. Indeed, there remain numerous other challenges related to fashion design, production, and disposal.

Do the dangers differ by geographical location?

While some chapters in this volume focus specifically on fashion dangers in the context of the United States, others present material from a global perspective. For instance, Chapter 8, "Exodus to Elsewhere," paints a grim picture of the impact of outsourcing apparel production on small communities across one US state, North Carolina. Yet, the experiences of these tiny towns built around textile mills are very similar to the fate of former textile workers in United Kingdom, Japan, or Australia. During the end of the twentieth century and early twenty-first century, when apparel and textile manufacturing was in sharp decline in the developed economies around the world, thousands of mills were closed and millions of workers were laid off (Kunz, Karpova, and Garner, 2016). Chapter 7, "A Look at Labor Issues in the Manufacture of Fashion," presents a global perspective on modern slavery, focusing not only on the United States but also the United Kingdom, Germany, Netherlands, and other countries. Many other chapters (e.g., 2, 6, and 14) illustrate dangers by providing examples of European fashion companies. The point is that, even though more examples might be presented from the US perspective, the global nature of today's fashion world means that fashion is more often than not generalizable and that points relating to America are equally applicable to most other countries and cultures.

Solutions to the dangers

The goal of the book was not only to discuss fashion dangers but also outline various answers to these dangers. While the volume presents many existing or conceivable solutions to empower consumers, companies, and nations to address the dangers, it is nearly impossible to propose "ready-to-go solutions" to all of the dangers. Most problems are very complex and pervasive; some are contentious and rarely have one right answer, such as, for example, the cultural appropriation of fashion, covered in Chapter 9, "Taking Offence," or Chapter 3, "Stealing Designs."

Each chapter includes a discussion of solutions to the exposed dangers. Some of these solutions are already employed by progressive countries, leading ethical businesses, and responsible consumers. For example, an important industry initiative, the Sustainable Apparel Coalition, is highlighted in Chapters 2 and 5. Other solutions discussed in the book are new and futuristic.

Chapter 2 offers food for thought for practicing and aspiring fashion designers to help them develop garments that do not harm the world we live in. In Chapter 6, the pros and cons of producing apparel domestically vs. outsourcing the manufacturing component are presented. The implications of these decisions might be of interest to fashion companies and current and future professionals in charge of this area—fashion buyers and merchandisers.

The dangers discussed in Chapter 9, "Taking Offence," and Chapter 10, "Striving to Fit In," might be amplified with the use of digital media. In these cases, solutions might require thoughtfulness, consideration, mindfulness, and responsibility—in other words, human qualities, not the latest technology. Chapter 12 shares best practices and provide tips to deal with the dangers associated with washing and drying your clothes.

The path forward

To help readers navigate this complex topic, we have developed a table that holistically summarizes the major dangers and suggests a path forward by outlining diverse directions and approaches for addressing them (see Table 2). Horizontally, the table first presents a summary of major, or key, fashion dangers discussed in the book (WHAT) and uncovers the causes, or sources, of these dangers (WHY the dangers exist). Next, strategies to address the dangers are examined (HOW the dangers can be solved). Finally, chapters where the dangers and solutions are discussed in the book are listed for ease of referencing. Vertically, the table is divided into four parts based on the magnitude or level of the dangers. In other words, who is affected by the dangers. Is it individual people? Company or organization? The whole community or society? Or, perhaps, our entire planet? Overall, the table presents a "helicopter view" of key fashion dangers and possible solutions, which allows the reader to consider them from different perspectives.

Some of the solutions presented in the table may appear to be too simplistic. In most cases, they are expanded upon in the respective chapters. The fashion industry is constantly changing and evolving, as are the dangers associated with it and so too, of course, the solutions to these dangers. New technological advances that are being introduced almost daily promise to solve many of the dangers but not all. In some cases, it will be up to the readers—current and future industry professionals, consumers, and society as a whole—to develop comprehensive and effective solutions to the dangers. Chapter 1 offers a useful framework for approaching a morally challenging problem, or danger, and for understanding the process of how and why we decide what is "right" or "wrong."

Paradigm shift

In respect of any danger, it is critical not only to develop innovative solutions but also to implement them. This will determine the quality of our lives and, more importantly, the quality of lives for generations to come. Who is "in charge" of seeing that these solutions are effected? Fashion companies? Government? Or, perhaps, ordinary people, like me and you? In the chapters of the book, these people are often referred to as consumers. We all are. We buy things, fashion-related or not, every day. We use these things and dispose of them. What role do we all play in minimizing or completely eliminating the dangers of fashion? In the words of Marie Curie, the nineteenth-century physicist, chemist, and twice Nobel laureate, "You cannot hope to build a better world without improving the individuals. To that end, each of us must work for his own improvement and, at the same time, share a general responsibility for all humanity." The authors

Figure Con.2 Moving from problem to solutions in the fashion business. Source: https://pixabay.com/illustrations/board-font-problem-solution-chalk-1521348/.

believe that grassroots consumer movements will play the biggest role in the changes to come (see Figure Con.2).

   To conclude, regardless of the danger level—personal, organizational, societal, or global (see Table 2)—it is clear that a paradigm shift is needed to develop new, alternative scenarios to current production and consumption practices. Some shifts are happening now. For example, the fashion distribution and retail industry is being transformed by the unprecedented growth of the rental and resale sectors (see Chapter 14). Will slow and sustainable fashion movements forever change the industry as we know it today *and* transform the way we shop, wear, and dispose of clothing? Instead of obsessing over and playing continuous catch-up with the latest trends in colors, prints, silhouettes, and other design details, will consumers recognize and accept sustainable trends as the most "fashionable"? The key solution is innovation and creativity to reimagine the existing practices of designing, manufacturing, selling, and consumption. Slow fashion will promote greater individuality and uniqueness of products that are locally produced by craftsmen and small businesses (see Chapter 2).

   Or, perhaps the paradigm shift will be found at an even deeper level—through questioning the values of a consumer society built upon the assumption of ever-growing consumption levels to continuously perpetuate economic growth. The very foundation of the capitalist economy—the infinite expansion of capital—contradicts the reality of the finite resources of our planet and the amount of waste and pollution it can handle. The business drive for profit at any cost should be questioned in the name of a sustainable future and fashion without dangers.

Table 2 The path forward—finding solutions to the fashion dangers

WHAT: Summary of Key Dangers	WHY: Causes or Sources of the Dangers	WHO & HOW: Solutions to the Dangers	Chapters in this Book
Personal Level Impact			
Physical and emotional dangers or harm: • physical pain from fashion; • eating disorders and body alterations to achieve ideal body image or beauty ideal; • low self-esteem; • negative body-image (dissatisfaction with one's appearance).	Promotion of particular body ideals by media and popular culture. Desire to be accepted as a member of a societal group (to "fit in"). Desire to be perceived as beautiful and fashionable at any cost.	Consumer education about the physical and emotional dangers of fashion. Systemic societal changes regarding beauty ideals and values placed on one's appearance. Representation of diverse body types, shapes, and colors in the popular culture, traditional and social media, and brands' advertising campaigns.	1, 10, 13
Increased consumer debt. Time and effort needed to manage the amount of stuff people own.	Overconsumption of fashion. Pursuit of materialism in search of happiness.	Consumer education about the reasons for overconsumption. Grassroots consumer movements, e.g., slow fashion and minimalist lifestyle.	2, 13
Company or Organizational Level Impact			
Illegal and unfair labor practices: • safety violations; • human rights violations; • child labor; • low wages; etc.	Drive for profit at any cost, often to satisfy company shareholders.	Transparent supply chain. Product traceability. Consumer education about unfair labor practices to increase demand for ethically made products. Third-party audit and certification. Government and world organizations' (e.g., United Nations) regulations and enforcement.	1, 4, 6, 7

(*Continued*)

Table 2 *Continued*

WHAT: Summary of Key Dangers	WHY: Causes or Sources of the Dangers	WHO & HOW: Solutions to the Dangers	Chapters in this Book
Company or Organizational Level Impact			
Illegal and unfair business practices: • small vendor abuse by powerful corporations; • design piracy; counterfeiting, etc.	Drive for profit at any cost, often to satisfy company shareholders. Consumer demand for high status designer products.	Transparent supply chain. Authentication and traceability technology. Consumer education to increase demand for ethically made products. Government and world organizations' (e.g., United Nations) regulations and enforcement.	1, 4
Community or Society Level Impact			
Disappearance of entire industries and economic shifts: • company shutdowns and layoffs; • loss of community identity.	Globalization of supply chain. Outsourcing production to low-wage countries.	Training people for the jobs in the fourth type of economy (knowledge- and technology-based economy). Entrepreneurial initiatives to create resilient communities.	6, 8
Cultural appropriation: • use of aesthetic elements from a culture without credit.	Ignorance of fashion designers, companies, or groups of people.	Education and public campaigns by non-profit groups, companies, education institutions, etc.	9

Planetary or Global Level Impact

1, 2, 3, 5, 6, 12, 13, 14

Climate change and pollution of air, water, soil, etc.: • production of fibers, fabrics, and garments (e.g., harmful pesticides and dyes); • transportation of materials and products around the globe; • clothing care (e.g., laundry, dry-cleaning, micro fibers in the ocean); • textile and packaging waste in landfills, especially non-biodegradable fibers such as polyester. Depletion of natural resources to produce and care for garments: • biodiversity threat; • use of non-renewable resources (e.g., petroleum for polyester; water).	Overproduction and overconsumption of fashion: • fashion = change (constant need for newness and latest trends); • fashion became a disposable commodity that is produced faster and cheaper. Linear (instead of circular) product life cycle when products are disposed of to landfills.	Innovative design and manufacturing practices: • circular business model/product lifecycle, or closed loop manufacturing (3, 5, 14); • zero-waste processes (2, 6); • clean energy use (5, 6, 13); • local or regional production (reshoring or nearshoring) (2, 6); • green and reusable packaging (5, 6). Buying less / reduced consumption: • consumer education about environmental impact of fashion (5, 2, 13, 14); • grassroots movements (e.g., slow fashion, DIY upcycling, fashion swaps, minimalist fashion, etc.) (2, 14); • burgeoning resale and renting industries (14); Extending clothing life cycle: • design and production of high-quality apparel that last (2, 12, 13); • creating emotional attachment to products (custom-made, sentimental value, etc.) (2); • repair and renewal practices (12, 14). Environmentally friendly care for apparel (2, 12). Government regulations and commitments (e.g., the Paris Agreement).

Consider the statement on an Everlane "Truth" T-shirt collection in collaboration with the *New York Times* (Truth):

What we buy.
What we put on our plates.
How we use our energy.
What we recycle.
What we waste.
How we travel.
How we stay informed.
What we talk about.
What we know.
How we understand climate change.
The truth is worth it.
The New York Times.

References

Brain, M. "Fast fashion has made some of the richest men on Earth." *Quartz*, August 2, 2016. http://qz.com/747242/fast-fashion-has-made-some-of-the-richest-men-on-earth/.

Firth, L. "Livia Firth: Every time you shop, always think, 'Will I wear it a minimum of 30 times?'" *Telegraph*, May 12, 2016. http://www.telegraph.co.uk/fashion/people/livia-firth-every-time-you-shop-always-think-will-i-wear-this-a/?curator=FashionREDEF.

Joint Economic Committee Democrats. *The Economic Impact of the Fashion Industry.* Washington, DC: United States Congress, 2016. https://www.jec.senate.gov/public/index.cfm/democrats/reports?ID=034A47B7-D82A-4509-A75B-00522C863653.

Kunz, G., Karpova, E., and Garner, M. *Going Global: The Textile and Apparel Industry.* 3rd edn. New York: Bloomsbury/Fairchild, 2016.

McGregor, L. "Cheap clothing created some of the world's richest people." *Sourcing Journal*, August 8, 2016. https://sourcingjournalonline.com/cheap-clothing-created-worlds-richest-people/.

"Truth. It affects us all." Everlane. n.d. https://www.everlane.com/nytimes.

Index

Page numbers in *italics* refer to figures.